GEORGIAN AFTERNOON

GEORGIAN
AFTERNOON

BY
L. E. JONES

RUPERT HART-DAVIS
SOHO SQUARE LONDON
1958

Made and printed in Great Britain by
William Clowes and Sons, Limited, London and Beccles

CONTENTS

GEORGIAN AFTERNOON

CHAPTER I

THE VILLAIN

THE villain of Victorian melodrama who, with a black heart and ingratiating manners, conspires, is foiled and scowls horribly in defeat is a figure rarely met with in real life. But, improbable as it may seem, I found myself, within a few weeks of my marriage, in the thick of a conflict with just such a stage-villain.

The hero, or shall I say the victim, in the melodrama which was to be my first taste of business was Mr Otis A. Mygatt, the American inventor of a prismatic glassware called Holophane. I had married on the strength of my employment by Mygatt as his "adviser." I also had a seat on the board of Holophane Ltd. The Villain was the managing director of that company, having successfully practised his ingratiating manner upon Mygatt in a First Act which I had missed. When I joined the board, in the middle of Act II, the plot was fully developed, villain and victim being already at arms' length.

The plot was simple enough. Mygatt, being short of funds, had pledged his controlling shareholding in Holophane Ltd to a financial institution as security for a loan of £10,000. The Villain knew this. He also suspected, rightly, that should the loan be called Mygatt would be unable to pay up. His plan was to induce the lenders, on the grounds that he, the Villain, was more likely than Mygatt to make a success of the company, to call the loan, foreclose upon the controlling shares and vote Mygatt out of, and the Villain into, the chairman's seat.

There was a certain piquancy about the casting of this petty drama. The Villain, for example, was brother to a kind and hospitable elder friend, for whom I had great regard, as well as to my own godmother; he bore a name much honoured in the City; he had won the D.S.O. for gallantry in the Boer War; and his reluctance to pay his debts had been forgiven in consideration of his having once, when out hunting, swum an icy river in boots and breeches to rout out from an eyot, and drive back to hounds, a draggled and half-frozen fox. He had courage and vitality; lived, in his own words, by favour of "the great god Tick"; was amusing, plausible, dissipated, and untruthful. In the course of Act I, still trusted by Mygatt, he had introduced to the board two friends of his own upon whose subserviency he could count. One was a retired colonel, with a diminutive skull enclosing the brains but not the lively reflexes, of a sparrow. The other, a major, and the brother-in-law of one of my wife's aunts, was a sheep in wolf's clothing. He had a fine head, an eagle face, bushy eyebrows, and a determined chin. His manly, weathered countenance was furrowed with the lines, you would have said, of decision, endurance, and command. In fact, behind that warrior-mask he was timid, wavering, and subordinate. He had an unconscious habit of assuming, at board-meetings, an air of the utmost ferocity whenever the point at issue was, as so often, too much for him—unable to decide, he

glared and glowered about the table, menacing us all
with a furious, uncomprehending eye.

Both these men, the pin-headed Colonel and the
masked Major, looked up to the Villain, the man who
swam the river, as lower-boys look up to the Captain
of the Eleven. They were never his conscious acces-
sories in villainy because neither could ever have been
persuaded that their *Führer*, demonstrably *sans peur*,
could conceivably be other than *sans reproche*. They
voted solidly and dumbly for the black they saw as
white. On the other side of the table sat Lord Ernest
Hamilton, Mr Fred Haggard, and myself. Lord Ernest
was an easy-going, unruffled man of the world, a little
inclined, like Mr Baldwin, to look at his watch and
discover it was lunch-time when things got difficult, but
staunch in a real crisis. His friend Haggard was equally
staunch, but disliked rows.

The frequent board-meetings were held in a first-
floor room in Carteret Street, and I shall never forget the
extraordinary and novel discomforts of those sessions.
Three years at the Bar had brought me into daily
commerce with men who were as intelligent as they
were upright, and I was naively unprepared for the
stress of contending with falsity and, even more
wearily, with hebetude. There is some satisfaction to
be had from fencing with a quick-witted rascal, but
the dreary iterations of a blockhead, stubbornly re-
peating by rote a formula he misunderstands, are exasperating. I disliked the Villain, but I could have
murdered the Colonel, a man without guile. I am afraid,
since on one occasion I made the Colonel cry, that I
must have been rude to him.

The Villain, accustomed to making conquests, had

received me with open arms. He talked of his "old friend Albert Grey"—my father-in-law who had been on rare occasions exposed, without enjoying it, to the Villain's company. He seemed to assume that the sound of the Christian names of common acquaintances would lull me into slumbering on sentry-go, for he could have had no doubts about the reasons for my appearance at that board-table. But I had been too well primed to be susceptible to blandishment and he quickly sized me up as a Balliol prig on whom it was useless to waste any more civilities. The cold war between us was on from the evening of the first day.

The Villain had every reason to be satisfied with his strategical position. Popular, *répandu*, and plausible, he had no difficulty in persuading the financiers to whom Mygatt's shares had been pledged that their security would prove to be a poor one unless he, the Villain, was placed in a position to manage and nurse the young Holophane company. Mygatt, as he well knew, was unknown in London, all but friendless, and in debt. The loan was called at a month's notice, and Mygatt, who had spent his fortune in founding Holophane concerns in America and Paris, was in truth at his wits' end where to turn for money.

But Mygatt had one friend who believed in him, Mr Herbert Smith, the City solicitor. This big, brusque, rather formidable man had made up his decisive mind that Mygatt deserved help and that Holophane had a future. My own links with finance were limited to one man, Mr Robert Benson, my wife's uncle by marriage. To him I now told the story of Mygatt's predicament. By good fortune Uncle Robin had not only a kindness for my wife and myself, but implicit confidence in the

judgment of Mr Herbert Smith. A few days before the
loan was due the Merchants Trust lent Mygatt the ten
thousand pounds. A banker's cheque for that amount
went into Mygatt's pocket book, and, made casual by
relief, Mygatt went into the country and I to shoot at
Howick. Whether the Villain, whose espionage department was efficient, suspected that Mygatt might have
succeeded in raising the wind, I do not know. What
he did discover was that we were both in the depth of
the country. He immediately sent out notices sum-
moning a special board-meeting for the following
Monday, the day when the loan fell due. He sent these
to our London addresses, knowing that we should
receive them too late to be present at the meeting. But
he had reckoned without Mr Ife. Mr Ife was the
secretary of the company, a secretive, faithful, uncouth-
looking man internally warmed by a dog-like devotion
to Mygatt and a smouldering resentment against the
Villain. Mr Ife took steps to discover our country
addresses, and sent off telegrams warning us to be
present without fail at Monday's meeting. I travelled
through the night from Northumberland and joined
Mygatt at Almond's Hotel. Mygatt, who had intended
to visit the City that morning and repay his debt, had
already learned from Mr Ife the purpose of the meeting.
It was for the board to pass the transfers for Mygatt's
shares, held by the lenders, into the lenders' own names.
We drove to Carteret Street in a taxi-cab. We were a
little late. As we went up the stairs Mygatt, who had a
sense of drama, took the banker's cheque from his
pocket. The Villain sat at the head of the table, in Mygatt's chair, signing and blotting share-certificates. At
his right hand sat a stranger, the representative of the

institution that had made the loan to Mygatt. Mygatt
waved the cheque and handed it to this rather surprised
person. And the Villain, knowing his little game was up,
scowled. He did not hiss "foiled again," with that knack
of hissing non-sibilants known only to villains, but his
empurpled cheeks took on a yet deeper hue, and his fat
low forehead contracted hideously over his bloodshot
eyes. I can see that scowl to this day. I am sure that the
gallery would have hissed. To me it was a most enjoyable moment, and although I tried to look prim I have
no doubt that I looked smug.

I did not enjoy the second round, which went to
the Villain. A rival firm had produced some prismatic glassware in imitation of Holophane and, when
threatened with an action, delivered the stuff to us to
be broken up. But the Villain, still managing-director,
thought it a pity to destroy glass which, from its
appearance, could well be passed off as Holophane.
He had the moulder's name ground off, and disposed
of the reflectors as genuine Holophane to our customers.
Mr Ife again, with "faith unfaithful," betrayed him to
Mygatt. There was a stormy board-meeting at which
the Villain was arraigned. Even his henchmen were
puzzled; the Major's ferocity, as he stared upon us all
in turn, was almost unnerving; but they remembered
the swim after the fox, and voted in vain against the
Villain's dismissal. For the Villain, not unreasonably, was
sacked then and there. He at once brought an action for
wrongful dismissal against Mygatt and the company.
It was tried before Mr Justice Bailhache and a jury. The
Villain's leading counsel was Mr Campbell, K.C., an
Irishman with a brogue. He opened his case as follows:
"The plaintiff in this case is Colonel Villain, a gallant

officer who won the Distinguished Service Order in South Africa. The defendant is a man called Moygut— I don't know of what nationality he is." The jury were a red-faced bunch of patriots; you could almost see them making up their minds about this Moygut who did not even have a country. Mygatt was not a good witness. Instead of explaining briefly that the bogus Holophane glass lacked the power of reflecting and diffusing light possessed by the genuine Holophane, he confused the jury with diagrams and long technical explanations of his cherished invention. The jury was bored with him. Mr Justice Bailhache wore a beard, a fatal bar to that judicial air which keeps juries on their toes. He also appeared to be bored. At any rate he left it all to the jury and said nothing in his summing-up to direct their minds to the very simple issue of honesty. The jury found for the Villain, who was awarded £400 and his costs. It was my turn to scowl. I hope I did not.

The Villain got his half-year's salary, but we were henceforth free of him, and although the Colonel and the Major continued, out of loyalty to a lost leader, to vote silently against all Mygatt's measures, they became harmless nuisances whose presence I, for one, would have missed. For neither of them understood balance-sheets, or words like "debit," "credit," "discount," or "c.i.f.," and I am afraid I amused myself at board-meetings by trying to discover what terms of trade or accountancy would most quickly transform the Major's features from serene strength to Achillean wrath. (The Colonel, I must admit, was poor game; his small tortoise-face had but one expression for all occasions, a look of puzzled aggrievement.) As for the Villain, he made one last attempt to get back on me for my support of

Mygatt. Two years later he heard, I know not how, that I had entered the employment of Helbert Wagg and Company, the investment bankers. The Villain went to call upon the partners, to warn them that they were taking a snake into their bosom. They replied that such a warning, coming from him, must be rated as a commendation. He had shot his bolt. The last time I saw him was many years later. He hailed me from the window of a taxi-cab in Threadneedle Street to ask if I would like a lift to the West End. The poor Villain was near his end through drink; I knew that it was the taxi-fare, not my company, that he was after; but I jumped in. He was affable and amusing, and after he had fumbled and I had paid in Pall Mall, we parted warmly and for ever. For all his black heart he is remembered by the few survivors of his rapscallion prime as "poor old V.! a jolly good sport." And if to be a sport is to live for years on "tick" in one county, go smilingly bankrupt, and begin the game again in another, then a sport he was. But I suppose them rather to be thinking of the fox, and the half-frozen river, and the top-boots and breeches in which so few of us would care, frost or thaw, to swim.

I had learnt, during a matter of months, in that troubled board-room where the gas-fire made the air as much over-heated as our tempers, many things for which I had been unprepared. I had learnt that stupidity is more intractable than malice. I had learnt, with feelings something like despair, how hard to bear is other people's tolerance of one's own enemy. I had learnt the uselessness of high words across the green baize. What I had not learnt was enough about the business of selling Holophane glassware to fit me for the post of managing director. For Mygatt, who had so unwisely placed the Villain in that post, now made the mistake of appointing me as his successor.

I had a small, loyal, and expert staff, with morning smiles for the representative of the cleaner, sweeter régime now in force. They were departmental experts, perfectly fitted to handle what custom there was, but in no position to increase it. I on my side, feeling that before I could direct I must understand, even to details, the work of the departments, lost many bright days as apprentice to skills I did not need. I visited the glass-factory at Gateshead, to watch a special sand from Belgium run molten into the moulds. I tried to grasp the laws of the reflection, diffusion, and refraction of light in the laboratory, and the break-down of overhead expenses in the costing department. But I could never have hoped, in so short a time, to achieve the *expertise* of the cheerful young men who wasted theirs in teaching me. What the company needed was a manager who knew how to sell things. Our product was good, but it was unknown; there were firms willing to handle it, but they had to be found, cajoled, persuaded, with all that curious, embarrassing, "have-a-drink-old-man" technique, in luncheon-rooms and bars, where half the time the talk is racy and irrelevant, but the range of permissible discount on each item in a varied catalogue must be carried in the seller's head, ready for quotation on sudden demand. I did not know the firms that dealt in such wares as ours, nor the streets, all east of Temple Bar, where their offices stood; I did not know the language of the buyers. The oblique yet personal manner required for approaching "our Mr Lysinski" was beyond my powers. And whereas the Villain had begun to build up a West End clientele by persuading his acquaintances and clubs to install Holophane, I was handicapped by my private opinion that our bowls and reflectors, having no aesthetic appeal, were fit only for offices and factories. If a customer said, "But I don't like the look of them," I could only reply, "No more do I." And that is not salesmanship.

I have written elsewhere that an honours degree in Greats should equip a man to earn his living in most professions. But I should have excepted the business of selling. The very habit of clear thinking, of careful appraisal, so serviceable in most walks of life, can be fatal to a salesman. He needs rather the religious temperament, capable of faith without scrutiny. Scepticism is fatal to him.

A man, provided he is efficient, need not like his job in order to be happy in it. But to do a thing badly is a wretched business, and I soon told Mygatt that I must look for another occupation. Through lucky chance, and a kind godfather, I was recommended to Helbert Wagg and Company, and for the next thirty years, except when we were at war, I was fortunate enough to earn my living in a calling for which I had indeed no natural gifts, but which blessed me with the best of good companions. I had no more language difficulties, and personal affections more than reconciled me to a path that ran well outside the boundaries of my private, interior world. And that, I dare say, is more than can be said about most breadwinning.

On reflection I must admit that, during my eighteen months in trade, it was the few spent in conflict rather than the greater number occupied by routine that I found the more exhilarating. I thought at the time that

the elimination of the Villain would bring ease and
relief, but in fact I missed him a good deal. There is a
fine simplicity, full of zest and savour, about fighting
in a good cause; it was a pleasure to return each evening
to our diminutive flat in Knightsbridge and retail, to
sympathetic and partisan ears, the varying fortunes of
the day. Victory, as we have since seen in two great
wars, can leave the victor rather at a loss. (The Devil,
in whatever guise, has been a great resource to mankind
and it is probably just as well that we are in no danger
of losing him.) I, at any rate, on looking back, am
convinced that for a spell of living intensely and at
speed, with all the joys of cut and thrust, I ought to
be much obliged to the Villain. For he alone, wily,
resilient and malicious, has turned, in my retrospective
eye, the hard white glare shed by Holophane reflectors
to a rosy and romantic glow.

CHAPTER II

BOOTS AND BREECHES

IN the third year of the first World War, I filled, for six months or so, the post of Chief Instructor at the Cavalry Machine-gun School at Maresfield in Sussex. I had a desk in the office of the commandant of the school, a "dug-out" from the regular cavalry, known as Lorenzo. Every Monday a fresh batch of officers would arrive to begin a month's course of training. These officers were of all ages and ranks, from major downwards, and many of them had seen active service in France or Palestine. Machine-gunning was not very popular with cavalry or yeomanry officers in those days; men who had joined the cavalry from love of riding and horses, and who saw themselves, on the day when the infantry were to break the enemy's line at last, charging through "the Gap" with sword or lance, cutting and slashing and sticking the flying Germans, had little inclination towards a weapon which could in no circumstances be fired from the back of a galloping horse. So that the task of the school was not merely to give instruction in the tactical handling of machine-guns; it included the weaning of reluctant officers from an outdated to a more modern and realistic view of how best to destroy the enemy, and the building up of an *esprit de corps* among machine-gunners, a pride in their shared mastery of a formidable weapon of war.

For the Machine-gun Corps had by then been formed; the regimental machine-gun sections were already grouped in squadrons under brigade command, and commanding officers who, in the beginning, had attempted to palm off their worst men and N.C.O.s upon the machine-gun squadrons were no longer tolerated by the Higher Command. Our job at the school was clearly to overcome prejudices and to persuade those who passed through our hands that the M.G.C. could be, and must be, a *corps d'élite*.

It was a pity, therefore, that the commandant of the school should be an old-fashioned cavalryman who disliked and despised machine-guns. Not that he disclosed this—he was too loyal for that—to the new arrivals who on Monday mornings were paraded before his office-desk, in groups of six or seven, by the adjutant. But Lorenzo's idea of how to welcome and reassure these rather disconsolate young men, and to discharge his duty towards them as well as to the school he commanded, was to make to them the following short, unvarying speech:

Well, gentlemen, this is a cavalry school, you know. In the cavalry we judge an officer by his boots and his breeches. What else could we judge him by? On Wednesday a first-class tailor and bootmaker from London will visit this camp, and you will all be measured for new boots and breeches. Good morning, gentlemen.

I wish it were possible, by some system of notation, to reproduce the very tones, the stresses, in which Lorenzo delivered this allocution, because only by hearing it, as I did week after week, could you realise the strength and simplicity of his own convictions. When he came to "What else could we judge him by?" the confidence, the certainty in his voice was absolute. He knew that there could not be in his hearers' minds, in anybody's mind, however wild or adventurous their speculative ranges, the remotest possibility of conceiving some criterion by which to judge an officer other than his boots and his breeches. Lorenzo had to be heard to be believed.

The rebellion that seethed in the breasts of the new-comers after this welcome had to be quickly put to sleep by my own irregular hints to them to take no notice, and by the adjutant's skill in delaying, in-definitely, the arrival of the tailor and the bootmaker. But my loyalty to my superior officer was even more sorely tried when he appeared in the lecture-room where I was summing up, chalk in hand, the lessons of that day's tactical field-exercise. My class stood to attention with a clatter that echoed in the wooden hut while Lorenzo, in impeccable boots and breeches, strode from the door and mounted the dais. He had some criticisms to make of the way the exercise had been carried out. He had noticed that the first rule in the selection of machine-gun positions for defence had been universally neglected. Although the line to be defended had in-cluded a number of bare hill-tops, no gun had been sited on these commanding spots. He had himself ridden to each in turn. Where the guns could have been hidden, God knew; not a single gun had he been able to discover. Now it stood to reason, didn't it? If there was a hill-top that was the place for your gun. "Don't let me see this happen again. Carry on, Major Jones." Lorenzo strode out, leaving me the delicate task, since in the army the higher in rank is always right, of reconciling my interrupted thesis that bare hill-tops are suicidal with the C.O.'s contrary dogma, expressed as an order. I could only point out that in war the best, owing to the resources of modern artillery, is sometimes the enemy of the good, and that we would now continue our study of the second-best method, that of concealing the guns from the enemy as we had, that afternoon, concealed them from the Colonel.

I was a temporary soldier, and under no compulsion to weigh my career against my convictions about the proper handling of machine-guns, but that I was taking a risk I knew from an episode in the past. A year or so earlier, the 9th Cavalry Brigade had carried out a tactical exercise behind the lines near Wormhout, in Flanders. At the ensuing "pow-wow" our red-headed Brigadier, Bob Greenly, a fire-eating student of war, was in the middle of a brilliant and incisive criticism of the day's work, when the divisional general rode up. Cis Bingham was a great gentleman, the most courteous and considerate of commanders, and enormously liked and respected. (His boots and his breeches were an example to us all.) But nobody could have called him a student of war. In his gentle, unofficial manner he said he would like to say a few words about the exercise. I have no recollection of what points he made, except that his views ran counter, in every respect, to those of Bob Greenly. When he had finished and ridden away Greenly said: "Well, gentlemen, you have heard General Bingham's views: naturally I have nothing to add." We were dismissed. I have often wondered what Greenly might have done had he not known, as he must have known, that no officer present could conceivably have accepted the general's rather woolly recollections of the Boer War as against his own

informed, up-to-date doctrines. Might he have winked?
I doubt it.

Greenly himself could, on occasions, be arbitrary to
the point of being irrational. My very first encounter
with the regular cavalry illustrates this. A few days
after my yeomanry's arrival in Flanders to complete,
with the 19th and 15th Hussars, the 9th Cavalry Brigade,
the whole brigade paraded together for inspection by
the brigadier. On the previous day my machine-gun
section had been issued (in the army's strange jargon)
with some new and bulky equipment, together with
some roneo-ed diagrams showing how the stuff was to
be packed in our narrow limbers. But the diagram
showed four limbers, and my section had only three.
By no means had we been able to make room for the
extra load ordered, and we went on parade without it.
Greenly rode up to my section, looked at the men and
horses, and ordered me to uncover the limbers.

"Didn't you get my orders about how to pack these
limbers?"

"Yes, sir, but we have only got three, not four.
There's no room——"

He cut me short. "Don't argue. Your business is not
to argue but to obey orders. Fall in behind and come
and see how the 19th Hussars have done it."

I rode behind him, inwardly boiling, to the next
section. The 19th Hussars had been his own regiment
and were the apple of his eye.

"Good morning, Reggie. 'Morning, Sergeant Hall.
Limbers packed all right?"

"Yes, sir." Jerry Hall's blue eyes were all candour
and innocence above his red moustache.

"All according to the plan?"

"Yes, sir."

"Good." Greenly turned to me. "Ask Settle to show you how it's done. And another time, don't answer me back!"

He rode away.

Reggie Settle, later to become my own squadron-leader and very dear friend, was a smart young officer indeed. But when I asked him to remove the tarpaulin and let me see how his limbers were packed, he only winked.

"We haven't got the stuff. It won't go in, not even into four limbers."

"You mean the sergeant just lied?"

"He had to. But we don't call it lying. We call it eyewash."

"But supposing the General had asked you to take the covers off?"

"He never would. He trusts us, you see."

I had not made a good start. Fortunately for me, my men restored me to Bob's favour. For, a few days later, the machine-gunners from the three regiments met in a gravel-pit for firing practice. Greenly rode up to watch us, and after a bit pulled out a stop-watch and said: "I'm offering a hundred francs to the team that can go into action in the quickest time." He then turned to me, quite kindly. "I think your yeomen would rather not compete, Jones. It would be a little hard on them, against these regulars. I don't want them to be discouraged. Let them watch, and see how it's done. These fellows are good, you know."

I knew what my men could do, however, and persuaded him to let them try.

"Very well. It's your funeral. Carry on."

My gunners, Slatter and Shelton and Mackenzie (who
was an old Harrovian), were all engineering-pupils at
Allen's works in Bedford; men of a different breed
from the private soldiers in the cavalry, physically and
mentally more alert, and all destined to get commissions. They won the competition hands-down, as I knew
they would.

The general did look a little rueful as he handed
over the prize; but he liked efficiency, gave some
generous praise to the men, and was nice to me ever
after.

There was a very dashing colonel in our Division
who shared Lorenzo's contempt for machine-guns,
although Lorenzo would not have approved of the
canary-coloured waistcoat which peeped out of the top
of this colonel's tunic; or of his rather long back-hair,
or of the four Sealyham terriers that continued to
flicker round his horse's legs long after the Higher
Command had forbidden officers to keep dogs. The
colonel was ordered, with other officers of all ranks
including myself, to attend a day-long demonstration
at a machine-gun school behind the lines. He watched
the deadly effect of fire from these weapons upon every
kind of moving target; he was shown the ease with
which they could be camouflaged and concealed, the
rapidity with which they could be moved from point
to point, the prolonged and continuous bursts of which
they were capable. At the end of the day the commandant of the school, after summing up the lessons
to be learnt from the demonstration, asked the senior
officers present to comment on what they had seen. The
colonel, whose boots and breeches would have been
outstanding in any company, spoke up. "All I have to

say is, I should like to see the machine gun that could stop a —th Hussar!"

It sounded very gallant. But the day was to come when the colonel, with his adjutant and two of his headquarters staff, would be killed instantly when attempting, on horseback, to charge a German machine-gun. His wish had been granted in full measure; he had seen a machine-gun that could stop not one, but four —th Hussars.

Another pair of elegant boots, of faultless breeches, belonged to a major in our brigade. This consummate horse-master, who knew not only the appearance, but the temperament, of every horse in his regiment, was second-in-command, and as such was sent ahead, in our many shifts of quarters, to discover and commandeer suitable billets for men and horses. It fell to me to do the same for the machine-gun squadron, and I grew accustomed, as I jogged along the tree-lined roads of Picardy with my Q.M.S., to the sight of the major's tall figure dismounted at a crossroads and bending over a map-case that he was turning this way and that.

"Hi, Jones, you can read a map; just show me where I am." He had never learnt how to set a map, this field-officer who, had his colonel become a casualty, would have been the responsible shepherd of six hundred trustful men and helpless horses. Nor had he any wish to learn. He could always ask somebody, as he now asked me. Horses couldn't read maps, and just look at the gloss on their coats! Lovely. A little linseed, but not too much, was the secret.

All the same, I was a little taken aback one day on arriving at a small, dusty school of red and white bricks, where I was to serve as junior member of a

court-martial. The major was president of the court,
which had been convened to try a Hussar for stealing a
fellow-soldier's cap. I dismounted and entered the tiny
school-room, smelling of ink and French boy, to find
the major thumbing through a sheaf of blue foolscap
papers.

"'Morning, Jones. You're the youngest, you have to
give your views first, you know. What shall we give
the fellow?"

"Hadn't we better first find out whether he did it,
sir?"

"If he hadn't done it, he wouldn't be here, would
he?"

"I think we must hear the evidence, sir."

"Oh, very well. As we're here. Bring him in,
Sergeant-major."

The "theft" turned out to have been a case of the
prisoner, during a route-march, and while marching at
ease, clinching an argument with his other half-section
by snatching the cap from his head and throwing it
over a garden wall. Even the major felt that this was
hardly "theft" and the charge was reduced to one of
destroying government property.

They were friendly, companionable men, these
regular officers who must invariably take precedence of
a yeoman of equal seniority. But it is hard to think of
them as warriors. They regarded the war not as their
very *raison d'être*, but as a tiresome interruption to their
chosen profession. Their thoughts and their talk still ran
upon hunting and polo; they walked and rode about
incessantly twirling short, loaded sticks to strengthen
their wrists; they made no pretence of any thirst for
fighting, gaily as they went to it when their turn came.

With rare and notable exceptions—such as Bob Greenly and Reggie Settle—they made no study of the skills, the adaptations, the ruses demanded by the novel predicaments and stresses of this new type of warfare. They were devoted to their men and horses, and looked after them; they were cheerful in discomfort and un-impressed by danger; but it was difficult to believe that these high-spirited young men, whose conversation consisted mainly of catchwords from Harry Tate's comic turn with his too perspicacious young son and a motor-car, were the trained, the selected, the professional guardians of their country.

It was, for me, a rather disconcerting change of climate when the brigade machine-gun squadron was formed, and I exchanged the stimulating talk of my yeomanry's colonel, Sidney Peel, that wise, great-hearted man, and the impish humour of our adjutant, Jock Crabbe, a Scots Grey of the Greenly-Settle school of fighting men, for the tags and commonplaces of the regular subalterns in our squadron mess. For as machine-gun officer I had lived with the regimental headquarters in the kitchen of a farmhouse at Wormhout, and shared Sidney Peel's delight in the conversation of our veterinary officer, a faithful, grizzled man who never let us down.

"I'm going over to see an old friend with the gunners this afternoon, Colonel. He *will* be surprised to see me! (A pause.) At least, he won't be so very surprised, because I met him yesterday and told him I was coming."

Sidney Peel's own boots and breeches, designed only for baggy comfort, were little short of a disgrace, and although his strong, lean brown countenance, with clipped moustache, was soldierly enough, his spectacles and thoughtful brow gave him a scholarly rather than a cavalry look. Indeed, on our first arrival in Flanders, the brigadier and his staff were inclined to think that they would have to teach his trade to this quiet, intellectual soldier-civilian. They little knew their man. Sidney had served as a private soldier in the Boer War, and on one occasion there had disciplined his own general. It happened like this. Sidney had been posted at a barrier with orders to allow nobody to pass without a written order from the Town Major. The Corps Commander and his staff came along, on a tour of inspection, and made as if to ride past without halting. Sidney barred the way, and asked to see the General's pass.

"Nonsense, my man. I'm your Corps Commander."

"I must see your pass, sir. Those are my orders."

"I tell you I am the Corps Commander. I need no pass in my own command. Now, stand aside there!"

Sidney aimed his rifle at the General's head.

"If you move forward I shall sh-shoot you, sir."

The General was helpless. One of the guard had to be despatched to the Town Major while the General and his staff waited, fuming, for the pass. To the General's credit, by the time the pass arrived he had recovered his temper and remembered the rules of the game. He congratulated the good sentry.

The little hesitation in Sidney's speech—it did not amount to a stammer—always seemed to occur before the operative word, as in "sh-shoot," and gave a distinctive flavour to his downright, pointed talk. In a very short time indeed the Higher Command learnt to

handle this unusual yeomanry colonel with circumspection, for his irony, if a staff-fuss over unessentials
was being made, could be withering, and they had no
answer to his respectful requests for guidance, so framed
as to expose the futility of many an order. It is only
fair to the regular cavalry to add that Jock Crabbe, the
adjutant, aided and abetted his colonel with gusto, and
had upon his desk, as a constant aid to efficiency, a card
inscribed: "Take not the slightest notice." For with a
Collinger-Buggins (as Sidney nick-named a certain staff
officer) daily harassing our regimental headquarters
with orders which were more often than not counter-
manded, training for war, which Sidney persisted in
regarding as his sole business, could hardly have been
carried on had notice been taken of them.

But if the generals became wary of him, the officers
of our two brigaded Hussar regiments took our colonel
to their hearts. It was interesting to see how the wisdom
and humanity of a salty man of the world, humorously
outspoken, appealed to these kindly but uncultured
young men. It was as if something starved within them
found nourishment in his experience and lucidity of
mind. They sought his advice, given with the authority
of character and conviction, from a background more
varied, both socially and intellectually, than any they
had known.

And it was not only from Sidney Peel that I was
parted when the machine-gun squadron was formed.
My brother-officers in the yeomanry, men like Alan
Lascelles, John Gore, Conrad Russell, Cuthbert Head-
lam, were all men of the world, literate and articulate,
each with his own brand of intelligence and, above all,
wit. They were people with whom it was fun to live,

who shared in a common pool of civilian memories, full of humour and speculation, keen, reluctant soldiers, knowing full well the values for which we had come out to fight, and the compulsion laid upon us to defend them. So it was small wonder if, on first joining the machine-gun squadron, I felt strange and isolated. I was many years older than my brother-subalterns, who sat round the linoleum-covered table in our temporary billets with nothing to exchange but the insignificant facts of the horse-lines or of polo long ago. But we did drink port after dinner, and I fell into the mistake, as I see it now, of talking to them as if they had been my late companions of the yeomanry, to the extent even of using irony or mockery, or worse still, occasional fantasy. It is only fair to say that Reggie Settle, our squadron-leader, was there to egg me on; but all the same it was unimaginative on my part not to detect sooner how detestable the subalterns felt this sort of talk to be. I discovered later that any form of irony was either unperceived by them and regarded as un-truth or condemned as "sarcasm." As for fantasy or mockery, the speaker was just "mad." I should have done far better to have lain low and entered into their own concerns, until friendship and liking were fully established, as in the end they were. For when Reggie Settle went on leave, and persuaded the brigade, with immense difficulty, to allow me, on the score of age and longer service, to act as squadron commander for a week, the subalterns took their revenge upon me in a highly disconcerting manner. They had been outraged, as regulars, at being placed under command of a yeoman; and they decided to show their feelings by doing much what trade unionists do when they "work to rule." They saluted and stood to attention whenever I spoke to them; they never went beyond "Yes, sir" and "No, sir"; they were completely silent in mess, and if I addressed a remark to them, would say no more than "As you say, sir." Their insolence was consummate, yet never a handle for official complaint did they give.

The result was wholly satisfactory. Reggie Settle, on his return, gave them such a wigging as left them generally ashamed, and I, for my part, felt I had much misjudged my juniors, since their conspiracy and its execution showed both a sense of humour and real histrionic ability. I had not thought they had it in them. Moreover, at the moment of the resulting *détente* we were ordered into the trenches for the first time as a squadron. Nothing establishes good-will and mutual confidence so well as responsibilities shared in danger; and the night of the Kaiser's birthday when the trenches at Vermelles known as "Big Willie" and "Little Willie" were severely pounded, completed the reconciliation. There were incidents and sights, that night, to shock us all into revaluations. We came out of the trenches as firm friends.

Reggie Settle himself I can only compare, as a natural warrior, with Julian Grenfell. He loved fighting for its own sake. (There was an occasion when he sneaked off to a flank where a small raid was going on, deserting his post with his own machine-guns, to spend a couple of hours in a forward sap hurling Mills grenades. He returned like a dog that has been hunting, guilty but wagging his tail. He should have been court-martialled; as it was, the infantry with whom he had joined in the fun recommended him for the Military

3

Cross, and it was given to him.) But a much rarer quality than pugnacity in this young soldier was his aptitude for command. He cannot have been more than twenty-three or twenty-four when I first served under him, but his handling of officers, N.C.O.s, and men, in all circumstances, was beyond criticism. He had, with easy, even jovial, manners, a natural dignity and authority that would have sat well upon a corps commander. There was *panache*, when he came on to parade, in the wearing of his cap, the management of his cane, the squaring of his shoulders, but no hint of swagger; his bodily motions were but the natural expression of innate assurance. He was as thorough as a Strafford, but his work, though incessant, was done with gaiety. He could bandy music-hall catchwords and hunting noises with his brother-officers of the 19th Hussars as if he shared their detached attitude to war; but I, as his second-in-command and confidant, knew the ardour and the restless activity of his pursuit of professional skill. It was Reggie's visits to Gunners and his study of range-tables and trajectories that led him to borrow a clinometer, clamp a Vickers gun on to some old railway sleepers, and shoot a machine-gun for the first time over the heads of our own infantry on to enemy communications, the gun being directed upon the chosen target by map and compass alone. There was much despondency and alarm in the front-line trenches, and a furious order to desist. But Reggie's patient demonstrations to colonels and brigadiers ended in permission being given, and the practice spread rapidly along the front, until "Indirect Fire" became a leading subject to be taught at the central Machine-gun School at Grantham.

Reggie Settle had strong, straight features, red hair inclined to curl a little, a clipped red moustache, an amused mouth. He lacked nothing that went to the making of a cavalry officer in those days; his boots and breeches were perfect; his belief in the worshipful nature of horses absolute; his hands light; his occupation on home-leave hunting, on Paris-leave a girl. Yet this gay, efficient, practical soldier, unprofessionally blood-thirsty, with unlimited ambition, liked nothing better, in the long war nights of waiting, than to question and cross-question me about philosophies, about thought, about the human predicament. He had a touching belief in the mental and moral equipment to be had from universities and from contacts with good minds: was I not a friend of Colonel Peel? Well, then. He pressed me about religion—did we have, or did we make, our souls? he would ask. His own education had been too fragmentary to enable him to detect the in-adequacy of my tentative responses; and the warmth of his enthusiastic affection blurred, for us both, the amateurishness of our discussions. He had, too, a delicacy of sympathy which could be comforting; he was the only bachelor brother-officer who ever hinted that he knew I must carry into battle the vision, not of simple death, but of a telegram on the hall-table of my London home and the breaking of a heart. He did not expect me to play truant, or to go bombing up saps in another sector of the line.

Reggie later won the D.S.O., became a colonel at twenty-six, and was killed in the great retreat of March 1918. His body was never found. Had he lived, he would have ranked, I can hardly doubt, among the Alexanders and Montgomerys in the second World War. For he

was a natural leader with the application and the
ambition to become a master of his trade; his questing,
expanding mind was large with generosities and sympathy. He seemed all set to become that kind of human
being to which great commanders, with exceptions,
belong.

When at long last, and in the infantry (to which I got
transferred only by unblushing wire-pulling at the
War Office), I had my own small command, I had
only to model myself upon Reggie Settle for success.
How would Reggie have spoken to a group of dumb,
demoralised men? How would Reggie have handled
newly-commissioned officers, socially diffident and
unconscious of their own basic capacities and fortitude? Would Reggie have approved this scheme as
"thorough"? If I made a good job of my command,
to Reggie must go the credit. His unresting, ardent
spirit, professional and precise, was in very truth commanding my machine-gunners through me.

In case it should be thought that in describing some
senior cavalry officers of the "boots and breeches"
school, and the rather unwarlike preoccupations of their
juniors, I have been reflecting on the regular army as a
whole in the first World War, it is only fair that I
should pay tribute to the infantry as I found it in the
last year of that war.

In January 1918 I was appointed to take over the
divisional machine-gun company of the 19th Division, then commanded by General "Ma" (now Lord)
Jeffreys. My Company took its orders directly from
divisional headquarters, and in this way I had the good
fortune to make personal contact with that distinguished
Guards officer. I shall never forget the warmth and

consideration of his personal welcome to me, and the atmosphere of his headquarters. There was an air of informality and ease which only a tradition of un-questioned discipline can afford. Moreover, every staff-officer, whether on the operations or Q. side, seemed to regard himself as the servant of the troops. My new command had been disorganised and neglected, and my first week was largely taken up in demanding equipment from the various supply departments. The sympathy, the helpfulness, and the speed with which my every demand was met were a real eye-opener. After the snubs, refusals, delays, and red tape of Collinger-Buggins and his colleagues, this human, swift, efficient response was astonishing to me. As a result the 19th Division was a fighting machine to which we were all proud to belong, and I look back to my brief service directly under its outstanding commander, or later under that fire-eating, single-minded warrior, Colonel Peter Winser, as the most exhilarating spell of living at full stretch in the course of my life. For being, like almost everybody else, a pacifist, I found a profound satisfaction, after the frustrations of the cavalry, in having all my energies liberated for playing a part, however exiguous, in the destruction of the disturbers of peace. There has always been to me something surprising in the claim to be "pacifists" made by men who refuse to lift a finger in defence of the peace they profess to cherish. To hate "war" in the abstract, but to take no part in resisting the makers of war, seems to be the height of absurdity.

The little group of writers and war poets who, during and after the first World War, wrote with such intensity of compassion for war's victims, must have shared this feeling, for most of them fought, and some,

like Wilfred Owen, lost their lives. So it is unfortunate
that they claimed, or have had claimed on their behalf,
the name of "pacifist," with its false connotation, not
of a lover of peace, but of one who will not lift a hand
to protect his love. Yet they can hardly complain if,
for all that they played the man, they are accused of
muddle-headedness. Of the profundity of their pity, of
the outrage suffered by their poet's heightened sensibilities, there can be no question. But they did allow
their *saeva indignatio* to fall upon the thing, the mindless
phenomenon called "War," rather than upon the
aggressors. They cursed the thunderbolt, not Jove. And
at times their very compassion appears to be shot
through with a strand of special pity for themselves as
artists. Readers, indeed, of Sir Osbert Sitwell's fine and
sensitive autobiography must be left with an uneasy
feeling that had the Kaiser or Hitler offered to protect
and cherish artists, writers, and poets in return for this
country's submission, he and they might have been
tempted to accept such terms. But could Sir Osbert
himself, whose broad humanity pervades his every page,
have written a single line of value with Henry Moat,
with Mark Kirkby, in chains? We know that he could
not. Great art has always been rooted in the primary
emotions, the shared and communicable sensibilities of
us all, and cannot flourish on a desert island washed, but
not watered, by the philistine seas. The artist creates,
reveals, and discriminates, pointing the way to the rest
of us, but he cannot live to himself. Like the rose tree,
to flourish he must be mulched with what may seem to
him to be the dirt under his feet.

It was, then, because they were true pacifists that so
many who fought in either Great War have been able

to look back upon their war service with satisfaction, not guilt. They did not contemplate the detestable sights of war, too well known for me to revive yet again, with cold, dispassionate eyes. Though not poets, they still could pity. But they did experience, for all the stark and tragic beastliness of war, a sense of living above their own level, and of straining, fit and hard as race-horses, to excel themselves, for once, in their allotted skills. For my own part, I certainly felt, in the infantry, this sense of exhilaration; but had I gone to the front as a lover of war, not peace, I should have been in no time shocked and appalled out of so unnatural an affection.

CHAPTER III

KRIEGSGEFANGENER

THE Spanish Ambassador to the German Empire in the summer of 1918 was a slim, elegant figure who took off his panama hat and made a most courtier-like bow to me as he entered the wooden prison-hut. My return bow to him, although low, was a clumsy one, because I was sitting, naked except for a very short zephyr-vest, on a peculiar throne which only those who have suffered from dysentery in a German lazaretto will recognise. It is not a perch from which bowing to an Ambassador is often expected; a fact which the Ambassador, with the rapid intuition of a trained diplomat, was quick to perceive, and his swerve away to the opposite bed, in the middle of his greeting to myself, was very sudden indeed.

It is to be supposed that the Pomeranians can be homesick for Pomerania, but to others those sandy and repellent plains have no appeal. I had thought, during the six weeks I spent in the constant twilight of a tall Gothic church at Anniches, six weeks during which March had become May with no faintest signal of spring given to us in these cold aisles, that any move at all, if only it brought a window and the sight of the sky, would be an inestimable blessing. I had lived, it is true, even in that sun-forsaken place, several days of joyful expectation, like a child before his birthday. For the one kind German nurse had promised to bring me young green leaves, or buds, to stand by my bed; it was a *wunderschöne* spring outside, she said, and I should have my share in it; and although, day by day, she forgot her promise, I trusted her and went on hoping, knowing that it could not be a twig of whitebeam, but secretly counting upon a chestnut spray, with the leaves not quite uncurled. At last my daily reminders took effect, and she brought me, stuck into a medicine-bottle, a sprig of privet. Grown men must not cry, but I was weakened by wounds and it was a very near thing. But when at last I was carried out into the sunshine, and placed in a most comfortable hospital-train that trundled along for three days and nights through Germany, often halting near bursting thickets loud with the descending semitones of willow-wrens, my hopes rose high. But at length green woods became scarcer and smaller, the country flat and featureless, with desolate wastes of sand; we were in Pomerania. At Stargard we were laid in rows upon the platform; I still had no clothing but a short vest (my blood-stained uniform, shirt, and underclothes had been cut off me with shears by the surgeon) and I felt humiliated by naked exposure to the sky. A brewer's dray was brought alongside, and its floor covered by wounded men, tightly packed. Then it was our turn. We were lifted and laid on the top of the first layer, upon their faces, upon their broken limbs. A whip cracked and the great dray-horses started off across the cobble-stones; the dray had no springs, and a most heartrending yell of pain went up from the men beneath us. We, the top layer, were the cause of their agony, but we were helpless, as we bounced and rocked above them. Mercifully the cobbled road changed, after a few hundred yards, into a sandy track, and the yells subsided into moans, to which we were by now accustomed, as people who live by the sea are accustomed to the continuous complaining of the waves. The track led away from the town into a vast assemblage of hutments surrounded by barbed-wire. It was a lazaretto, a prison-hospital for several thousands of "other ranks" of many nationalities, British, French, Serbians, Russians, and Italians. There were fifteen British and two or three Russian officers. Between the huts grew potatoes. Beyond the wire, except for a few birch-trees and the severe, rectangular town on one side, a dreary flatness stretched to the horizon.

There had been two occasions, not many weeks before our arrival at Stargard, when I had every reason to believe that my end had come. The first had been when I "came to" from a total "blackout" caused, I imagine, by loss of blood, almost immediately after I had been shot in two places. (Incidentally, being hit by a rifle-bullet is not at all as one would imagine—there is no sting or sharpness, but the sensation of being clubbed by an enormous sledge-hammer.) I had a certainty that I was done for, but was filled for a few moments with a sense of ineffable happiness and exhilaration. As soon as this faded, I lost the expectation of death and was resolved, if possible, to live.

The second occasion was in the middle of the following night. I still lay where I had fallen. In spite of the hard frost, I had been semi-delirious from thirst, seeing endless processions of butlers carrying trays of cool drinks, who came within a yard of me and then swerved away. But in an interval of clear-headedness a torch flashed, and I saw two German officers, in long grey greatcoats, stooping over me. They exchanged a few words; then one drew a small revolver from his holster and said to me "*Machen die Augen zu.*" I managed to raise my head and to say "*Nein, nein!*" in quite a strong voice. Whereupon he spoke to his friend and replaced his revolver in its holster. That, again, was just a momentary fright, too brief to rank as a case of looking death in the eye with full comprehension.

But now, in the noisome hut to which we were first carried, I had a feeling, for the first and last time in my life, of something like despair. For we had been laid, or rather thrown, into wooden bunks, to lie, half-naked, upon coarse blankets stiff and stinking with dried excrement. There were no orderlies, and all down the line wounded men were crying out for bottles or pans, and succumbing, with shame and disgust, to the necessity of doing without these luxuries. I had been taught to believe that open wounds must, above all, be kept clean, and saw no escape for any of us from gangrene and death. And when after an hour or two there was wheeled along the gangway a great iron tank, out of which a thick, viscous, black bean-porridge was ladled into iron basins, encrusted with the cement-like remains of former meals, I foresaw starvation as well, for to eat the stuff was impossible. I have to confess that I did lose heart, and was angry and embittered at the thought of having survived so many weeks only to perish at last in squalor and beastliness.

But in fact this foul place was only a "reception-hut," and after five or six hours I saw a British officer, cool and casual, come strolling along the gangway, stopping here and there to speak to the British wounded. It was Captain Gilfillan of the R.A.M.C., a Lowlander

to whom I think I may fairly say that I and many
others in that camp owe our lives. He was a quiet,
humorous, self-contained Scot, slow of speech, deliberate in his movements, whose very presence was reassuring. With only local anaesthetics, no antiseptic
lotions, and paper bandages, he operated and dressed
wounds for most hours of the day, but when his work
in the dressing-hut was over, he strolled among us
with an air of amused insouciance that disguised his
watchful concern. Gilfillan told me long afterwards
that in that hot summer, with clouds of flies buzzing
between the wards and the open latrines that lay
between them, he expected daily an outbreak of typhus.
But it never came; and when, after many months of
cutting and dressing in the filthy dressing-hut, he had
had no cases of serious sepsis, he was forced to the
conclusion that modern hospital precautions must be
grossly overdone. Indeed, my own observations in that
dressing-hut, to which I was carried on a stretcher every
third day to lie upon the floor, waiting my turn, in a
Scutarian stench, led me to the opinion that a man is
harder to kill than the proverbial cat. For I saw upon
the operating-table, week after week, men so emaciated,
and with such stupefying injuries, not to be described,
that I began to feel, on their behalf, that Death is less an
enemy to be feared than an intolerable laggard of a
friend, the most heartlessly procrastinating of guests.
Not that Death had any reluctance to visit the camp at
large. The hut in which the coffins were knocked up
adjoined our own, and the hammering went on all the
time. We reckoned that not less than a score were
carried out daily. But those who did die perished, according to Gilfillan, mostly from starvation, and from

a resultant form of dysentery caused by the irritation set up, in their starved, enfeebled guts, by the stony grit in their ration of black bread. Their only other food was hot water with an occasional turnip floating in it.

We, the officers, had black bread that was coarse enough but fairly digestible, and canary-seed soup in the middle of the day. Canary-seed does not swell in water; it remains like the grains of sand in a spring, very much itself at the bottom of the soup-bowl, but it does tinge the water, like Aunt Jobiska's lavender-water, pink. The men's sporadic turnips did not colour their hot water at all; to that extent the difference of rank was marked by the punctilious Germans.

On my first arrival I could not eat even the officers' brand of black bread, but, fortunately for me, there was a little assistant-doctor on the German staff who was not a professional soldier. He was a librarian at Munich who not only disliked all Prussians, but had an aunt at Ventnor in the Isle of Wight, where he had been used to spend his holidays. Kind little Doctor Tautz, appealed to by Gilfillan, ordered me white bread, and when I still remained so thin that the camp barber refused to shave me ("You cannot shave bones and hollows"), two eggs a day were added to the régime. But I should have quickly lost my two eggs—and who knows what else as a result?—had it not been for Conrad Russell. It happened in this way.

Conrad Russell, a brother-officer in my yeomanry, had shared a billet with Hugh Dodds, John Gore, Tommy Lascelles, my wife, and myself at Hatfield Peverel, before our regiment embarked for France. Conrad was the only man I have ever known who was

able, by sheer personality, to relate anecdotes at the
breakfast-table, on a dark winter's morning, not merely
with impunity, but acceptably. He did not even have
to make them à propos or relevant to what was being
said; indeed, during those early, hurried meals before
parade, nothing was being said. We ate in silence, until
Conrad, with grave and courteous deliberation, would
ask us: "Shall I tell you an anecdote?" Because Conrad
was Conrad, our assent was warm and genuine. "Shall
I tell you an anecdote about King Ludwig of Bavaria?"
"Yes, please, Conrad." Then followed the story of how
King Ludwig, after the Battle of Mühldorf in 1322, sat
down to supper with four of his knights. There were
six eggs for supper, two of them upon King Ludwig's
plate. But Ludwig, with a gesture which must often
have brought tears to the eyes of Himmler and Goering,
handed one of his eggs to a knight called Schweppermann, exclaiming: "To every man one egg, but to the
pious Schweppermann two eggs."

Conrad's anecdotes, because of the tones, the articulation, and the tempo of the telling, stuck in the memory.
So that when, three years later, the chief surgeon at
Stargard made his rounds and, seeing two eggs upon a
stool by my bed, demanded furiously why the devil a
British prisoner was being so indulged, I was able to
answer, thanks to Conrad: "*Ich bin wie der fromme
Schweppermann: für mich zwei eier.*" The chief surgeon
was a Prussian brute; his forbidding, leathery countenance was criss-crossed with duelling scars; he was heart-
less and unapproachable; but for once he was amused.
His fury vanished; he slapped his thigh and roared with
laughter, looking round upon his staff and shouting:
"*Gut! gut!*" The colour returned to little Tautz's white

face, and I swallowed my two eggs daily (raw) until the barber consented to shave off my beard.

Because of a wound in the back, and bed-sores on my hips, I had to spend six weeks at Stargard lying upon my face, a very awkward position for eating and drinking, and one that forbids reading. So my thoughts had to wander a good deal then; and I propose to let them wander now, or rather, to remain poised for a moment upon Conrad who had done me, unwittingly, so good a turn. If I was lucky to have by me, out of Conrad's store, a sally that could save me from starvation, Conrad, on an occasion when his pride was in jeopardy, had to save himself. It was in the years after the war, when he had begun farming, and was still inexperienced. He was taking a train journey, and a local farmer, with whom he was acquainted, suddenly posed him the question: "Is your wheat at all winter-proud, Mr Russell?" Conrad had not the ghost of an idea what "winter-proud" could mean, but Russells do not care about owning up to ignorance, especially touching their chosen profession. He was greatly embarrassed.

"What did you say, Conrad?"

"I looked at him rather angrily, and said: 'Winter-proud? I think there's a great deal of nonsense talked about winter-proud wheat.'"

The farmer tapped him on the knee, and said: "I'm inclined to agree with you, Mr Russell."

"Beautiful" is an epithet usually reserved for women, not for men, but Conrad's face was truly beautiful, with a fineness both of line and modelling fit for a cameo. His height enhanced the effect of his Mercury-like head; only in the feet had nature served him

shabbily, as she had served Lord Byron cruelly. For
Conrad was flat-footed. The looked-for winged sandals
were not there. What were there, to his hebdomadal
indignation on Sunday mornings, were spurs. "I can
understand the reason for a lot of foolish things in war,"
he used to say, "but what I shall never understand is why
I have to wear spurs in church." He was not really cut
out for the cavalry. "If you walk in front of them they
bite you, and if you walk behind them they kick you"
was his verdict on the horses in his troop. It was not how
Long Tanner of the 19th Hussars would have spoken.

Everything that Conrad said was made arresting by
his most individual locution. His utterance was delibere-
ate; and he gave full value to every syllable, allowing
himself time, as most Englishmen do not, to bring out
the sound of each consonant. Without a hint of pre-
ciosity, he drew, in ordinary conversation, upon a
vocabulary wider than ours. He spoke, as others write,
in a highly individual style, and in one that compelled
attention. His mind was pocketed to hold recondite
facts; his reflections were his own, and his humour
all-pervasive.

To digress, as I have just digressed, to indulge
vagrant thoughts and memories, was, for many weeks
together, my only resource at Stargard. Sleep was hard
to come by, partly from hunger, partly from flea-bites.
In these I was encased, from crown to toes, as in chain-
armour. There was no unbitten spot upon my skin. The
arrival, after many months, of a hair-brush was a major
event. To spend the night brushing yourself all over,
again and again, is both exercise and an occupation. As
for the hunger, it did this to us: it confined our conversation to the subject of food. In early days we used to plan

our first meal after liberation; it was always to be eaten at Simpson's in the Strand, for the sake of the juicy steaks, the rich red sirloins. But later, from bio-chemical promptings, we abandoned Simpson's for a village sweet-shop. Sweets and sugar obsessed us, as I have read that they obsess Arctic explorers. When, after four months, our first parcels arrived from home, we pooled all sweet things and divided them among our-selves with jealous exactitude. We could not have borne to watch a companion with half a teaspoonful more sugar than ourselves.

There were fifteen British officers in the hut, some bedridden, some mobile, in various degrees of invalid-ism. We came from the most diverse homes and back-grounds, and spoke in many accents. In the eight months that we spent together we never had a quarrel. Nor did we once talk bawdy. This was, I suspect, due to the variety of social strata from which we were hewn. Fifteen public-school boys would, on occasion, have swapped smoking-room stories. Fifteen ranker-officers would have done the same. But respect for un-known backgrounds imposes, as was proved in our case, an absolute ban upon that form of humour. It seems that prudery, non-existent in a Robinson Crusoe, and rare among the like-minded, is the product of a hetero-geneous society. Or was it simply that the propinquity of so much suffering, of that daily procession of coffins, of the surrounding stenches and beastliness, made us all fastidious? We laughed a lot, especially after the influx of food-parcels began, but it was at the Germans, and especially at the camp interpreter, who alternately blustered or fawned upon us, according to the news from the front. For he was a German-Canadian who had been visiting Germany when the war broke out, and pressed, reluctant, into the German army, and we never tired of describing to him the details of his execution by hanging after Germany's certain defeat. As the news of reverses thickened, the poor man grew more and more flustered, and begged us to give him a testimonial. But we said no; on the contrary, we should all, if possible, attend his hanging. He was a huge, burly fellow, both bully and poltroon, and was a constant entertainment to us.

But our comfort, if such a word can be used of a rather harsh existence, depended upon our hut-orderly, Giovanni. He was an Italian, with whom none of us could converse; a stocky, fair-haired, blue-eyed man whom one would have taken for a Breton. He served us British officers, with no communication but smiles, with unwearying and devoted attention. He was our single-handed sick-nurse, bed-maker, and housemaid. He carried and emptied and swept and dusted with smiling alacrity, deft, quiet-footed, and watchful. When Giovanni was taken away, and two British Tommies took his place, we knew the difference indeed. They were unhandy, noisy, and forgetful. They must have found us uncommonly peevish and hard to please. For we had become accustomed to the service of a near-saint.

The impression made upon us by the German officers and N.C.O.s was quite unexpected by myself. Apart from the chief surgeon, who was a callous, pompous man of the starched Prussian type of every caricaturist, they appeared to be all suffering from neurosis. They were given to screaming. The Commandant screamed and waved his arms when a sick prisoner, digging potatoes, collapsed from exhaustion. He beat the fallen man with his scabbard, and ordered a sentry to pound his ribs with a rifle-butt until the blood spurted.

It was the sound of screaming that called us out of our hut to see the camp sergeant-major run amok through several wards, lashing at each bed as he passed it with a swagger cane, and knocking or kicking over a few cripples who stood on crutches round the doors. But it was not the wounded men who were screaming; it was the German N.C.O.

We were visited on one occasion by an inspecting general, von der Golz. This enormous man was the one German officer, besides Dr Tautz, to show us courtesy, and even kindness. He stood by my bed and enquired, through an interpreter, if I had any complaints. (Being a major, I was the senior British officer.) I complained, first, of the men's food. He promised that it should be improved, and it was. I next complained that a British officer had been kicked on the behind by a German sentry. For this insult to the British uniform I had demanded, as I explained to the general, a written apology from the commandant and the punishment of the kicker, but had received a verbal message that nothing would be done. General von der Golz turned to the camp commandant and questioned him, too rapidly for me to follow. The commandant began to explain; but the General stopped him with an impatient gesture, saying "*Nein, nein.*" He then turned to me and, through the interpreter, informed me that the camp commandant offered to me his profound apologies, and undertook that nothing of the sort should occur again. The commandant, standing behind the bulky general and out of his sight, took off his cap and slammed it down upon a table, clenched his teeth and both fists, and danced with rage. This little furious pirouette, performed so close to a formidable superior and among the stiff, expressionless members of the general's staff, all standing to attention, gave us much pleasure. But, for all that it was done in silence, it was another case of that improbable neurosis.

But the oddest and most surprising of these neurotic outbreaks took place, not at Stargard, but in a train. A few weeks before the Armistice I'Anson and I were discharged from Stargard and sent, escorted by an Alsatian corporal, to Karlsruhe. According to the Geneva Convention we had first-class travel-warrants. However, the guard of the express by which we had been ordered to travel refused to carry British prisoners. He hurled our kit-bags back on to the platform and pushed us out after them. We had to wait many hours for a slow train to Berlin. We again climbed into a first-class carriage, this time unseen by the guard. But there was a German colonel in the next compartment, who immediately came into ours and ordered us out again. The corporal began to descend, but the guard came along blowing his whistle; the train started; the guard gave a shove and the corporal tumbled in again at the colonel's feet. The colonel was, according to the corporal, an officer of the Imperial Guard. He was a most distinguished-looking man, tall, grey-haired, handsome, with every appearance of good breeding. But, on finding that our escort and ourselves were now committed to his carriage, although not to the same compartment, he began to scream. He waved his arms. The words "*Schweinhunde von Engländer*" recurred many times. The corporal stood at attention and said nothing.

We prisoners probably looked as amused as we felt. But it did not end there. The colonel, who could hardly order us out of a moving train, retired growling to his own compartment next door. But at the first stop he leant out of the window and the high scream began again. A small crowd gathered round him. I could catch enough of what he was shouting—this Guards colonel addressing a knot of shabby civilians —to understand that he had been twice wounded for his Fatherland, and yet was expected to travel next door to two swine-hounds of Englishmen. The little crowd did not appear to mind this as much as the colonel did, if at all. They shifted their stance a couple of feet to the left and had a good look at us, but their faces were quite expressionless. Because our corporal was a nice chap who hated the Prussians, we gave in to his urgent, whispered pleas that we should stop laughing. At the next stop the same thing happened. The colonel screamed out of the window, a small crowd collected, and the story of his two wounds for the Fatherland and of the swine-hounds next door was repeated, word for word. And so on for three or four stops. After that the colonel, exhausted, went to sleep. But one has only to think of, for example, Lord Jeffreys, or any one of our more distinguished-looking Guards officers (whom outwardly the Prussian colonel did, surprisingly, much resemble), behaving like this at the stations between Paddington and Oxford, to realise the immense, the unbridgeable gap between the British and the Teutonic temperament. On the platform at Berlin another officer forbade our escort to carry my kit-bag for me, but my final impression of the German people, and this time of the civilians, was of a different kind. We had been taken

to a small prison-camp for officers in the middle of
Karlsruhe, and when the Armistice was signed, and
every German officer in the camp had suddenly appeared in plain clothes, we naturally came and went as
we liked. A fellow-prisoner and myself hired a carriage
and drove about the town, which has many most
delectable eighteenth-century buildings, roofed with
brown tiles. It was our first whiff of freedom; the war
was over, and we were in high spirits. Coming home,
we found the main-street blocked with marching troops,
returning defeated from the western front. The crowd
on each pavement was welcoming them with cheers
and a flutter of waving handkerchiefs. Bouquets and
wreaths, which the troops twined upon their bayonets,
were showered upon them; it had every appearance of
a triumphant and victorious home-coming. Our cab-
man, who wished to drive down that street, turned into
a gap between two platoons, and we joined the procession. The crowd, seeing two British officers in uniform,
seated in a small Victoria, taking part in this rather
pathetic "victory" march, redoubled their cheers and
agitated their handkerchiefs more violently as we passed.
The swine-hounds had become heroes overnight. We
stuck out our chins and looked straight before us, as
forbiddingly as we knew how. Our hearts could not
have been colder towards these curious people, suddenly
fawning upon the representatives of the nation they had
most hated.

My personal exit from Germany had a touch of
drama. An important Dane, who was a friend of my
father-in-law, worked some spell with the Berlin
authorities through the Red Cross, and a few days
after the Armistice the camp commandant, still in

civilian clothes, told me I was to go, with an escort, to Kiel. The long bridge across the Rhine from Kiel to Strasbourg was held, at the German end, by a ragged, lounging group of German machine-gunners. The bridge itself was deserted. I walked across it slowly and alone, followed by a German corporal bent beneath my kit-bag. As I approached the French end, I found myself looking into the muzzles of a row of French machine-guns. Every gunner wore a brand-new uniform and steel-helmet. A huge tricolour flag was draped about the stone-work of the approach to the bridge. I waved my stick and shouted: "*Vive la France.*" The machine-gunners roared back: "*Vive l'Angleterre!*" The German corporal dumped my bag and slouched back to Kiel, while I stepped, all but embraced by Pétain's hand-picked and newly-equipped redeemers of Alsace, on to the soil of France.

Strasbourg was celebrating. Every woman and girl was in Alsatian dress. All the flags were out. Friendly people helped me with my kit-bag to the foot of the great flights of stairs that lead up to the railway station. I asked an official if there were any trains for Paris. "One train a day," he said, adding, as he glanced at the clock, "but today's train was due out a few minutes ago. Run, all the same, it may still be there." I tried to run up the stairs. I fell down three times. I was picked up and half-dragged on to the platform. A train still stood there. The roofs of its carriages were covered by swarming French soldiers. The corridors were packed to bursting. "*C'est un prisonnier anglais,*" shouted one of the kindly Frenchmen hustling me along. At once a door was opened and I was dragged, somehow, into the train. I sat, panting, on my kit-bag, low down in a thicket of serge trousers. The train started, and I wondered if, after all, I was to survive. But there was no end to the generosity of these Frenchmen. The word was passed down that an English officer, a prisoner and a *blessé*, must be found a seat. Someone, whom I never even saw or thanked, gave up a corner seat, and I was pushed and squeezed along the corridor and into this refuge. I had no money of any kind, neither ticket nor warrant, but was given hot food and drink whenever the train stopped. We reached Paris two days later. Whatever the faults or the ingratitude of the French, I shall never forget my debt to those good-hearted men.

I do not think that I made much profit out of my eight months as a prisoner of war in Pomerania. Unwounded prisoners have the excitement of planning escapes; there was no question of anything of the sort for us. Nor had we any opportunity of drawing worthwhile conclusions about the German character or way of life. We did, it is true, verify the old commonplace that to impress a German you must shout at him. There were one or two comical scenes when I myself, although still unable to sit up in bed, was able to turn the offensive bluster of a German N.C.O. into subdued acquiescence merely by hammering on the bed-table with my fist and shouting. But we met no German civilians and, at that stage of the war, when man-power was already stretched to the limit, it is probable that the soldiers we had to deal with would have been looked upon as very poor specimens by the Germans themselves. Our sergeant-major was clearly abnormal, and the commandant regarded by a visiting general as a man to be snubbed in public. Only the colonel in the train can, to judge from externals, be fairly regarded as a precursor of the Nazis, given to hysterical yellings. It is curious to reflect, nearly forty years later, that I returned home to tell the story of that screaming colonel as if I had heard and seen something extravagantly out-of-the-way. Since that time millions of men and women have heard the screeching of Hitler himself. When did Germans, once reputed to be so ponderous and bovine, first have their *crises de nerfs*? When will they cease to have them? No, I did not become an authority upon the Germans through my spell of captivity; indeed, beyond learning that the German for "retreat" was "*Hindenburgstrategie*," I did not even add much to my schoolboy scraps of their language. But was there no private, interior profit to be drawn from the confinement, from the calls upon one's stock of patience and endurance, from the round-the-clock companionship, *à huis clos*, with fourteen other captives?

I certainly had to be patient. Through the long nights of sleeplessness and hunger, the weeks and months of waiting for news from home, the bouts of pain or illness, there was no choice in the matter. But enforced patience did not, in my case at least, become a habit that endured when the compulsion was removed. I have been no less impatient since than I used to be before my German adventure. Nor can I honestly credit my character with any improvement due to such suffering as I had to put up with. Even moderate pain makes me peevish and self-centred; intense pain (such as I never felt in Germany but only ten years later, as a result of the same wounds) I found unbearable to the verge of despair, and was saved by heroin, not fortitude. I shall never prescribe suffering for the good of any living soul; and while it may be true that pain, in some of us,

begets sympathy for the pain of others, I have found a
depth of compassion in persons who have known neither
pain nor griefs. Suffering can easily make a man self-
regarding, whereas pity belongs to those who look
about them; besides, it is a gift and a grace, not a lesson
to be got from a beating. And when clergymen talk of
God's use of suffering as a means of bringing us to Him,
I do not believe them. But if captivity did no character-
building for me, nor hardened me for future mischances,
it did teach me some facts of life. I learnt, for instance,
that nervous irritation can be almost as insupportable as
physical agony. There was one hot afternoon when two
Serbian prisoners decided to play and dance outside our
hut. The dance was a mere shuffling of their feet, in
rope slippers, to and fro in the white dust; but the tune,
of about four bars, repeated over and over again, all
but sent me crazy. For the musical phrase ended upon a
note which, in its context, the human ear refused to
accept as an ending: it demanded, it insisted, that
relief should be given, a solution reached. Relief was
given, and to the ear's satisfaction; but, unhappily, this
relief consisted in a repetition of the first bar of the tune,
which led, inevitably, to the fourth bar and to that
same unacceptable note, left hanging in the air. I suppose
that the dancers, who played that torturing tune on
some sort of mouth organ, were themselves inhibited
by that expectant, interrogative last note from coming
to a stop. At any rate they went on for a couple of
hours or so. By this time my head was under my pillow
and my fingers in my ears, as I writhed in real agony.
The place where it hurt most was not in the head, but
in the solar-plexus; I have felt something like it under
a dentist's drill. It is a sensation very close indeed to

despair, and I have never again underrated the misery which can be inflicted upon the human organism by a noise alone, not necessarily one loud or discordant, but of a shape, or a shapelessness, for which the nervous system can provide no receptacle.

Another fact of life learnt by me in those months of enforced intimacy with accidental, not chosen, companions is of more general interest, and is one too often forgotten, or suppressed, by political and social theorisers. I was fortunate indeed in my fellow-prisoners. I had from them, when I most needed it, nothing but kindness and consideration and, in convalescence, unbroken good humour. We shared many jokes together, as well as our food-parcels; we had a very real liking and respect for each other; we became friends. We swore, on parting, to hold an annual reunion in London, and although, in the event, only the gentle Leadbetter turned up at my house for the first, and last, of these, the failure was mainly due to geography, and to the widespread scattering of us all.

All the same, we lacked the first prerequisite for full satisfaction in companionship, which is a common stock of ideas. I can remember no exchange of thoughts, except with Gilfillan, about any of my main preoccupations, and I have no doubt that others were in the same case. Egalitarians, and those who believe in "getting together" as an infallible ice-breaker, too often forget that our profoundly lonely human souls can communicate only by reference to shared experiences. To people accustomed to read, the bulk of those experiences, or at any rate those to which they attach most importance, are not the day-to-day happenings of ordinary life, but the far more engrossing adventures found in books.

Ideas, characters, speculations, a free ranging in time and space, backwards and forwards—all these ingredients fill the common cistern from which readers draw their refreshment and much of their nourishment as well. One reader can exchange ideas with another because each can honour the currency proffered by his fellow. But between those who read and those who do not there can pass only the small change of commonplaces. And reading, apart from newspapers, magazines, and "shockers," is still the resource of a minority. It is true that the non-reader can often interest and charm the reader by his practical knowledge and skills, by his humour, by his knowledge of men and the world, and by the fascination of human personality, however illiterate. The reader can and does look up to and admire the non-reader as a far better specimen of humanity than himself, as well as one more accomplished in the art of living. But what he cannot do, in a little community indifferent to books, is to subdue his secret cravings for some birds of his own feather with whom to flock. My spell in a prison-camp, for all the good fellowship there, left me persuaded that cultural strata will long survive social and economic ones. And that comes, I suppose, to no more than this: that the egalitarian State will still have its high, middle, and low brows who must somehow manage to stick together. If they do not, many will perish from sheer boredom.

I had some fairly narrow escapes at Stargard: from starvation, from Spanish flu, from blood-poisoning, and so on. That I did escape them I owe to Dr Gilfillan. But even he could do little for me when, on my first arrival, the bed next to mine was occupied for a time

by a young officer who, although recovered from his
wounds, neither read nor walked nor talked nor
played cards, but sat upon his bed and sang "Someone
is coming to tea on Sunday" over and over again. It was
the only line of a song that his not very capacious mind
could remember; and even that one line was not true.
There was no tea in our hut to which "Someone"
could come.

Do Frenchmen read more than we do, or have they
some art of picking up, out of the air as it were, a
thought here, a phrase there, which gives to their casual
talk a faintly bookish savour? There was a ward for
French prisoners, into which, after convalescence, I
sometimes strolled. The wounded here were mostly
young men, and although not officers, they were
aspirants—cadets already chosen to become officers. I
could still talk a little French in those days, and although
there was one among them who liked to talk to me in
English ("My foot he kick me all the night") it was
French that we spoke together. And I must confess that
I found those visits a refreshment. Laughter rippled
down the ward, caught up from bed to bed; scraps of
wit or near-wit flew about; words were used for fun
as Englishmen might use a ball. These Frenchmen had
fewer parcels than we did, and their anxieties were
deeper than ours, for they were not, as we were,
optimists about the war. But, to entertain a visitor,
they put on their gaiety as if dressing for a party, and
expressed it in easy, flying phrases which could have
come, among Englishmen, only from the literate. It was
with a Frenchman, again, at Karlsruhe, that I was able,
for the first time, to exchange ideas inspired by literary
and not merely personal experiences. He was a major

in the Gunners, sensitive, intellectual, and profoundly sad. I enjoyed our long walks round and round the gravelled compound, but learnt from them, not only the refreshment to be got from another man's intelligence, but the comfort I had owed to the hopefulness and good spirits of my British hut-fellows at Stargard. The best company after all, I reflected, in a prison-camp is that of the simple, the unquestioning, and the optimistic.

I have already mentioned the deep impression made upon me, through things seen in the dressing-hut, by the toughness of the human body and its stubborn reluctance to accept death. It must have been this, I think, that led, in my own case, to a minor, but profitable by-product of captivity—the cure of a secret neurosis about illness. Ever since the death from pneumonia of an elder brother at the age of fourteen, I had been liable to panic when told that anybody of whom I was fond had a "high temperature": or even "a temperature." I can remember, in my middle twenties, being unable to enjoy that admirable comedy *The Great Adventure* because, in the first few moments after the curtain goes up, the hero's servant dies of pneumonia. That word sent a chill, a cold fear, through me which spoilt my whole evening. Had the servant been run over I could have been perfectly happy. But ever since my sojourn at Stargard I have assumed that people who have temperatures will recover, and have been more afraid, in my own case, of living too long than of being cut off too soon. It has been a pleasing change for the better in the character of that close companion, my "subconscious self."

Lastly, I imagine that I am at one with all other ex-captives in having acquired, through my experience, a strong determination never again, if it could be avoided, to suffer separation from the centre of my affections.

An unwounded prisoner of war has but one duty: to escape if he can. When escape, as in the vast majority of cases, is impossible, he has the heavy burden to bear of being able-bodied yet useless, while his countrymen are fighting. We wounded prisoners were far more fortunate. We had not "surrendered"; we were physically incapacitated from any more fighting; for those of us not dangerously ill the risks of war were over; our ultimate return home was, from Germany in the first World War, almost certain. Whatever our trials and privations, we had, from the moment when anxiety over the issue of the war itself had been allayed, good reasons for a profound inner peace of mind. If there was a combative side of us that fretted at not being "in at the death," there was, in my own case at least, another side that was more than content with the prospect of a safe return to private felicity. No, the burden of our kind of captivity is not laid upon the captives. We had been posted as "wounded and missing"; but we were not missing to ourselves. It was upon our homes that the shock of that sinister phrase fell, to be followed by a gnawing suspense of uncertain duration. Of all tribulations, anxiety is, in my experience, the worst. Most of us can summon up courage enough to face a known catastrophe, but to meet and to master the eroding crescendo of suspense demands gallantry of a rarer kind. Such fortitude was, in the event, not found wanting; it was amply displayed, but not by us. We were the lucky ones.

There are long periods, as I have said, when a prisoner

has no resource but his thoughts. I imagine that mathematicians and musicians, as well as writers of the creative kind, can set themselves problems and find amusement in solving them. But those of us who lack the gift of invention or analysis must fall back upon memories. And here I was fortunate indeed. I was near enough to my Eton days to miss no detail, in my retrospect, of the fascinating and sunlit activities that had filled them. I was still nearer to my years at Oxford. The Balliol gallery offered me an almost inexhaustible choice and variety of pictures to recall. If the landscapes were not too reliable, since, as in the case of Eton, they were uniformly bright with sunshine, the figures in the conversation-pieces were always true to life. Believing in their survival, unchanged, I was under no compulsion to see my dead friends in heroic postures. I could be amused at their portraits as I had been amused in their company. The English countryside, in eternal summer, was spread out before me; I could hear the hum of insects and the song of birds; I could even, in our malodorous camps, recall the smells of an English garden after rain. (For memory has not only sight, but sound-and-scent-tracks.) I could, above all, recall a courtship in bluebell-time, and the unshakeable reassurance of my home.

In looking back upon those eight months of captivity it is only fair to remember that for all the heat and the stench and the weariness, the scenes of suffering and brutality, I possessed this great store of enlivening memories from which to draw comfort and consolation. And draw them I did.

CHAPTER IV

BEAULIEU

IN the prison-camp at Stargard, in the days after our food-parcels had arrived to appease that constant obsession with hunger, our thoughts returned again and again to our home-coming. My personal daydream, careless of times and seasons, foresaw my arrival, in full bodily vigour, upon a day in May and in the English countryside. There would be bird-song and the scent of fresh lawn-mowings, and all the buttercups would be out.

The reality was different. The winter that followed the November armistice was long and dreary. I had my share of spoiling, for I found myself in an officers' hospital, of which my wife's sister Sybil was commandant, in Dorchester House. The doctor had said, casually, "You are going to have this cough for quite a time," but they put me into a pneumonia-jacket and I had my suspicions. The spoiling came from Rose Hammond and Lucy Tritton and other wartime nurses whose professional skill was softened by all the graces. And I remember a visit from my uncle, a much-loved Bishop of Lewes, who had made a vow, when I was reported missing, to restore to me, should I return to safety, my grandfather's gold watch. As a young man he had pocketed the watch, after my grandfather's funeral, before the astonished eyes of his elder brother, my father. It appears that Heaven hears a bishop's vow, since I was preserved, and now the Bishop completed his part at my bedside. He told me of the vow, without mentioning how he had come by the watch. I knew this already from my father, but gave no sign, I trust, to my friendly uncle of scenting, in his kindly action, an admixture of vicarious restitution.

I lay snug, and more than cosseted, in a warm and cheerful ward; but outside it was a winter of discontent. There was much trouble over demobilisation; and I can remember how, at night, a sudden series of back-fires in Park Lane was so exactly like the sounds of the rifle-shots I had heard in the streets of Karlsruhe when the German régime had cracked in defeat, that my heart sank within me like lead. Had it really come to this? It was absurd, of course, and I only recall it because such a reaction, even of a sick man's nerves, does illustrate the general malaise and disillusionment of that sombre winter. For spring lagged badly, and in the third week of March the tops of the elms in Hyde Park had still not thickened and grown red. And then, suddenly and as if miraculously, my Stargard daydream came as good as true. At shortest notice I was told to get up and put on my uniform, a thick bundle of tickets for two was put into my hand, and twenty-four hours later my wife and I awoke to see the sunshine striping the walls of our bedroom through the slats of a *jalousie*, to hear the shrilling of swifts over a garden of mimosas, a southern voice singing *Santa Lucia* to a guitar beneath our balcony, and the knock on our door of a waiter in a striped jacket bearing a tray with coffee and *croissants*. There are moments in life when happiness is absolute. This was one of them.

The fairy godmother who had waved her wand over us and worked the miracle was quite unknown to us. She was Lady Eva Wemyss, a rich red-head with a heart as big as herself, who owned a white, green-shuttered villa at Beaulieu. She had the imagination and the generosity to invite, through the Red Cross, a certain number of wounded officers, with their wives, to spend three months convalescing on the Riviera. Some stayed with her in her villa; others, like ourselves, at Bond's Hotel hard by. For all alike everything was paid for, including the journeys.

How we came to be selected as recipients of this largesse I do not know. There may well have been hundreds who needed it as much or more, but there cannot have been a couple more sensible of their good fortune than ourselves, or more ready to savour it to the full. Consideration for the wounded bodies of fighting men is common enough : care for the wounded spirits of their wives is rare. And there can be few ordeals more racking to the spirit than the blank and menacing silence that follows, often for many weeks, upon the posting of a husband as "wounded and missing." So that we shared, the pair of us, a blissful sense of healing and relief as we walked, that first morning, to call upon our unknown benefactress, between her blazing flower-beds, beneath her Judas trees in bloom. The sun dazzled us; the Mediterranean was at her brightest and bluest between the shaggy palm-trunks, and the air was that of summer. We found our hostess, at eleven o'clock in the morning, playing bridge out of doors.

Lady Eva was delightful. Beneath an enormous shady straw hat and a mass of curling red locks, her eyes twinkled with merriment and enjoyment. She could hardly have been fatter. She told us, indeed, that although she could not swim a stroke, it was her custom in summer to be rowed a quarter of a mile out to sea, and there to be lowered into the water by her boatman, and left to float. "I'm so fat, you see, that I cannot sink." She made us free of her garden; she asked us to lunch (where my wife once disgraced herself by taking the whole of a *langouste*, intended for six guests, upon her plate); she exuded friendliness and hospitality. But I fear that we were a sad disappointment to her. She liked to play bridge from breakfast to lunch, and to gamble at the Cercle at Monte Carlo in the afternoons and evenings. She liked to talk about stocks and shares and to be given market "tips." We did not play bridge; we had neither the money nor the inclination for gambling; we disliked the crowds and hot rooms of Monte Carlo; and I knew, as yet, nothing about stocks and shares. We wanted only to be let alone, to be out-of-doors all day, and to be quiet. She was giving us perfect contentment and we, alas, had nothing to give her in return. It was a one-sided bargain, and a bad one for Lady Eva. She was far too kind to show it, but she must have written us down as a very dull young couple indeed, with no capacity for enjoying good things to be had for the asking. Fortunately for her, she had other protégés on whom the delights of bridge and baccarat were not thrown away, and there was a young man, on half-commission with a firm of stockbrokers, who had the post-war gambling-counters of the Stock Exchange at his finger-ends. It is to be hoped that he enabled her to recoup her lavish expenditure on the rest of us.

I am sure that Lady Eva made all allowances for the

rather pale and limp soldiers from Bond's Hotel, who,
still wearing uniform, sat or lounged about the remoter
parts of her garden, not exactly skulking, but avoiding
the broader vistas commanded by the bridge-table.
Any faint unease in the relationship of beneficiaries to
benefactress was on our side. The one right and acceptable gift that a guest can make to his hostess, where the
conventional exchange of hospitality is ruled out, is that
of himself: of his thoughts, his talk, and his humour.
Where there is little or no common reference for
thoughts, few shared topics for talk, and different
standards of humour, the guest is virtually empty-
handed. He must put up with a situation where he does
all the taking and makes no return at all. It is a situation
that does make for a certain amount of discomfort;
a faint sense of guilt. I fear our consciences did not
trouble us overmuch. I have always thought the French
Riviera, for most of its length, an overrated resort. The
agglomeration of heavy white masonry that lines the
coast-line for miles and miles, weighing down the feet
of the mountains at the very point where they should
be curving with natural grace into the sea, is displeasing.
If you are on the shore and want to visit the hinterland
of stone-pine and *maquis*, of olive and myrtle, an
impenetrable barrier of Hotels Métropole bars your
way. If you are among the foothills and wish to bathe,
you are in like case. The esplanades and boulevards have
been denaturalised with date-palms and fleshy grey
aloes; there are prickly pears round the very bandstands.
And on three days a week the mistral, that implacable
trouble-maker, rattles the shutters, whirls up the dust,
and hunts you from one windy spot to a windier.

But Beaulieu is, or was, different. Either the mistral

has blown itself out before it reaches that narrow strip between mountains and sea where the unassuming hotels and villas keep their distance from one another among the trees, or the hills themselves, rising suddenly from the plain, ward it off. Beaulieu is umbrageous, not glaring; a place of gardens, not boulevards. And a few miles to the west lies a most enchanting pleasure-ground. This is the small verdant golf-course of Cagnes, bounded by the sea on the south and on the west by a river, haunted by blue wagtails and yellow. The river flows out of a gorge from which the little town of Cagnes, old and brown and native, climbs steeply up to crown its own independent foothill. The course itself is short and flat, ideal for convalescents; the fairways are divided by groves of umbrella-pine or poplar; a hedge of pink roses ran inland from the clubhouse; and H.R.H. the Duke of Connaught, playing in uniform, zigzagged slowly away from or towards his pretty little partner, Mrs Doubleday. And, better still, high in the branches of a white poplar, but not too high to escape notice, a lesser grey shrike sat upon her nest, while the cock-bird justified his name of Excubitor, "the Watchman," by perching on the topmost twigs.

This was in the early days of our "bird-loving," and I cannot pretend that it was without recourse to the bird-book that I was able to distinguish, by the black band upon his forehead, the lesser from the greater grey shrike, whom I had seen once or twice when riding the rolling plains of the Pas de Calais. And I was too much of a novice then to make such a list of birds seen as I did nearly a decade later in a garden at Ciboure near St Jean de Luz, where the Pyrenees peter out into the Atlantic. On that occasion the same wounds that had brought me to Beaulieu sent me, far more enfeebled, to Ciboure, and once again bird-watching proved to be the best of resources for an invalid. The bookseller at Bayonne had declared that the very good reason why he had no book about birds was that in that part of France there were no birds; all the same, without leaving the villa garden, I listed sixty-three species during the winter and spring. At Beaulieu, not knowing what to look for, we saw fewer kinds, but, being in the path of the spring migration northward, saw and heard birds in large numbers that are usually seen or heard singly. There was a day or two, for instance, when every clump and covert round the golf-course and upon the hills above was ringing with cries of "kew kew kew". The criers were extraordinarily evasive and hard to see, and for a couple of days we could only call them the "kew kew birds". They were wrynecks. Another morning the orange-trees in the garden of Bond's Hotel were alive with warblers; by next morning they were gone. But the bird with whom we got on better terms than with any other was the hoopoe. For we made occasional excursions to Mont Agel on the heights above Monte Carlo, to play golf upon one of the roughest and most beautiful golf-courses in Europe. You played along stony fairways that wound among bleached rocks, and to keep your eye on the ball needed determination indeed, so entrancing was the prospect. For snow still lay deep on the sharp, dramatic peaks of the Alpes Maritimes, and nothing catches the eye like a snow mountain; it not only distracts a golfer, but is apt to disenchant him with the game of golf itself. There is something absurd about putting in the presence of magnificence. And when there is a hoopoe strutting on

the putting-green, crest erect, flashing orange and white
and black at you, your interest in the game sinks lower
still. There was a day when the sounds of "hoo hoo"
pervaded the course, and the hoopoes who, unlike the
wrynecks, were tame and confiding, alighted within
twenty yards of us while we lunched. Close at hand, a
hoopoe is almost as difficult to believe in as a Mandarin
drake. "*On dirait artificielles*," as the flower-woman at
St Raphael used to say in praise of her roses.

I am not sure that it was not on "hoopoe day" that
we also found the jumping spider. He was a large hairy
grey spider with a death's-head adumbrated in a darker
shade of grey upon his back, and he caught flies by
leaping upon them. The flies were settling, as flies love
to settle, upon Bunt Goschen's felt hat, which lay by
his side while we lunched. We did not see the spider
arrive, but suddenly he was there, sitting on one edge
of the crater made by the pushing in of the hat's crown.
You might have thought that the flies would have seen
the large, menacing creature, but if they did they must
have underrated his agility. For they settled freely on
the opposite side of the hat's crown, or upon the brim;
and if they settled within five inches or less of the spider,
their chance of escaping his leap was about one in four.
The fact that he was not infallible, that he sometimes
missed, somehow seemed to enhance, not to diminish,
our admiration for his skill. Had he been infallible, we
should have ascribed his powers to "Nature," and given
him no personal credit. But seeing him on occasion a
trifle too slow, so that the fly was up and away while
the jumper was in mid-air, brought home to us the
difficulty of his feat, and when next time he brought it
off, we praised him to his face. We also had to praise

him for his patience and good temper, since—I have to confess it—we rather unkindly robbed him of his flies before he could eat them, so as to leave him lean and avid for another jump. He probably thought, like a bishop, that his trials were sent to him by Providence, and must be endured humbly. He can hardly have guessed that his special Providence was thrilled by his agility and prowess and determined to prolong the show.

Gerard Goschen's hat was there to interest the flies because Goschen himself was there. There are a handful of people still living who will know what that meant to us in terms of gaiety and fun. Bunt was another of Lady Eva's bedesmen: he had suffered, a prisoner of war with a severe head-wound, solitary confinement and especial ill-treatment as the son of a former Ambassador to Berlin. So he, too, was in a mood to savour the sights and sounds and scents of a Mediterranean spring and, as always, to share and communicate his pleasures. It is not everybody that a young couple, lately re-united after a long and anxious separation, would welcome as a permanent third, both at the little round table in Mr Bond's dining-room and on their daily excursions. It is possible that Bunt alone could have been so welcomed. But he had the tact, the sensibility, and what I can only call the "dearness," to play the part perfectly. Like Sidney Godolphin, he was "never in the way and never out of the way."

There was one morning, indeed, when it seemed that we must play golf at Cagnes without Bunt. For there was a little train with wooden seats that must be caught soon after breakfast, and when the time came to leave the hotel Bunt was missing. I found him still asleep in his room. Bunt's wits were about him instantaneously when roused, as had been proved years ago in Bedford Court Mansions when Alan Lascelles woke him on the morning of King Edward VII's coronation and Bunt exclaimed gutturally as he opened his eyes: "They crown me today, Ponsonby, what?" But with only five minutes to go before the train was due to start we wrote Bunt off for the day. All the same, as the guard was blowing his whistle a dishevelled figure came bounding along the platform and shot into our compartment. Bunt's hair was unbrushed and he wore only a shirt and trousers and a pair of brogues with laces flying and tripping him as he ran. He trailed a golf-bag in one hand, and in the other grasped a coat and waistcoat and a long string tie which flew out behind him. He cannot have looked, on his way to the station, every inch an officer upholding, as the Duke of Connaught upheld them, the best traditions of the British Army in the country of our brave allies. I have little doubt that when the stringy tie had been knotted, and his shoe-laces tied, Bunt must have asked, to calm and to fortify his spirits, for the story of Sir John Horner and the lesser spotted woodpecker. It was a story of which he never grew tired and, like a child, he insisted on absolute verbal accuracy in the telling. Not a syllable must be changed. The story was first told me by Sidney Peel, who had met Sir John Horner in the bird-house at the Zoo. In the cage was a lesser spotted woodpecker and, for something to say, Sidney asked Sir John whether he had ever seen one wild. "Indeed I have," said Sir John, "on three occasions, and what is more, I clearly recollect each of them. The first time I saw one was at Mells. I was dressing for dinner when one of the children called to me: 'Come down quick, Father, there's a lesser spotted woodpecker on the lawn.' I ran downstairs, just as I was, but by the time I got there it was gone. That was the first time I saw it. The second time was also at Mells. One day my keeper said to me: 'I saw an interesting bird in the drive this morning, Sir John—a lesser spotted woodpecker.' 'Why, Jarvis,' I said, 'that must be the bird I saw yesterday, but I thought it was a cuckoo.' That was the second time I saw it. The third occasion on which I saw it was—God bless my soul, I've clean forgotten!" This story, provided the teller was word-perfect, always left Bunt greatly refreshed.

Bunt's susceptibility to young women was prodigious. In trams, in trains, in hotel corridors, he was everlastingly encountering "the nicest woman I know." Big eyes, a little pallor, a hint of delicacy, were irresistible to him. There was a girl who sat with her parents in the dining-room, with a pretty, weak face whom he christened "Little Blossom." Her trivial gestures, her comings and goings, were closely watched; he longed to comfort her although, to our eyes, she appeared to be in no need of comfort. I don't think he ever spoke to Little Blossom, any more than to the young French bride on her honeymoon. That the French bride needed comfort was clear enough, for her odious young husband, a French officer with pince-nez, read the newspaper all through meals. Bunt was torn between an itch to sock the husband on the jaw and an even stronger one to take the little bride in his arms. He did neither, of course, but his preoccupation with this minor tragedy was genuine. The case of the lady golf-professional at Mont Agel was different. Bunt paid her five francs to

play a round with him, and for a day or two she was
"the nicest woman I know," in spite of her looks,
reminiscent of Queen Victoria, which led us to suspect
that she carried a spare golf ball in each cheek. But
there came a day when Bunt challenged her to a match,
and the lady professional, noticing that Bunt had teed
his ball one inch in advance of the plates, said nothing,
allowed him to drive off, and then claimed the hole.
For the first and only time in his life Bunt made a
woman cry. The very nicest of all the women he knew,
we never saw. Bunt met her, I think, in Nice, and disappeared for three days. He had been, he confessed, on
a wild-goose chase into the Provençal hinterland—I
believe as far as Draguignan. Whether he had even
spoken to his charmer we never knew. He was reticent,
but chastened, on his return to the fold. There are
difficulties in the way of comforting young women
who are already quite comfortable.

Even in that first winter after the war the Riviera
was, as nowadays, full of smart people. We had little
inclination for such society, but when my wife's Aunt
Susan (Lady Holford) wrote to say that we must not
fail to go over to Cap Ferrat, where "darling Johnnie
and Jeanie are longing to meet you," we felt that it
would be churlish to leave such flattering and unexpected longings unsatisfied. Sir John and Lady Ward,
a daughter of Mr Whitelaw Reid, the American Ambassador, were very smart people indeed, and so was
the white-coated manservant who told us, on our
arrival at the Villa Rosemary, that we should find our
host and hostess on the tennis-courts. The approach to
the courts was highly exposed, across a vast lawn, and
we were watched every inch of the way by a group of

exquisitely dressed, but glassy-eyed, strangers. Both
darling Johnnie and darling Jeanie were playing tennis,
and not until the set was over had we a chance of
introducing ourselves to that tall and handsome pair.
On doing so, we realised that either Aunt Susan had
been mistaken, or that the two darlings had succeeded
in mastering their longings. Their handshakes were
casual, their expressions blank; they introduced us to
nobody; they did not ask if we would like tea. They
went back to their game, and we wandered away over
the lawn and back, through the house, into the road,
the richer by a "darling Johnnie" joke which amused us
for some years.

Perhaps we were solaced by a belated tea at the Villa
Maryland, which lies further out towards the point of
Cap Ferrat. For here we were warmly received by two
Edwardian notabilities, Mrs Richard Ward, better
known as Miss Muriel Wilson, and her mother, then a
very old lady, Mrs Arthur Wilson of Tranby Croft.
The garden of Maryland in late April or early May
stands out among the wonders I have seen. It may not
have been a gardener's garden, full of rarities, but for
sheer breath-taking beauty I have not seen its equal.
The backcloth, so to speak, was the Mediterranean
contrast of cypress and olive, with the sea showing
between the trunks of the olives. That is common
enough, although, thanks to the subtle colours of an
olive-grove, turning from green to grey with any
slight movement of the air, the pleasure of it never palls
through custom. But what made you gasp and stare was
the multitude of flowers between, beneath, and climbing
up the trees. Red roses fell in sprays from the tops of
the olives. Our English April, May, and June appeared

to be blossoming as one month in extravagant splendour. We really did stand astonished. The Villa itself, designed by Mr Geoffrey Peto, with patio and slender arcades, was admirably and precisely fitted to its surroundings, as well as to the southern good looks and bright attire of our younger hostess. Was it the contrast between that vision and the landscape of the trenches, of Pomerania, and the darkness of that winter in England, that made so enduring an impact upon my mind? I do not think so. Maryland needed no foil to her singular radiance.

It was June, and the rose-hedges white with dust, before we returned to England. We have never again visited the French Riviera, nor had any wish to do so. But in a lifetime of many windfalls, we have had none better timed, or more imaginatively generous, than that for which Lady Eva shook the tree. I wish we could have repaid her in some sort. We never could, and I suspect that our spoken and written thanks struck her gay insouciance as a trifle flowery and overdone. But gratitude endures; and I must hope that in the Elysian Fields there may be some game, simpler than bridge, in which I can join, some form of celestial roulette in which I shall be, at long last, her excited companion.

CHAPTER V

GLENLOCHAY

M R EDWARD WAGG, known to his own family and to all his friends as "the Laird," was the younger of two brothers, senior partners in the City firm of Helbert Wagg and Company, when I first entered its service in the summer of 1914. He was already a little old gentleman, white-haired and rubicund, with a slight stoop and short legs which I fear Mrs Gamp would not have hesitated to call "bandy." His face was clean-shaven, and he had a frog mouth as wide as, but less impish than, Lord Beaverbrook's; his expression was misleadingly mild for a man of so much character and decision. His voice was gentle, and his manners so courteous as to risk being wrongly called "old-world." (They were, on the contrary, the natural expression of his own civilised nature, whereas "old world" manners were, in most cases, inculcated as a protective device in a tetchy and quarrelsome society.) He was a bachelor with, I suspect, fond memories: could his proposals, if any, have been so polite as not to have been understood? In his leisure hours the Laird was an avid reader of history, biography, and memoirs; in the City he enjoyed a flutter, especially in such esoteric forms as "giving for the Put and Call." He was at all times imperturbable. When the famous "Baring Crisis" shook the City the Laird was on holiday in Scotland.

His partners in London, not immune from an epidemic of "jitters," telegraphed to him: "Barings in difficulties. Return at once." It is necessary to have some inkling of the power and prestige of Baring Brothers in those days (long since happily restored) fully to savour the Laird's reply:

"If by returning can save Barings will come: otherwise propose finishing holiday." He did finish it.

When I first joined H. W. & Co. in the summer of 1914, the Laird and his elder brother, Mr Arthur Wagg, sat side by side at two enormous knee-hole writing-tables at one end of the lofty partners' room in Threadneedle Street, facing the door. They shared one characteristic: a capacity for sitting almost motionless. Since they had lately abdicated from active management in favour of the two junior partners, Alfred Wagg and Adolph Schwelm, I, who sat in a corner by the door to pick up what I could by watching and listening, got an impression of two restless, cigarette-smoking figures crossing and re-crossing in front of a pair of benevolent Buddhas. Schwelm in particular, slim and white-faced, with dark, smouldering eyes, was always on the move, endlessly walking and talking. Alfred contradicted everything Schwelm said, and Schwelm contradicted Alfred. The Buddhas said nothing. By the end of the morning the chain of contradictions ended in agreement, the Buddhas nodded, and another step had been taken in the business of the City of Ottawa or that of the Constantinople Trams. I was learning dialectics.

I think it was during those few weeks before the war that the Laird gave me a little book on *Options* to study. For a brain like mine it was a harder nut to crack than

Kant's *Critique of Pure Reason*, but the outbreak of war, and the telegram on my hall-table: "Mobilise," saved me from the embarrassment of any questions from the Laird on a subject which, to him, was a simple and amusing pastime.

The war and my consequent convalescence kept me away from the City for something over five years, but H. W. & Co, with an habitual generosity, kept my place open for me. I returned to find many changes. Mr Arthur Wagg was dead: Schwelm was in South America, where he eventually founded a new European colony on the Parana river; there were two new partners, Nigel Campbell and Bernard Barrington; Alfred Wagg was now the head and front of the firm. But there was the Laird, sitting at the same desk as before; still a little old gentleman, but no older; still fond of a flutter; tranquil, rosy, and polite.

This time he did not ask me to renew my study of the "Put and Call"; he asked my wife and myself to stay with him in Scotland. It was a visit that led to rare delights.

The Laird had two country houses: the Islet, a rococo, red-brick villa which he had built for himself at Maidenhead, and the shooting-lodge of Glenlochay in Perthshire. The gables of the Islet rose from lawns and rosebeds on the right bank of the river Thames to a height sufficient to catch and to irritate the eye of Mr Waldorf Astor (at that time still an American Senator), who had lately bought Cliveden, standing aloft among the woods on the opposite bank. One day the Laird received a note: "The Hon. Waldorf Astor wishes to know whether Mr Wagg will sell his cottage." The Laird wrote back: "Mr Wagg wishes to know whether

6

the Hon. Waldorf Astor will sell his palace." No
business was done.

As for Glenlochay, the Laird in his early thirties had
taken from Lord Breadalbane a fifty years' lease of that
enchanting glen, believing that half a century would
either see him out, or at any rate outlast his taste for
Scotland. It did neither. It was with real regret that the
Laird, well on in his eighties, had to abandon for the
begonias and weeping-willows of Maidenhead the
everlasting hills of Perthshire.

But neither at the Islet nor in Glenlochay did the
Laird, a lifelong bachelor, live alone. On a fishing visit
to an hotel at Killin he had met, in the distant past, a
stockbroker twelve years younger than himself, called
J. K. Edward. He later invited this casual acquaintance
for a Saturday-to-Monday visit. J.K. came, and remained for fifty-five years. It was a rather surprising
friendship. J.K. was an old Etonian, not without family
pride, for it was a dire offence to call him "Edwards."
But his appearance and intonation did not suggest Eton,
or indeed anywhere in particular unless it be the Silver
Ring on some obscurer racecourse. In late middle life,
when I first knew him, he was a gross-looking man with
a husky gruffness of a kind that, but for J.K.'s temperate-
ness, would have been called a "whisky" voice. He wore
loud checks and addressed young women as "little
lady"; had an immense knowledge of social scandals,
past and present; enjoyed risqué conversation, and took,
on the whole, a low view of human nature. A man of
coarse and common clay, you would have said, and the
most improbable life-companion for the little, tranquil
Laird, all gentleness and courtesy. But in fact there was
in that common-looking clay which was J.K. a vein of

fine gold. For his devotion to the Laird was absolute
and unselfish, active with delicate consideration. In so
far as the Laird, during his prolonged old age, had to
renounce more and more of the activities in which he
had delighted, J.K. renounced them too. He shortened
his paces to keep step with the older man, and geared
down his full-blooded way of life to match the dimin-
ished beat of the Laird's own slower rhythm. When
the weather was too rough, or the butts too distant, for
the Laird to join the shooters, J.K. also stayed behind.
He took a morning and evening stroll up the Glen,
towering in a flapping cape over the little old man at
his side, at a rate which must have been exasperating
to one of his stride, for the Laird crept, in his last years,
like a snail. He drove with the Laird : he sat with him :
he watched over him : he stood between him and all
petty annoyances. And it was all done from sheer
affection. J.K. had his own business ; he was comfortably
off ; he paid his share of the household expenses. His
attachment, that exacted so much real self-sacrifice, was
as genuine as it was touching.

Would the Laird, on his side, have been capable, had
the case arisen, of a like devotion to J.K. ? I have no
idea. For seven years running we spent a fortnight each
autumn at Glenlochay, and from time to time were
summer guests at the Islet. The Laird was invariably
the most courteous and considerate of hosts. But I never
succeeded in penetrating the veil of his kindly formality
to the core, or indeed to the outer layers, of his
mind and character. He said very little, and most of
what he said was the small change of polite conversation ; questions on the day's sport, fears and hopes for
the weather, the punctual recurrence of his standing

observation that the hills did not get any lower. His mind must have been well stocked from his massive reading, but he rarely mentioned books, and never discussed ideas. He could be merry enough after dinner at the bridge table, especially when his old crony Daddy Ford was a guest. Daddy Ford was a card-player of deliberation; he liked to ponder well before committing himself, and when Daddy made one of the Laird's four, a bell, a trumpet, and a toy drum were placed upon a shelf beneath the card table. The Laird himself was a quick player and when Daddy's hesitations began to irk him, the bell was tinkled as a first warning. If Daddy, his indecision only aggravated by this hint, still fingered first one and then another of his cards, the little drum was beaten. Whereupon, as a rule, Daddy laid down a card, for there was a sense of fate, of finality, in those drum-taps. But I have known occasions when Daddy's frantic efforts to recall which suit was trumps, or whether the ace of hearts had yet been played, could not be stayed or brought to a decision even by the drum. The toy trumpet had to be blown. One blast was enough; Daddy played whatever card he happened to be touching with his finger-tips; and his opponents gathered in another trick.

All this was great fun to watch from the ingle-nook, whence a great log-fire threw "warm gules" on the Laird's amused old countenance, making the rosy rosier. But Daddy Ford was a traditional butt, and his visit a kind of minor Saturnalia in the customary calm decorum of the Laird's existence. He did not chaff, or jest with, his other guests; his humour was reflective, and included no personal sallies, no dart-throwing to provoke, or to betray, his or their sensibilities.

But the main reason why, after so long an acquaintance, I am still in the dark as to the Laird's real nature,
and unable to answer my question: Would the Laird
have been capable of J.K.'s selflessness? is the extraordinary atmosphere of sanctity in which the Laird
lived. I have visited many and diverse homes in my day,
but I have never met with anything comparable to the
hushed circumspection with which the Laird was
treated by his household and guests alike. It was not
quite the atmosphere of a Court, for while Royalty
must of necessity be gently handled, the constraint laid
upon courtiers, in the main out of loyalty and respect,
has in it none the less a little pinch of fear. For Royalty
can, on occasion, turn "ratty." But I never detected a
trace of apprehension where the kindly old Laird was
concerned. We breathed, in his homes, the air of a
temple rather than of a palace: the Laird might have
been a "holy man," or the Incarnation of a Buddha.
We were not, but felt that we might well have been,
asked to take our shoes off when we entered his front
door. In most English houses the routine, however well
starched, is softened or bent to suit the visitors, there is
an implicit conferring of a "freedom" in the welcoming
handshakes; the hostess will even wait, after dinner is
upon the table, for a tardy guest. But at the Islet or
Glenlochay it was the guests who had to shed their free
and easy ways; it was the host, the little holy man,
silver-haired and benevolent, to whose habits all must
conform. It was not for him, on the stroke of eight
o'clock, to count heads, or to make sure that the
principal lady guest was present, before going into
dinner. If she was not down, that was her affair. The
Laird rose and led the way into the dining-room, ahead

of his guests. Once there, he carved the joints or the birds with a craftsman's attention; so that the principal lady might well hope to slip unnoticed into the chair at his side, and so to escape the loss of "a life." But if she did so hope, she had forgotten J.K. For there was a tradition at Glenlochay, imparted by the seasoned to the novice guests, that to each newcomer so many "lives" were allowed; when these had been lost, it was the end of you. You were not asked again. To be late for a meal cost a life; to knock out your pipe on the metal-work of the wagonnette cost another. You very properly lost one if you omitted to tell the Laird that it had taken more than one shot to kill your stag, or forgot to confess your misses. The notches against you were made and counted in J.K.'s head. But nobody ever pretended to discover just how many "lives" were allowed, or whether the allowance was the same for all.

I lost my last life, after seven years of punctuality and of truthfulness about the day's stalking, by falling ill. It was true that I fell ill with a certain lack of consideration. A specialist from Edinburgh had to be sent for and given a meal; I was carried out of the Lodge on a stretcher and put into an ambulance; there was a good deal of fuss and agitation. All the same, when two years later I had completely recovered and was stalking again on other forests, it was a shock to discover there was to be no forgiveness for me. I was never invited again. Both the Laird and J.K. must have known that stalking in Glenlochay was the high, bright peak of my holidays, for I had never been inarticulate about the intensity of my enjoyment. But they were not thinking of me or of my fun. J.K., I have no doubt, was thinking of the Laird, whose peace I had once disturbed. And

the Laird, I suppose, was thinking of himself. Or had
J.K. a veto? Could he obstruct the motions of the
Laird's own amiable heart? We shall never know. For
it is one of the consequences of being preserved in
cotton-wool, or existing in a little home-made Lhasa,
that the object of all that care and reverence cannot be
weighed on any scales. J.K., whom it was difficult to
like and easy to weigh, would have needed pure gold
and plenty of it, to counterbalance his rough, devoted
heart. And perhaps, after all, in the fidelity of that gruff
watchdog was to be found a true index to the character
of his charming, spoilt old friend.

To this day, when two or more Glenlochayites meet,
and after notes have been compared about guest-
behaviour under the impact of J.K., the same old stories
are likely to crop up. There is the one about the young
stockbroker, not bred to the country, who shot a white
cock-pheasant and brought it in consternation to the
Laird: "I'm dreadfully sorry, Laird, but I'm afraid I've
shot a seagull." There is the cautionary tale of the very
old friend indeed who, having been regularly invited
for the grouse-driving for more than twenty years,
confused probability with certainty and allowed his
cartridges to reach Glenlochay before the customary invitation had reached himself. He got a postcard from the
Laird: "Some cartridges have arrived for you: where
do you want them sent?" That was, not undeservedly,
the end of him. There was the Russian lady married to
an Englishman who, after two days of pheasant-
shooting, decided that she was not amused. She told
J.K. that a telegram had come with the news that her
small son was seriously injured and that she must
return to London at once. What she did not know was

that telegrams were brought by a boy who walked two miles from Killin and was consoled by Mrs Pheby, the woman-butler, with cake and ginger-beer. Mrs Pheby was under bond to report all such incidents to J.K., who thus knew that no telegram had arrived and that the lady was lying. He expressed his sympathy, and said that as he, too, had to travel to London that night, he would have the pride and pleasure of escorting her. The lady decided that a fortnight at Glenlochay was more endurable than ten hours tête-à-tête with J.K., whereupon her mother's intuition told her that her son's injuries were, after all, but slight. She stayed.

But our favourite story was that of the Yorkshire parson who, "following round," peppered the Laird in the next butt. He returned south, and getting several weeks' start of his victim, put it about that the Laird had peppered him. This came to the ears of the Laird, who sent for the parson and asked him to explain himself. "I'm most awfully sorry," said the parson, "and I really did not mean to tell a lie, but I was so terribly upset by the whole affair that I honestly couldn't remember whether you shot me or I shot you."

Glenlochay, through which the river Lochay runs and falls, now silvery, now amber-coloured, with all the tricks and graces of a highland stream, stretches away towards Rannoch Moor and the Black Mount from the western end of Loch Tay. The Laird's ground, extending to about fifty thousand acres, took in the hills, of respectable height, on both banks of the river, and was about twelve miles in length, from the Lodge to the farthest beats. The Lodge itself, low and long and whitewashed, lies snugly backed against a wooded

foothill in the mouth of the Glen. It faces south-west
for comfort and looks over the heads of garden flowers,
unnaturally bright as are all Highland blossoms, to a
hayfield and the river. The river, here placid and
deliberate, is fringed with alders that, to my Norfolk
eye, seemed more than life-size. The hayfield I remember for the bright greens of the aftermath between the
belated haycocks, but more memorably, at my first
sight of it, for the flying form of Muriel Gore, racing
with her hair unloosed. Why she raced I no longer
recall, unless it was that she was eighteen and felt like it;
but her hair was pale gold and flew out behind her as
she ran. She was slender, too, and I thought of dryads,
but did not say so to J.K. Muriel and her sister Kathleen
were great-nieces of the Laird, and it was reasonable to
hope, after that early enchantment among the haycocks,
that one or the other would be commonly found enlivening, with her beauty and charm, that bachelor
lodge. But it was not so. They were rare birds at
Glenlochay, scared away, I feel sure, in spite of their
affection for the kindly Laird, by the crudities of J.K.,
whose tap-room gallantry and wheezy archness repelled
their straightforward young minds. Indeed, but for an
exception like their sister-in-law Margery (now Lady
Earle), eyed and ankled like a gazelle, who sped up the
hills to kill deer with the skill and enthusiasm of the
seasoned stalker that she was, Glenlochay was not a
place for women. They were too palpably "the ladies";
there was a faint suggestion of cloakroom segregation
in their banishment to the formal upstairs drawing-room
in which no book was to be found. They were not
permitted to join the guns until lunch-time, since J.K.
must be free to change his shirt in his butt. They were

asked if they would care for a drive in the afternoon, and they were wise to care.

But for a man, or at any rate for myself, Glenlochay was paradise. The early, solitary breakfast, with cold grouse on the sideboard; the punctual crunch of the dogcart on the ground outside: Gregor Macdonald at the door to ask if Misterr Jawnes had his bullets: old John the coachman, bearded and morose, but watching the signs of the weather as keenly as if the day's fun were to be his, not mine; all these unchanging preludes to pleasure filled me, for all their familiarity, with a vast contentment. The seven-mile drive up the Glen was a slow one, for it was mostly uphill and the pony, who was to climb the hill later on, husbanded his strength by walking, but never too slow for me. When, on occasion, I was whirled up the Glen in twenty minutes by some visitor ready to risk his car on that narrow, stony track rather than rise early, I realised how much of the day's enjoyment was held in the gradual unfolding of the hills, and in our pony-paced emergence, clop by clop, from a country of forest trees, of larch and elm, alder and sycamore, into the bare and open glen. Besides, if one went too fast, how could Cameron (pronounced Carmeron with the first syllable long-drawn-out), the enormous farmer, wish us good luck from his front door, and allow Jimmy Menzies to make his recurrent joke: "Yon man would make a grand beast"? For Cameron must have weighed twenty stone at least, a much greater weight than his few small fields seemed to be capable of nourishing. But no doubt he ran sheep on the hills, the sheep that so excitingly, and at times exasperatingly, complicated the stalker's approach to the deer. For Glenlochay had never been a recognised

deer-forest; in the earlier years of the Laird's tenancy
the grouse-shooting was the thing, with pheasant and
blackcock in November, and the spying, stalking, and
shooting of a single stag an event to be celebrated even,
I have been told, to drunkenness. But gradually the
deer increased in numbers, drifting over from the Black
Mount, and wandering on both sides of the Glen; the
keepers became stalkers, Ben Chaluin at the head of the
Glen was reserved as a sanctuary, and about forty stags
were killed each season on one or other of seven "beats."
But the sheep were never taken off the hill; the Glen
bottom was dotted with "fanks" used at the gatherings,
and many a ragged old blackface has alerted the hinds,
and spoilt a promising stalk, by "whustling" through
his nose from the crown of a knoll. It was an intricate
task to approach deer without disturbing sheep, and
demanded much patience and such use of dead ground
and cover as won concealment not from one direction,
but from two or more at once. For mountain sheep,
even if not startled, will draw together when men are
about, and the deer miss nothing of the sheep's behaviour.

Another advantage to be had from that slow progres-
sion up the Glen was time to watch the weather. The
choice of beat, the point of departure, the plan of cam-
paign—all these depend, in deer-stalking, upon the
direction of the wind. For although the red-deer have
keen sight and are, especially the hinds, naturally
watchful, it is upon their noses, not their eyes, that
they mostly depend for safety. At the taint of men
upon the breeze, even from a mile away, up go their
noses, and they are off and away. And the breeze that
carries the taint can be slight indeed—sometimes barely

perceptible on a wetted forefinger or by tossing a wisp of dry grass into the air, so that, on a windless morning after rain when the under-edges of the clouds draping the hill-tops were smoking and writhing in indecision, moving a trifle to the west on Meal Gurdie ("but it will be whurrling in yon corrie"), drifting slowly eastward on Ben Heaskernich, seeming to lift over Ben Clach but to sink into Misty Corrie, it was no loss for us to have an hour and a half in which to see the weather establish itself, for good or ill. And even when "the wall" was reached, where the road ended and the pony was taken out of the shafts and saddled with the deer-saddle, there were often another three miles to walk, up the treeless, flat-bottomed head of the Glen, before we turned to the hill, on this side or that, and the day began. But after the trees had been left behind, and before the wall was reached, the switchback road had passed beneath a bare green hummock on which stood William Macdonald's cottage, and William himself, spy-glass slung, staff in hand, waiting before it. William had the face of a snipe, fine-drawn and eager; searching blue eyes, and a small, lithe figure, very neatly dressed in a good tweed. He was the stalker for the far beats, and no relation to Gregor Macdonald, the head keeper. Gregor was a master of the art, and regarded William, I think, as inclined to be impulsive; and indeed William's speed on the hill was remarkable. But I only once knew him to blunder through haste, and his intense, un-professional enjoyment of the job he was paid to do delighted me. He rarely smiled except at the first greeting; he hardly ever spoke; but his keenness was as unmistakable as that of a fox-terrier ratting, and declared in much the same way. For every movement

of his small, wiry body expressed the eager concentration of a dog hunting. And when, as often happened,
Jimmy Menzies came with us to carry my rifle, my
happiness was complete. Jimmy was a younger and
stronger man than William, with every gift of the born
stalker, and the pair of them worked together, when
William was in command, in complete accord, both
enjoying the game for its own sake. But Jimmy was
less taciturn than the run of Highlanders, and liked to
recall past adventures; he would pause, as we climbed,
to point out "yon awfu' green patch" below Ben More
beside which Misterr Jawnes had killed the "twins," a
pair of eight-pointers of like colour and all but identical
heads and weights, or the white stones in Larig na
Veachig where we had broken the spell after seven
blank days in rain and snow. The eighth day had been
the worst of all, with mist as well as rain, and we were
returning, chilled and discouraged, in a murk almost
too dim for spying, when a last look up the Larig,
which lay gloomy as a Hell pictured by John Martin,
disclosed beasts among the stones. We stalked them in
the gloom, and I shot a heavy black stag and a second
galloping away, and thereafter the luck turned. But
memory is strangely reluctant to hold pictures of blank
days, or even of the sombre magnificence of the hills,
all purples and indigos, under the dark canopy of
storm-clouds. I have been, I feel sure, more stirred at
the time by the menace and mystery, the sudden reces-
sion into lurid obscurity, of the familiar corries in bad
weather, than by their serene loveliness in sunshine.
But it is always with the sun on our backs that I now
see the three of us, William, Jimmy, and myself, beginning the climb from the Glen, while George Macdonald

or Dan or Ebb Steel is leading the pony away by gentler slopes to the spot from which our signals should be seen. There has always been, to me, a palpably sensuous pleasure in the mere planting of a foot on a Scotch mountain: an agreeable "give" and a yielding to pressure in the bog-fed mosses of the lower slopes, a wiry spring in the short heather, and a firm, rubbery resilience where the black peat itself is exposed among the hags. And when the main climb is over, and one can stride out upon the short, firm turf of the tops, where the ptarmigan crouch and skulk among the stones, the good, swift going, over such commanding ridges and summits, in so brisk an air, is sheer exhilaration.

But if Misty Corrie was our beat, even the first slopes, through waist-high bracken, were steep enough, and I have not been sorry when a pair of wheatears made an excuse for a momentary pause. But William and Jimmy were not interested in wheatears, or in twites either; like other gamekeepers and stalkers I have met, they did not know the names of quite common birds and flowers, although always on the alert for a sprig of white heather.

So unless the eagle himself appeared, I got few breathers until the first spying-place was reached, and by that time the sweat was running down my back and chest in big drops, a sensuous pleasure unknown to women. But at the spying-place we all threw ourselves upon the heather, backs to a stone, and our telescopes came out of their leather cases. The eye-lens of my own would be misty at once, from the steam rising from my eye-sockets, and there would be a good deal of wiping of eyes and glass in turn, but William remained cool

whatever the weather, and his glass swept the hillsides
with rapid certainty. Spying is an art in which the
amateur, unless bred in the Highlands, cannot hope to
equal the professional. For the approach to deer, an
experienced rifle can live even to excel the stalkers,
especially if he has had a soldier's training in the "use
of ground and cover." (I have myself on more than one
occasion reached a position for an easy shot by a route
which the stalkers declared to be impracticable. "Ye'll
be in full sight of him all the way," but in fact there
was a subtle slope, and the ground across which I
wriggled was, I could see, dead ground.) But to "make
good" whole hillsides before an advance, lest some stray
hind with calf, lying perdue in the heather, should be
startled into betraying us to beasts still out of sight,
requires, if it is to be done quickly enough, a close
familiarity with every feature of the corrugated scree-
strewn slopes. Speed is essential, or you will lose the
day, and accuracy more so, or you will lose a stalk.
And when beasts are spied, it needs long experience to
make sure, at a great distance and across the shimmer of
a heat-haze, that a shootable stag is among the bunch.

We expected little from the first spy, which was of
the routine "making good" sort, and were soon
climbing again. For deer, when resting, lie facing downhill, and if you can stalk them from above, you greatly
lessen the chance of being detected. Once on the high
ground, we strode freely, and if the breeze was steady
felt that we had the mastery, and it was a great moment
when, after a spy, William shut up his glass with a
snap, and said : "He'll du." And now the fun began. To
get downwind and, if possible, above our chosen stag
might on occasion demand a couple of hours of alternate

descents and climbs; there were sheep to outwit, as I
have said; it might be necessary to crawl up a burn,
kneeling on sharp stones, or, worse still, to creep
through patches of burnt heather, which excoriates the
wrists; and when the chosen spot for a shot is reached,
and heads cautiously raised, inch by inch, for a peep,
the deer may have grazed away out of sight, or a
treacherous little wind, swirling in the hollows of a
corrie, may call for a retreat and a fresh plan. Or the
deer may be there, but lying down, the shootable stag
at ease behind a rock, with only his antlers showing,
and the hinds dispersed about him, their big flap-ears,
like the twin blades of a dicotyledon, erect and alert.
In which case there is nothing to do but wait until the
stag stands up. There are only two ways of killing a
stag dead; you must shoot him through the heart or
through the neck; with a bullet through his body, if
the heart be missed, he may go far, and die miserably.
To wound a beast is the one fear of a stalker, and even
when the stag is on his feet and at an easy range, no
shot may be fired until he turns so as to expose his
heart. Equally the shooter must make sure that his own
position is comfortable and secure; that he does not fire
when blown or panting from his crawl, that grasses do
not obscure his sights: that the weight of the rifle is
supported, not by a tremulous elbow, but by the earth
itself. The rifle-barrel must be motionless when the
trigger is squeezed; for this, contact with the shoulder
must be of the lightest, and the left hand cushioning
the barrel from the earth, relaxed and inert. To make
sure of this, in the presence of these watchful hinds, is
the shooter's responsibility; the stalker has brought him
to the spot, and can do no more for him. The slope of

the ground, tufts of heather, rocks, grass—there are
many awkwardnesses and handicaps to be overcome
before that barrel is aligned and at rest, and the wrig-
gling, the shifting, the adjusting of body and rifle, must
all be done so quietly as to be imperceptible to those
percipient and sensitive hinds. Modern rifles have so flat
a trajectory, that at any range up to two hundred yards
a motionless barrel and a fine sight should mean a clean
kill. But the rifle itself leaps at the shot, and the stalker's
"got him!" is always a welcome sound. Triumph is
inevitably followed by a pang of pity for a kingly stag
lying dead upon the heather, but it would never do to
confess this to the stalker or ghillie, and there is the
business of the gralloch, and of signalling to the pony-
boy, to be attended to. All who go stalking should
learn to do their own gralloching, with speed and neat-
ness, although the first plunge of the arms, elbow deep,
into the hot entrails, is an ordeal for the queazy. But if
the pony is far away, or there is mist about, time can
be saved if both stalker and ghillie can be released while
the shooter cleans up. And there is humiliation in
remaining incompetent to do a necessary job through
fastidiousness.

Luncheon is curiously ceremonious on the hill. It
always went against the grain with me to sit, after the
shared labours and excitements of the stalk, apart from
the others, chewing the breast of a cold grouse. I should
have liked to chat with those keen, friendly men; to
discuss the plans for the afternoon; to be told the
names of distant peaks and ranges; to recapitulate the
morning's adventures. But the unwritten rule was
absolute; the rifle must eat solitary and aloof, until the
moment came to hold up the flask of whisky. Then

William walked across, cap in hand, and took the flask to Jimmy, and both drank to further successes.

And yet, perhaps, these twenty minutes of solitude among the great silent hills were justified. There were some things that all three could not share. The pleasure in the sight of the wheatear was one of them, and the profounder satisfaction to be got from the shapes and colours and ever-changing moods of the hills was another. For, ultimately, the pre-eminence of deer-stalking as a sport does not lie in the hard exercise, the conflict with storm and steepness, or in the fascinating business of circumventing, by skill and stratagem, the most alert and wary of quarries. The fun in all these is enormous; but the crowning enjoyment is of the ineffable beauty of the red-deer's home. For grace of outline, for depth or delicacy of colour, for the allure in their folds and corries, Scotch hills must surely, despite their lack of scale and of the greater mountain splendours, be hard to match. No doubt the "sweet influences" of these enfolding hills were felt throughout the day, but the business of stalking deer demands strict attention, and to relax and gaze, possessed by beauty, was a profitable interruption.

There was, besides, the fascination of the red-deer themselves. If deer had been seen and watched, a blank day mattered little. It is provoking when a stalk goes wrong: when the breeze unaccountably swings round and you feel it upon the back of your neck as the noses of the deer go up: when an old cock grouse explodes from the heather shouting "Go back, go back!" just as you are crawling in for the shot; or when the blasted sheep run together, like the black-faced fools they are, upon the opposite slope. But to see the deer springing away and up the hill, making nothing of gradient, however severe; easy and elegant, on legs so slender you would think their slim fetlocks could never carry weight up to twenty stone or more—to see this is to see the very perfection of rhythmic motion. And the head of a stag, when the spread of the antlers is wide and even, as he pauses for a moment to look back upon what disturbed him, is a noble sight indeed. And in the last days of September or early October, when the rut is on, there are fresh excitements. For now the stags are unappeasably restless, night and day; either circling their bunch of hinds, jealous and possessive, or travelling incessantly in search of hinds to be won from a weaker than themselves. From time to time they stretch out their necks, now shaggy and dark with hairy masculinity, and roar a challenge. The roar of a stag echoing in the hollows of a corrie, and breaking the customary silence of those remote and solitary hills, has a peculiar thrill in it. If one thinks of lions, it is not of course a true "roar"; it is nearer in kind to the bellow of a bull, but lower and hoarser, and with unexpected carrying power. And if the roar is answered, there is hope, with a little luck, of the sight of a battle. Challenged and challenger meet head to head, antlers clashing, but body-weight is what seems to count rather than armament, for a "hummel," or hornless stag, if his body be the thicker, can meet and defeat a royal beast, pushing him downhill with bare forehead alone. I am ashamed to confess that on one occasion, not to disappoint the frantic urgings of William Macdonald, I shot a heavy beast at the moment of victory over a lighter, but plucky, antagonist. The astonishment and delight of the smaller stag, when his formidable antagonist fell

dead at his forefeet, could almost be seen. I thought of
Lord Randolph Churchill and Lord Salisbury. It was
dusk when the fight took place, and the combatants,
locked together, stood out black against an orange sky.
I made a picture of the scene in chalks as a Christmas
card for William, and it had a place of honour in his
sitting-room until his early and lamented death.

But a shot so late in the day as that must have caused
William grave anxiety. For the Laird held his stalkers,
not his guests, responsible for seeing that the guests
were back at the Lodge in time for eight o'clock dinner.
I have no idea what the sanctions for a breach of this
rule may have been, but there was no doubt at all
about the stalker's dismay if it became a near thing, so
it is likely that in this case the gralloched stag was left
on the hill till the morning, with William's handker-
chief tied to his antlers to keep away the foxes. This
meant a very early rising indeed for some ghillie and
pony-boy next morning and a loss of weight for the
entry in the stag-book, but nothing mattered so long as
the rifle appeared in the Laird's sitting-room, bathed
and in evening clothes, before the stroke of eight. And
of course I told my host that a beast had been left on
the hill: to have concealed it would have meant the
loss of a "life."

For seven seasons running I spent a fortnight on the
hills that grew yearly more familiar, with stalkers and
ghillies with whom I became ever more intimate and
companionable. It is small wonder that Glenlochay, for
all the slight restraints and eccentricities at the Lodge,
stands first among my pleasure-grounds. Here, and here
alone, did I ever win the privilege of doing my own
stalking—a sign of confidence not lightly given to other

than Highland-bred rifles by those cautious stalkers. But it would be ungrateful not to remember many other days of happiness on the hills, more especially at Lochluichart in Ross-shire. At Lochluichart, with Lord and Lady Northampton, all was fun and gaiety, warmed by longstanding friendship and shared affections. If Duncan Fraser, the head stalker, who looked, with his fine aquiline nose and small imperial, like some high-bred French general in the Crimean war, was at first faintly intimidating, the feeling did not last long. And no ghillie was ever more human and endearing than Sandy Urquhart, cheerful even when a lady-fisherman, while fishing from a boat, persisted in catching her fly in his ear. And young Kenneth Campbell, on the romantic West beat, was a stalker after my own heart. He was serious and unsmiling, but his enjoyment of the day was never made stale by habit. He loved the game for its own sake, and once his confidence was won, became a companion as well as a guide. Kenneth's sense of humour was of the proverbial Scotch sort. When his employer told him the well-known tale of the man who, by mistake, shot his own father on the hill and was ever after known as "Baghdad," Kenneth said: "That was a verra' good idea, my lord." He then went apart—for they were lunching—to drink in the burn. On his return he gravely formed up again: "And what for did they call him Baghdad?" Kenneth, unhappily, was stricken with a fatal disease, and died in the flower of his young manhood.

Above the loch, and delightfully accidented with hummocks and knolls and miniature ravines, was a grouse-moor where we shot over dogs. Even forty years ago this fascinating form of sport was going out of fashion, and a great pity it was. The shooter who moves only from butt to butt, necessarily skirting the great spread of heather and hag and rock and bracken where the grouse have their home, misses a great deal. He sees the coveys only on the wing. "Dogging," on the other hand, brings intimacy with both moor and birds; one sees the tender young heather, induced by burning, on which they feed: the sunny banks and hollows where they dust themselves: the knolls from which an old cock will have a furtive look round. And the systematic quartering and ranging of a good setter or pointer, attentive to the keeper's whistle, are a joy to watch. Then there is the recurring excitement of a determined point; the breathless haste to get into range before the dog looks back over his shoulder: the suspense as to just how and where and when the birds will explode from cover: it is all, under the hot sun, sweaty and strenuous and exhilarating work. For a good shot there is of course no tax upon his skill to compare with that to be had from driven birds; but the compensation for that lack, in the close acquaintance with the terrain, the hard exercise, the constant movement, and the fascination of the dogs, is not to be despised. If Nora was at times given to ranging too wildly—and I can still hear her name being shouted by an infuriated keeper—the Lochluichart setters were good dogs, who did not take us sixty yards uphill for a lark or a twite. And we had walked all day like men. They were happy days indeed, passed in the company of kindred spirits, and although later a curtain fell, never to rise again, the remembrance of them, and gratitude to those who provided them, abide.

Of the majestic hills of Fannich, and of Vernon

Watney, their fortunate possessor, I have written elsewhere; and in the forest of Glen More, which leads one
imperceptibly, by easy rolling crests, to the summit of
the Cairngorm, I had little luck. All the same the giant
Scotch firs rising above the silver-white sands that edge
the loch, and the sight of crested tits within a hundred
yards of the Lodge, helped to make up for blank days
and misses and inauspicious winds. And the fun and
high spirits of my hostesses did the rest.

The present generation, in the unlikely event of it
reading these words, will no doubt be offended by the
confession of a man, claiming to be civilised, that he
has found his own height of enjoyment in a sport which
involves the killing of a harmless and beautiful wild
creature. The athletic, sport-loving young men of today
prefer to stalk animals, whether red-deer in Scotland
or bigger game in Africa, with a camera rather than
with a rifle. It is a great advance, and one of which
I whole-heartedly approve. But were I to become
physically young once more, but with the memories of
my killer-days still fresh, could I be one of them, and
carry my cine-camera through the scrambles and crawls
and drenching and exhaustions of a long day on the
Misty Corrie beat, without a single regret for the
culminating moment, for the triumphant shot? I wish
I could say yes. There ought to be no question about it.
But the ancient, atavistic hunting instinct in us is stubborn and deep-seated. On the day I no longer want to
chase a rat I shall count myself among the camera-men.
But that day has not yet arrived. And there are other
considerations. One is that of the outlook of the Highland stalkers. These delightful characters were hunters:
they pursued the stag for his meat, as is proved by the

rule that on the day the sleepless, rutting stag has
fretted away his weight until his haunch is no longer
worth the winning, all stalking ceases. Unless stalkers
have changed out of all knowledge, their zest and
persistence will still demand, and expect, the reward of
a kill. And I must add, for candour's sake, a wholly
discreditable consideration, personal to myself. Great
as has been my delight in all forms of shooting, I have,
through inherited incompetence to hit a fast-flying
object, whether ball or bird, with bat, racquet, or gun,
never been a good shot. I have always minded this.
And the discovery that I could be an accurate shot with
a rifle and was born with a good eye for country was
vastly comforting to my vanity. Here was a sport in
which I could excel. I am not saying that I could ever
have killed a deer from vainglory alone. But I am
pretty sure that even today, given a couple of my
former companions, and the return of youth for a day,
I should be up and away to the hills again with a rifle,
not a camera. And I should have secret, shameful hopes
that old John the coachman, when he met me at the
station with the dog-cart, would repeat the old formula,
so comforting to a poor grouse-shot: "The stags *will*
be a-feared when they hear that Misterr Jawnes has
arrived!" Having confessed to this measure of blood-
thirstiness (as the opponents of sport will have it), I
must add that there was one aspect of deer-stalking
which, even while I revelled in it, left me uneasy. It
was the monstrous inequity of reserving such enormous
tracts of the loveliest country in these islands for the
pleasure of a mere handful of individuals. To every
rifle and his party anything up to 15,000 acres of
mountain and moor was allotted for the day. No man,

or woman, or child might invade this privacy, for fear
of disturbing the deer. The deer-forests of Scotland,
forty years ago, covered hundreds of thousands of acres
of the most delectable playground for all who love
scenery, walking, or climbing. No degree of pleasure
for the few can justify so great a deprivation of the
many. The Access to Mountains Act has, I believe,
already mitigated the evil: but I see no answer to those
who would have the Highlands as a whole made free
to hikers and to climbers. I would, however, make two
conditions. First, that motor-roads should not be
allowed to penetrate and destroy the lovely, the remote,
and the unspoilt glens. And, secondly, that sufficient
mountain sanctuaries should be set aside, forbidden to
the footsteps of man, to assure that the red-deer, under
skilled protection, should live their lives in quietness
and security. It is easy to say this now that my stalking
days are over. I believe that, if pressed, I must always
have said it.

I have had many unforeseen windfalls in my life. Few
can have been less easy to foretell than that Threadneedle
Street would prove to be a gateway into the Highlands.
My long association with Helbert Wagg and Company,
begun with an eye to a livelihood, has brought me in-
numerable blessings, quite unconnected with money-
making: affections, friendships and fun, and an object
for those day-to-day loyalties so essential to one
accustomed, as I was, to the incentives and obligations
inherent in membership of a school, a college, or a
regiment. These could have been hoped for, if not
counted upon. But that the same fair wind that blew
me, in bowler hat and pin-stripe trousers, into Threadneedle Street should also have blown me, in the oldest

of old tweeds, on to a Scotch mountain was hardly to have been expected. Yet so it was; and among my many unrepayable debts to H. W. & Co. I must reckon those long days of sheer delight given to me, with such unrewarded generosity, by the little old Laird, the only one of my partners I never got to know.

CHAPTER VI

REXINGER

I HAVE called this chapter after a man who played but a minor part in my City life because the paradox of his personality makes him no bad symbol for the City itself as I found it. Just as in Rexinger appearance and reality were wholly at odds, so did I find the actual City far different from the idea of it held by outsiders.

Rexinger's real name was Ernest Rechnitzer, but Mr Arthur Gairdner, the Scottish managing director of the British Overseas Bank, with whom at one time Rechnitzer had close relations, decided that his name was Rexinger. Gairdner, who once confided to me, after a second glass of port, that he was the only man in the City of London who understood banking, was, for all his bonhomie, tenacious of his opinions, and once his decision had been taken about Rechnitzer's name, nothing could shake it. So Rexinger it had to be, at any rate during business hours.

Rexinger then, of Jewish-Hungarian origin, was a good and loyal friend of the firm I served, but his outward appearance certainly belied his true nature. To say that he looked like an International Crook would be unfair to international crooks, who are much too cunning to look their parts. What Rexinger looked like was the Hollywood conception of an international crook. His beaky nose, his deep-set, hooded eyes that

moved incessantly from side to side, never resting upon
your own; his dubious silences; his immaculate purple
shirts embroidered with strange devices; his general air
of furtive conspiracy: all these combined to make
Rexinger, at first sight, too bad to be true. In fact he was
a simple, straight-thinking man, with an overriding
passion for fencing. His mind was fertile and ingenious
in what may be called the machinery of international
finance, but he was incapable of subterfuge.

Rexinger was concerned with the firm I served, and
with the British Overseas Bank, in some major trans-
actions with the Government of Roumania. Roumania
found herself at the end of the first World War with
a heavy burden of short-dated borrowings, Treasury
Bills and so on, held in many countries. She had no
means of repaying these at due date. The amount was
around twenty million sterling. The finance Minister,
Vintila Bratianu, a huge, sombre, bearded xenophobe,
had no intention of defaulting, but it was essential that
his country should have time to pay. Accordingly he
came, reluctantly, to London to negotiate a funding
operation, by which all his creditors would be asked to
accept long-dated bonds, at low interest, in exchange
for such I.O.U.s as they then held. I was too junior in
the firm to be present at all the negotiations with Mr
Bratianu, but I was often enough in attendance to
realise the part played in these difficult talks by M.
Titulesco, the Roumanian Ambassador in London. The
contrast between Finance Minister and Ambassador was
striking. Bratianu was slow, obstinate, and suspicious
of bankers; Titulesco, who looked like a Chinaman,
with his smooth yellow face, broad cheek-bones, and
sleek black hair, was all wit and sparkle and flexibility.

I imagine that Rexinger was kept out of sight; at any rate the confidence of Bratianu was eventually gained and, once given, remained unshaken.

Before, however, an operation on so great a scale in so many countries could be begun, provision had to be made for the expenses. The Roumanian Treasury was empty, and in order to raise the wind a preliminary loan, called the External Loan of 1922, was to be issued in the London market. It was to settle the detailed contract for this loan, and more especially to make sure that it was well and truly authorised by Roumanian law, that I was sent on my first journey to Bucharest in, I think, July of that year. Looking back, I find it a little surprising that I was sent single-handed on so responsible a mission, for although I was far from young in years, my experience in the City, owing to five years' absence during the war, was meagre. But at that time my firm's experience of long-distance negotiations abroad was also small, or they would assuredly have given me a secretary to help in the task of coding and decoding lengthy cables in the intervals of my sessions at the Roumanian Ministry of Finance.

Not that I travelled alone. The British Overseas Bank was our partner in the business, and they, too, sent a representative to Bucharest. But he was oddly chosen. He was a retired colonel, who had served with credit in Intelligence during the war, but knew nothing at all of finance. He was, I gathered, sent "to show the flag" of the B.O.B. (as the bank was known in the City).

I was introduced for the first time to the Colonel at Victoria Station. Before the train had left the station he asked me whether I had brought my medals. I had to admit that it had not occurred to me, since my business was to be financial, not ceremonial. He said that we might be invited to banquets. I thought it unlikely, since we were neither of us partners in our respective houses, but underlings, and said that in any case I felt equal to facing a banquet without medals. He then observed that it was a question of prestige. Prestige is too airy a thing to be argued about, so I turned to the morning papers and the Colonel went down the corridor. He did not return, and when later I followed him upon my lawful occasions I came upon him in another compartment displaying a case of miniature medals to two admiring, or tolerant, old ladies. Our prestige, it seemed, was being established even before we arrived at Dover.

During the four days' journey in the Orient Express the Colonel told me things, but I have forgotten them. On arrival at Bucharest we drove to the Athenée-Palace Hotel, where the porters were magnificently dressed, but the water, in a temperature of about 90° in the shade, was wholly cut off except for a few hours in the morning. The Ministry of Finance was less than a quarter of a mile from the hotel, but after a first humiliating visit to pay our respects to the Chef de Cabinet that ended in our rising from our gilt chairs to find that we had left pools of sweat upon their silken seats, we made the daily journey in a tiny Victoria, so low-slung that you had to step up but an inch or two to enter it.

In the afternoon we had our first meeting with the Finance Minister himself. He told us that we were just in time, since the law authorising the loan was to be passed by the Chamber next day. I asked to see the text of the law. The big, bearded man pulled out a

pencil and, after a moment's consideration, scrawled a
couple of lines in French on a piece of blotting paper.
He tore it off and pushed it across to me. "Will that
do?" he asked. Since I was under strict orders to have
the law scrutinised by a first-class lawyer before agreeing
to it, I said I would give him an answer in the morning.
He readily agreed, since the Chamber was not to meet
until the afternoon. He invited us both to be present at
the session.

This was not the sort of procedure I had expected.
It was decidedly more slapdash. We hurried off, the
Colonel and I, to the British Embassy. The Embassy
was a large and pleasant white villa standing among
really noble catalpa trees. The Ambassador had been
warned of our arrival and of our business, and I confidently rang the front-door bell. We were directed to
a side-door which led into the Chancery. Sir Herbert
Dering did not keep us long waiting. He was kind and
courteous—distant at first, but in the end inviting us to
lunch. He warmly commended to me the Embassy's
own lawyer, a Mr Rosenbaum (or some such name).
With a note of introduction from His Excellency I then
sought out Mr Rosenbaum. He was a charming man,
in appearance much resembling the late King Edward
VII. He was friendly, twinkling, and prompt. He
looked at my piece of blotting-paper, sat down at his
wide writing-table with the flowers and the silver
frames, took a half-sheet of note-paper, and wrote upon
it that the proposed law, if passed, would be entirely
valid, constitutional, and binding. We parted with the
warmest expressions of mutual regard. The next day
we attended the Chamber. Several of the deputies wore
peasant costume. One man was dressed in a long white

nightgown. Bratianu made a very short speech, and the law was passed unanimously without any debate.

That evening, as I sat at dinner in the hotel, a note was brought to me. It was from Mr Rosenbaum enclosing his bill for services rendered. It was for £2,500. I had not expected, of course, that I should get off with five guineas. I was prepared for twenty-five. Had it been £50 I should have felt robbed, but should not have protested. But £2,500!—for an opinion scribbled out of hand in my presence. I went back to Sir Herbert Dering. He was profoundly shocked. He swore that never again would the Embassy employ Mr Rosenbaum. He advised me to call upon the rascal and make my protest in person. I did so. I asked him if the amount had been expressed in sterling by error, being intended for lei. This suggestion shocked Mr Rosenbaum in his turn. He explained that the tariff on a case like this was based not upon the amount of work involved but upon the amount the bankers were likely to make out of it, and it was obvious, he said, that on a loan of this amount the bankers were likely to do very well for themselves. (In this he was not far wrong.)

I was acutely distressed. I felt that, on my first mission of trust, I had let the side down badly. I had to cable the dreadful news to H. W. & Co. I expected to be recalled, if not sacked. Nothing of the kind. The directors could not have been more merciful and forgiving. They only remarked, mildly, that another time I should ask the price before buying a legal opinion in a foreign country. They said they would handle the matter themselves. I think Mr Bratianu's aid was enlisted; at any rate a lesser, but still outrageous, sum was eventually paid to the voracious and winning Mr Rosenbaum.

Then came another shock, a cable from H. W. & Co.:
"Have you provided in the law for the issue of a dollar
tranche?" I had not. To do so had not been in my
instructions, but again I felt that I should have had the
foresight to ask for such provision. The law was now
passed, and I recognised for the first time the force of
the expression "sweating blood." I hurried to Mr
Bratianu. He said the law would do quite well as it
stood, if the bankers felt like issuing a tranche in dollars.
I consulted another lawyer, with the heroic name of
Diomedes (after enquiring what his fee would be: it
was something like five guineas). He confirmed what
Mr Bratianu had said. But my directors were adamant.
Dollars must be specified in the law. Mr Bratianu was
quite undisturbed; he scribbled on another piece of
blotting-paper, went down to the Chamber and
amended the law. But I felt that my career was now in
real jeopardy.

My spirits were not improved by my general situation. The heat was exhausting, and I worked about
eighteen hours a day, partly at the Ministry, but usually
in my hotel bedroom. My principal affliction was the
coding and decoding of cables. The Roumanian Post
Office was quite incapable of transcribing correctly
groups of four capital letters. After sending solid chunks
of the draft contract I would receive a message: "Your
cable incomprehensible repeat," or I would spend hours
over some lengthy despatch in code which, when
decoded, made no sense.

Meanwhile the Colonel sat in the lounge of the hotel
in deepening depression. He flatly refused to lend a
hand with the coding or the decoding, on the grounds
that he knew nothing about banking. When I pointed

8

out that I needed a de-coding clerk, not a banker, he mentioned prestige. His depression was caused by the strange lack of invitations to banquets, or even of a summons from the Queen Mother. For he was obsessed with the notion that it was Queen Marie's amiable habit to invite all British army officers to pay her a visit, which might, who knows, lead most agreeably to this or to that. I am not sure that he had not dreams of a medal. But not a sign came from the Palace. Our only invitation was to lunch at the Embassy, where Lady Dering playfully betrayed the rather revealing fact that, before our arrival, the Ambassador had been under the impression that bankers were not people to be received socially.

Finally the Colonel disappeared altogether for three days without warning to his colleague. He reappeared in high fettle. It seemed that he had, under Providence, scraped acquaintance in the hotel bar with the Roumanian Navy. The Royal Roumanian Navy at that time consisted of a smart launch on the Danube. The Colonel had been for a trip in the Navy, had been the guest of honour at a pocket banquet on board, had worn his medals, and had made a speech. Prestige had come into its own, and the Colonel was a new man.

My second trip to Bucharest, in the following spring, was upon the business of the Consolidation Loan. This time my companion was Rexinger himself, whom I knew but slightly when together we boarded the Orient Express in Paris. I was still but half-accustomed to his hooded side-glances, and felt a little self-conscious as we paced the platform before the train started. It was a relief when a bearded young man, whom I had met casually on some forgotten occasion, accosted me

without seeming to notice Rexinger. "Are you expect-
ing a romantic adventure on this train?" he asked. His
plump lips shone red and wet under the arc-lamps.
Heavy with responsibility, I had to admit that I was not.
"I always find a romantic adventure on the Orient
Express," he said. His curly young beard jarred me and
I did not wish him luck. Whenever I saw him later,
he was always alone and asleep.

In those days the Orient Express took four days and
nights to reach Bucharest, and I had leisure to become
acquainted with Rexinger. When he was not talking
about coupons and talons and tranches and the
mechanics of a large-scale issue of Government Bonds,
he talked about his beloved fencing. I also discovered,
I forget how, that he was a devout and practising
Catholic. A good, rather simple soul.

We were traversing Europe in early May, a thing I
had not done before and have not done since, and I was
transported by the sheer beauty of the countryside. I
have often told myself that an English spring, say in
Kent or Devon, is unrivalled, but I must admit that in
point of mass and multitude, of variety and surprise,
the wild flowers and trees of Switzerland, Northern
Italy, Jugoslavia, and Transylvania are more exciting
still. I was ravished and astonished by such super-
abundance. But I could not share my delight. Rexinger
did not look out of the window. He had seen it so often
before, he said. He liked better to fix his eyes upon
the minute-hand of his watch, and to calculate, by the
number of bumps made by the train each minute, the
speed of our progress. If you know (as he knew), he
explained, the length in metres of each separate rail, the
calculation is easy. For as the wheels cross the point

where rail meets rail, each carriage makes a slight, but to Rexinger's trained ears a perceptible, bump.

There was one rule enforced upon this transcontinental journey which struck me as tiresome. In the dining-car no wines were served except those of the country through which we were passing. For an adventurous palate that is fair enough. The tiresomeness occurred if you passed a frontier during meal-times. For then all the bottles, even if still three-quarters full, were swept away by the waiters, and you must either order a new bottle of a new country, or go without. It is one thing to be compelled to buy a native wine; it is quite another to be debarred from drinking what you have paid for unless the soil beneath your carriage-wheels has actually produced the contents of your glass.

We arrived at Bucharest after midnight, and the next day being Sunday, I took a long lie. But when I met Rexinger at lunch, I learnt that he had risen at seven to attend early Mass. This capacity for self-discipline, beneath that dubious façade, impressed me.

Rexinger's adroit and professional cooperation allowed me leisure to look about me. Bucharest, physically, is no more exciting than Nice, but it afforded two pleasures which never palled. One was the sight of the white oxen that drew the municipal water-carts. I have seen splendid specimens of these lordly and impassive animals in Tuscany and Umbria, but none to equal this Roumanian strain. The span of their great curving black-tipped horns was immense. A pair of such heads could make a side-street impassable. During the midday siesta they lay down, side by side, in the shade. Whatever their thoughts, if any, the look in their eyes was mild and magnanimous.

The other pleasure was to drive under a long avenue of lime trees in full flower to eat caviare out of doors. The caviare was red, not black, and was not served, as in this country, in small, grudging dabs. It was ladled out of a great bowl into a soup-plate, with fine, free swings of the ladle, and you could ask for more. There were no trumpets, but the scent of the limes was accompaniment enough. It would also be ungrateful of me not to remember the hospitality of Mr Adams, the Commercial Attaché, and a youthful English couple, the Ralph Carlisles. How this young pair came to be living in Bucharest I cannot remember, but it was refreshing, in that rather garish city, to be accepted with kindness in a cool grey flat where each picture, each piece of sculpture, was choice and cherished. As for Mr Adams, he flourished too early, for in those days commercial attachés were decidedly looked down upon by the regular diplomats. He was a man of great ability and trenchant speech, who found it hard to conceal his impatience with what he considered the superficiality of the Chancery. He had made it his business to study the economics of Roumania with thoroughness, and but for him I should have found it difficult, if not impossible, to collect the facts which it behoved us, as sponsors of Roumanian Government Bonds, to know. His printed reports seemed to me masterly and statesmanlike documents, but he confessed to me sadly that as far as he knew nobody ever read them. If somebody did read them he returned no sign of having done so to the author. The Commercial Attaché was not asked to dinner at the Embassy. Had he been, he would have enlivened the company, for Adams could be witty as well as sagacious.

Vintila Bratianu himself, although a stubborn fighter over every clause, every line of the contract, was kind and friendly. He was at heart a countryman, and drove me on one occasion, by atrocious roads, to an oak-wood renowned for its golden orioles. It was a most tantalising visit. The great wood resounded with flute-like calls, but so thick was the foliage that I got but one fleeting glimpse of an oriole. The fluting might be immediately overhead, but we craned our aching necks in vain.

It must, I think, to judge from the state of the crops, have been on the occasion of my earlier visit that Bratianu took me to see his own farm. Bucharest stands in the middle of a flat alluvial plain, and for many miles we drove past fields of stunted maize and short, wispy rye. The houses were apparently built of mud; the peasants were lean, stringy, and sunburnt almost to blackness. Suddenly we turned up a side-road between fields of Indian corn higher than our heads. A great farmstead was crowded with tractors and machinery. There was an enormous barn containing the latest American corn-drying plant. I asked my host if the splendour of his crops compared with the miserable growths of the peasants' was due to fertilisers. No, he said, only to deep ploughing. The peasants, who used wooden ploughshares, could only scratch the surface.

"Then why not, Excellency, if your soil is so rich . . .?"

"We have no capital."

"But foreign capital, to transform this whole plain into a farm like your own . . ."

The old xenophobe frowned at me. He looked almost savage. "Never, never, never!" he said. So that was

that. I do not know whether the Russians have yet
extracted the wealth from that rich earth. It is unlikely,
even if they have, that those thin peasants are any the
fatter for it.

On our return journey in the Orient Express I learnt
something new about locomotives. We were still on
the Roumanian plain when our engine broke down.
We all descended from our carriages and sat among
the wild flowers, waiting for a breakdown gang to
come and do repairs. After an hour or so a small engine
bustled up with a crew of experts in the tender. They
swarmed round our enormous engine. They began
removing from it all those fascinating steel shafts which
joint together the fore and rear wheels of an engine,
and make gestures, when the wheels are running, like
those a man makes when cranking up his car. After
stripping the wheels of these connecting-rods, and
removing various minor contraptions, the tough little
men made a faggot-like bundle of the lot and hoisted
it, with pulleys and levers, on to the buffers of the
engine.

"*Tiens!*" said a French passenger. "*Donc tout cela, ça
ne sert à rien!*" It seemed that he was right. We were
told to climb in, the whistle blew, and the enormous
train went on as cheerfully as before.

I began this chapter by saying that Rexinger's
personality, in which the apparently complicated and
mysterious turned out to be simple almost to naiveté,
might stand as a symbol for the City itself. Certainly
outsiders, in those days, knew little of what went on
there. One often heard that a father or an uncle was
"something in the City." Who ever heard of a man
being "something at the Bar" or "something in

Medicine"? When I first joined Helbert Wagg and Company I had, as a full-fledged barrister, a smattering of Company Law, and I could read a balance-sheet. I had also, at Eton, done those sums we called "Stocks and Shares." But I knew nothing whatever about banking, about the money market, the creation of credit or the foreign exchanges, and next to nothing about the Stock Exchange or investment. During my year's convalescence after the war I attempted, by reading, to become acquainted with these subjects. My Director of Studies was my wife's uncle by marriage, Mr Robert Benson. Uncle Robin was a Merchant Banker—a profession of rather ill-defined scope which includes neither trading nor banking. He was also a theoretician with views about currency. He liked, after dinner, when the ladies had left the room and the port was going round, to ask us: "What is a pound?" It seems that Sir Robert Peel had first asked that question, and that it had never been answered to either Sir or Uncle Robert's entire satisfaction. These discussions with a man who went daily into the City and had made a fortune there greatly increased my sense of the quality of learning and expertise that would be required of me in my new calling. I read Uncle Robin's annual speeches to the shareholders of the Merchants Trust, in which he talked of "hard" money and "soft" money, with wonder at their erudition, and even more wonder at the intellectual standard of the shareholders who presumably could understand them.

Uncle Robin began by placing me, as it were, in Fourth Form to read the works of Mr Hartley Withers. For lucidity and readableness these unpretentious books are unsurpassed. They uncover, in clear, almost colloquial language, all the mysteries of the money market, of banking, of the Stock Exchange, of the acceptance houses, of the foreign exchanges. I felt, after reading them, greatly encouraged. I was heartened, I remember, at learning that no banker might become a Director of the Bank of England. If the greatest bank in the world could be run by men with no previous experience of banking, finance must be easier than I had thought it to be. But the overriding and most stimulating impression made upon me by Hartley Withers was that of a mighty, smooth-running machine, of closely interlocking parts, and perfected by centuries of experience, which was day by day sustaining and replenishing the life-blood of our own country and of all those with whom we traded. I was almost persuaded that all the constituents of this great machine, the bankers, stockbrokers, bill-brokers, acceptance houses, arbitrageurs, and the rest must be expertly and responsibly aware, as Hartley Withers himself was aware, of the public benefits flowing from their respective skills. And I developed a profound respect for Gold, and for Gold's manipulator, of almost automatic sagacity, the Bank Rate.

When I reported back to Uncle Robin, and thanked him for having introduced me to an interpreter who had made all plain, he appeared to be a little flustered, more especially when I spoke of my new devotion to Gold and to the Bank Rate.

"But what is the good of fiddling with the Bank Rate when Rome is burning?" he asked. As for Gold, was it Gold that enabled France to pay her war indemnity after 1870 with a rapidity that astonished and alarmed Bismarck? By no means, he said; the French

paid with *"titres."* Claims—might not claims on goods
and services be as good as gold? He moved me up into
Fifth Form and gave me more advanced reading. There
was the great Marshall. There was a book on Banking
and Currency by an author I have forgotten. But I do
not think it can have been Uncle Robin who introduced
me to R. G. Hawtrey's writings. Hawtrey had been an
Eton Colleger in my time, and was now a Treasury
official with a fabulous reputation. It was Hawtrey
whose brains Winston Churchill, when Chancellor of
the Exchequer, was determined to pick. The higher
Treasury men, so the story went, demurred. "They keep
Hawtrey in a dungeon," complained Sir Winston, "but
I insisted on having him brought before me. He still
had the straws in his hair."

These were stiffer studies for me, and I developed
doubts and hesitations. Was Hartley Withers's beautiful,
beneficent machine as reliable as I had been led to
believe? Could it, after all, creak? Uncle Robin
welcomed my indecisions as a sign of progress. He made
further sly digs at the Bank and its Rate. He even shook
my faith in the Governor himself. It was Lord Cunliffe
who had given Lloyd George the figure for German
reparations, that fantastic amount demanded by the
Treaty of Versailles. Uncle Robin, staggered and
sceptical, had asked Lord Cunliffe how he had arrived
at such a total. "It came to me in church," was the
Governor's reply.

The nearer the day approached when I should be
passed fit for duty, the more complicated and confusing
became my mental picture of my new profession. I
read a book on Arbitrage, which renewed the self-
mistrust induced in me, five years earlier, when Mr

Edward Wagg had advised me to master a slim volume on Options and "The Put and Call." I began to wonder whether I was not, after all, too thick-headed for the City. I confessed my misgivings to Uncle Robin. He was most comforting.

"Nobody," he said, "understands Arbitrage and Foreign Exchange unless born a Jew or an Armenian. These races do not even have to be taught such subjects: they understand them by the light of nature. And they can be hired. You will hire them, my dear Jonah." I could not, at the time, see myself hiring anybody, but I was consoled none the less. Incidentally, Uncle Robin was wrong. But perhaps he could hardly have foreseen the career of a young Anglo-Saxon, then at school, who was later to join Helbert Wagg and Co, as a junior clerk. Today he is Sir George Bolton, a Director of the Bank of England and envied throughout Jewry and Armenia for his mastery of Foreign Exchange.

About a year after the Armistice I was declared to be fit, and I returned to Threadneedle Street. And here I should perhaps explain the nature of Helbert Wagg and Co's business. We are described in the reference books as Investment Bankers, but are known in the City as an Issuing House. Our main business is to bring together those who need capital and those willing to supply it. Our service to those who need it is to see that they obtain it on the best terms, as to rate of interest and conditions of repayment; in the most suitable form, as by the issue of bonds, shares, or debentures: and, more especially, to guarantee, by underwriting, the subscription by investors of the amount required. Our service to those willing to supply capital is to vet the capacity, standing, past record, and probable future of the people raising the money. By putting our name on a prospectus as Issuing House we tell the public, in effect, that we have had a thorough look at the business concerned and believe it to be a sound one. For these services the capital-seekers pay us a commission. Helbert Wagg and Co. have other activities: arbitrage, the management of investment trusts, the loan of spare cash to the discount houses, and so on. But their main function is that of "issuing" to the public, through a prospectus, or placing privately with such insatiable but wary investors as the great insurance companies, shares and securities of all sorts. The business is a responsible one and demands a variety of skills, some exact, some psychological rather than scientific. The probing of a would-be borrower's past record is largely a matter of trained accountancy. But the forecasting of his future performance may entail a broad study of the whole field in which he operates, and many diverse lines of enquiry. To take a simple example: a client proposing to increase his capital may have made a fortune hitherto out of a particular machine. His record of profits is one of steady increase; his name and status are first-class. But what if a new invention is on the brink of being commercially proved, one that will put our client out of business? Alertness, imagination, and research will be called into play, and above all a capacity for judging character. For in the last resort figures and balance-sheets are but the recording-charts of human qualities. Gifts for accuracy, research, and a sure instinct for the quality of a fellow-creature are not always found in the same person. Hence the advantage, in an issuing house, of team-work, and it was as a team that the firm I served achieved success and even prominence.

My entry into this new world of the City was un-
conventional; owing to my maturity I was not asked
to begin, as I had begun my military career, in the ranks.
I never licked a stamp, kept a ledger, handled securities,
or gnawed an apple in the face of the present Lord
Salisbury when he dropped in to borrow money for
the discount house for which at one time he worked.
(He did not much like the manager of our Money
department. "He eats apples at me," he mildly complained, "and shouts 'No money, no money!' before I
am through the door." I don't think we much liked our
money-man either, but it was typical of H. W. & Co.
to decide that if an old servant is too rough-hewn to be
recommended to others he must be retained for life.)

I sat, from the first, on a thick carpet in the partners'
room, and "listened in" to all that went on there. I had
plenty of time on my hands, for in the first year or two
after the Great War there was small demand for the
services of a careful, conservative firm like ourselves.
The war-profiteers, and in particular the shipowners of
Cardiff, that "city of dreadful knights," were busy un-
loading their factories and fleets upon a credulous public
through mushroom issuing houses, long since sunk
without trace. Values were monstrously inflated, but
every offering was over-subscribed. We had to sit with
folded hands amid the rush and bustle of money-making
all round us. At dinner-parties in the West End I was
sometimes congratulated on being in an issuing house
at such a moment of opportunity. My head-shakings
were politely, but patently, regarded as signs that our
own grapes were sour.

And now I was beginning to discover in the City, as
I had discovered in Rexinger on that journey to

Bucharest, the contrast between a distant and a nearer view. A fact of life that I learnt early was that Uncle Robin himself was far from being a typical City man. The shareholders of the Merchants Trust were not, after all, on his intellectual level; the bulk of them did not even attend the Annual Meetings at which he read those speeches about Peel and the Pound which had taken so many weeks of careful preparation and re-vision. In truth, during the whole of my career in the City I came across a mere handful of men who were in any sense students of monetary or economic problems. There was Robert Brand of Lazard's and the Bank of England. There was Oswald Falk of Buckmaster and Moore. There was the great Maynard Keynes. There was Mr Coutts, who managed the Provident Mutual. Albert Palache, who later was one of our partners, was a profound student of these high matters. But in their casual contacts with their business associates such men did not betray their learning. It would have been to small purpose had they done so. For to the vast majority of those daily occupied with the manifold branches of financial business, theories and doctrines were of no concern. City men might be cogs in Hartley Withers's beneficent machine, but they were unconscious cogs. What they did know was that they were in the City to make money.

For some years I continued, in my spare time, a course of reading which might some day, I hoped, qualify me to talk on equal terms with the Robert Brands and the Oswald Falks. I did not like the idea of being a mere smatterer in the principles that governed a system of which my own calling was a part. It would be, I felt, a humiliation if my thoughts about the Gold

Standard, about "managed" currencies, about the exchanges, about investment, about the money market,
about Keynes, about the Treasury, about Sir Montagu
Norman, were to be for ever beneath the level of the
thoughts of the best minds. But gradually, as the years
went by, I grew discouraged. I lunched from time to
time with Falk, and he did not even reply to my tentative remarks about Gold—he chewed in silence and
changed the subject. I realised again what had been
revealed to me at Oxford—that a second-class mind
cannot, by wishing, become a first-class mind. Nor had
I any natural interest in these complicated matters—my
interest was a forced one, self-induced by my dislike of
not understanding the whole of which I was, by trade,
a part. And my discouragement was not made less by a
growing conviction that, so far as the practice of my
trade went, study and knowledge counted for nothing.

I had only to look about me. There was no man in my
own firm with a better nose for business, and a readier
capacity for doing it, than my late partner and friend
Sir Nigel Campbell. A Scot of distinguished lineage,
he had made his way in early life with the very mini-
mum of education. He had left Eton while still young
to go prospecting for minerals, with knapsack and
hammer, in the Rocky Mountains. Failing to discover
the right sorts of mineral, he sold bonds from door to
door in the United States. Knowing his pertinacity, I
have no doubt that he kept his foot in every doorway
until the householder bought a bond to get rid of him.
In any case the firm he served, William A. Read and
Company, made him a partner, and on his return to this
country Alfred Wagg, with his sure instinct for team-
building, offered him a partnership in H. W. & Co.

Now it would be unfair to call Nigel illiterate, because he could read and write, although his spelling was uncertain and his meaning, on the rare occasions when he put his thoughts down in writing, not easily discovered. But when he arrived, morning after morning, and said "I have been thinking in my head, Alfred," there was no question of the force and justness of his appreciation of any business that might be on the tapis. He had the imagination to foresee broad combinations, and the ingenuity to make them practical. His simplicity and integrity made him trusted, and he achieved many notable successes.

Yet Nigel had never, as far as I could discover, read a book in his life except shockers, which he devoured on holiday and on train journeys. Of economic or monetary theories he knew nothing. Devotion to an American wife of rare charm and intelligence, and to three pretty daughters, sweetened his background and provided the motive for his untiring activities. For Nigel, despite his single-minded attachment to money-making, could never be called a money-grubber. He enjoyed the game more than the prize. But it is small wonder that working daily under, and later as partner of, such a man, I gradually lost interest in theory and turned my attention to performance.

My observations, from my desk in the partners' room, of other City activities, confirmed my increasing suspicions about the relevance of my studies. A stream of stockbrokers made regular morning calls upon our chairman, Alfred Wagg. They came, of course, in the hopes of netting an order to buy or to sell, but they were always welcome, some for their cheerful and amusing company, and all for the information they could give about the movement of markets and prices. Of all these alert, friendly men I can call to mind only a few of whom it could be said that they were serious, thorough-going students of the intrinsic values of the securities they bought and sold for their clients. Nor were these few outstandingly prosperous. One of the most successful brokers, whose income in good times was said to touch six figures, was almost absurdly ignorant of the quality of his wares. I can remember an occasion when he had been pressing Alfred Wagg to buy a certain American share during the great boom in the late 1920s. When asked the nature of the business in which he was so anxious that we should become shareholders, he was almost indignant. "I haven't the slightest idea," he replied. But he kindly offered to ring up one of his clerks and find out. This man's prosperity was due, not to any professional knowledge, but to his wide social connections. He had a remarkable knack of getting rich people, with whom he dined or shot or spent his Saturdays to Mondays, to invest or to speculate through his firm. His fellow-brokers were not always kind about him.

"Good morning, X. How's the Duke?" enquired one of these, in ringing tones, on the floor of a crowded House.

"Er—which Duke do you mean?"

"Oh, any old Duke."

There is, I suppose, no more harm in collecting dukes than in collecting stamps, but the supply being limited, it cannot be everybody's hobby, and X might have been wiser to keep his pet amusement to himself. He was a man who did many kindnesses of which he did not speak.

9

Then there was Berdoe Wilkinson, a partner in the firm of Mullens, Marshall, the government brokers. He was a figure of irresistible flamboyance. Tall, portly, dressed up to the nines, with an enormous buttonhole, he came sailing into the room like a latterday Beau Brummel, with the malice left out. Breezy and bawdy and big-hearted, he did us all good. Business, for all his shrewdness, was a great game to him, to be transacted with laughter and humanity. I have always wondered how he talked to Mr Governor at the Bank, and coped with the infinite reserve, the settled austerity of Sir Montagu Norman. Could that face creased with amusement, those twinkling eyes, ever achieve gravity? Did the Governor feel, as we felt, greatly refreshed by the visits of this all-conquering charmer?

And here let me digress for a moment. During the greater part of my City career Sir Montagu Norman was a tremendous, but an enigmatic, figure. With his long, pale, handsome face, his dark, pointed beard, his broad-brimmed, soft black hat, his cloak and cane, he looked to be every inch not a banker. He looked like a Spanish hidalgo, and a conspiratorial hidalgo at that. It was in keeping with this outward appearance that he had a taste for travelling incognito, as Mr Skinner. But, like Aircraftman Shaw, he took care that the world should know who Mr Skinner was and where he was going.

I never met Monty, as he was universally known, officially, and only twice, I think, at private dinner parties. But there he was, during the greater part of my City career, ruling over us all. He had not, of course, a scintilla of legal authority; he could never command, only request. Yet his requests were taken as commands, and complied with to the letter, often at a real sacrifice. A summons would come to Alfred Wagg, who must put on a top-hat in which to obey it, for the wide-brimmed soft hat that hung outside Mr Governor's room would tolerate no rival. Mr Governor would be exceedingly gracious, but his quietly spoken words might cost us many thousands of pounds.

It is surprising that, after so many years spent under the absolute but sanctionless rule of this man whose re-election by the Court, year after year, was accepted as inevitable, I should be quite unable to give any account of him. That he had what is called "personality" in the highest degree is certain. But what was his real stature? That he worked hand-in-glove with the Treasury was the common belief, but did he or the Treasury give the lead? Was he a profound thinker and an economist, or a magnificent puppet whose strings were pulled, conceivably even from the dungeon in Whitehall where R. G. Hawtrey languished upon his straw? It is on record that, when giving evidence before the Macmillan Committee on Finance and Industry in the economic blizzard of 1930, the Governor's replies to questions put to him by the wide-ranging minds of Keynes and Ernest Bevin showed a marked degree of rigidity, even narrowness, in his own views, as well as an aloofness, almost amounting to indifference, in his attitude towards unemployment. Is it possible that his reserve, his reticence, were the defences of a man who could say his piece, but durst not go beyond it? If this was indeed the truth, the Treasury were more than fortunate in having so imperial-seeming a spokesman. For there is no question but that his immense prestige in the City was all his own, and but little related to his office. I was once given, by a sister of Monty's, some memories of her brother's early life, and, to those who knew him in his glory, they are unexpected enough to be worth setting down. He was, it appears, what is now called a problem child. He was uncouth; he was unkempt; he was sullen and intractable; above all, he was subject to outbursts of uncontrollable rage. He was unhappy at Eton and left early. He was unhappy at Cambridge and went down after one wasted year. His despairing parents placed him, at the age of about twenty, in the care of a Lutheran pastor in Switzerland. The Lutheran pastor set him to work in his garden and on his small farm, and made him sweat. Young Norman loved it; for the first time in his life he was happy. After a couple of years or so the Pastor sent him home—a changed character. He was tidy; he never lost his temper; he was intelligent and ambitious. A place was found for him in the house of Brown Shipley and Co. in New York, in which he rapidly rose to responsibility, and from which he was later transferred to Brown Shipley and Co. of London. I forgot to ask Mrs Balfour whether the Lutheran pastor lived to see that impressive, bearded figure, with his air of secret brooding over great affairs, with his calm, his dandyism, and his authoritativeness. I hope he did, for then he must have felt himself to be, when he recalled the clay from which he fashioned so much splendour, an artist indeed.

Since writing the above words I have been shown an unpublished impression of Sir Montagu Norman written in March 1932 by the late Geoffrey Madan, and by the kindness of Mrs Madan I am allowed to print it here:

This morning I saw a remarkable sight. I came up to the City in the Underground rather late, about half past ten. At

Bond Street a man got in whom I just know, and have spoken
to three or four times in my life. He wore loose clothes, a ringed
and jewelled tie, a crumpled black hat. His general presence
made a most distinguished effect, suggesting all manner of
romantic things; a Restoration poet, an historic French admiral,
a bearded nobleman of Spain—the ideal which everyone would
like to think his own great-grandfather attained, to adapt a
famous obituary phrase. This strange being was in a state of
high tension. He lay back looking half strangled, as if fallen
from a great height, or praying to be supported in some heavy
trial; darted a glance away, focusing a distant passenger and
slowly dropping his chin; glared round with the queer look
of a man swelling with laughter and longing to share it with
someone else: or groaned aloud in pain. The carriage was half
full. A woman rose to get out at a station. He started and
stared in horror, lifting both hands with delicate fingers, and
crooning a song as if to calm a child. Then he fell back, with
forehead deeply lined, a flicker of splendid hands, and a
magnificent eye wide open. Two or three people recognised
the Governor of the Bank. In the inestimable English tradition
they smiled faintly, assumed all to be somehow for the best,
and let it go at that.

The train scraped round the rails at the Bank station, and
emptied itself. Last but one, out of the carriage, strolled this
enigmatic figure. He struck out now in some odd rhythm,
half jaunty, half defiant: bent idly down to peer all round an
empty carriage: then slid past a group of people at a double
pace: only to halt for a leisurely and mournful study of an
advertisement on a wall. At the end he paused again, gazing
nobly into the distance, like some fine old Swiss guide watching
the signs of a storm. Soon he strode on and mounted the
escalator, alone, like the bridge of a ship, striking a glorious
pose-portrait of an admiral in China seas.

> Even in the presence of an enemy fleet,
> Between the steep cliff and the coming wave.

I thought of the Treasury saying, that the Bank of England acts
like a commander in the days before strategy was thought of.

He had no ticket at the bar: and the same instinct which would not stare in the train, would not ask a question as he left the platform. As well demand a passport from a Czar. But the ticket was found at last by its imperial owner, stuck in the back of his soft dark hat. Still the drama continued; a chuckle, a tormented backward glance, a sudden scrutiny of forbidden entrances. At the top, one last proprietary gaze at the vulgar novelties which pressed on the old symbolic temple of Threadneedle Street. The traffic was in full flow: it was instantly reined back as he approached: three men saluted. But the mysterious grandee had already tripped and sauntered out of sight, chin in air.

But I must return to my muttons. My belief in the profitableness of book-learning, weakened by my daily observation of how successful were those who had none, was still further shaken by the story of the Independent Investment Trust. Trust companies, according to the British as distinguished from the American usage of the term, were, I believe, invented in Scotland, but have had a long and prosperous career in the City of London as well as in Edinburgh, Aberdeen, and Dundee. They are designed to carry out the simple and sensible idea of "spreading the risk." It is impracticable for a widow with a hundred pounds to spread her risk over more than half a dozen securities, and even to do that is highly inconvenient. But by buying shares in an investment trust, with a portfolio of, say, six hundred securities, from the bonds of governments and cities to the ordinary shares of industrial or commercial concerns in all parts of the world, the widow can see to it that not six but six hundred investments must go bad before her capital is lost. And not only that, but in the directors and managers of most investment trusts the widow has canny and experienced men to select her multifarious holdings for her. It is a sensible system that has worked well, and not only for widows. Now, about the time that I went into the City a new Investment Trust was formed, called the Independent investment trust. The board was to consist of three directors only, of whom one, the great Maynard Keynes, was already a legendary figure, commonly reputed to have amassed, by sheer intelligence, tidy fortunes for both King's College, Cambridge, and the National Mutual Life Insurance Company. When therefore Keynes, in association with the economist Oswald Falk and one of the leading lights of the Scottish trust company world, announced, in a prospectus, that he and his friends intended to manage an investment trust on new lines, there was quite a stir. I have forgotten in just what language these new lines were described, but what it amounted to was that the directors intended to use their brains. And since their brains were undeniably first-class, I for one was duly impressed. I subscribed for a few shares for my wife, and I persuaded my fellow trustees of the Balliol Endowment Fund to buy more than a few shares for Balliol. The result of this reliance on brains was disappointing. When other investment trusts, managed presumably by rule of thumb, were standing up well to the chances and changes of the 1920s, the "Brains Trust" lost a substantial part of its capital. I felt a most uncomfortable responsibility towards my old college. Ultimately the three highbrows took a most unexpected step. In a becoming fit of modesty, or repentance, they asked Helbert Wagg and Co. to undertake the management of the Trust, and my partner Bernard Barrington to become chairman. Under this lowbrow and commonsense management the losses were made good and the Independent Investment Trust is now a flourishing concern. I recall the amusement with which Bernie Barrington used to describe his earlier experiences at the board meetings, before either Keynes or Falk had resigned. The clash of brains sometimes led to an excited waving of arms, and on one occasion the chairman, who sat between this distinguished pair, felt his own nose to be in jeopardy, so wide-ranging were their gesticulations. I think this object lesson in the fallibility of experts in their own chosen field of endeavour was the last straw, so far as my own dwindling faith in study was concerned. As I have said, I had no natural interest in economics; I was in the City to earn my living, and once I became convinced by what I saw going on around me that a knowledge of economic and monetary theory had no bearing on money-making, I turned away with relief from my homework. I banished some thickish and rather repellent books to a top shelf, and soothed the dying struggles of a defeated conscience by reading the *Statist* and the *Economist*. What a pleasure it was, after working hours, to turn to Joseph Conrad, to Macaulay, to Scropes's *Days of Deerstalking*, or, for serious study, to my perennial preoccupation with what is so misleadingly called Theology.

Not that conscience for ever ceased to rear its tiresome head. At the general election that followed the formation of a National Government in 1931, despite my distaste for politics except as a mildly cynical spectator, I felt bound to go down to Norfolk and to do my best to unseat our Labour member. I led off with an article in the *Eastern Daily Press* in which I demonstrated with, as I thought, irrefutable arguments that if this country was driven off the Gold Standard it would starve. I followed this up by speaking night after night in draughty, dimly-lit village halls, introducing myself as a non-party banker, and trying to put the fear I honestly felt into the hearts of the cautious, suspicious, but attentive and ruminating villagers of North Norfolk. Even "Friday" Layton, the bearded, "larned" radical of my own parish, who was accustomed to down all opponents with his book-larnin', found himself at sea over the Gold Standard. The whole question was new to them; the old familiar heckling-guns were useless against my technical, non-political attack, and I used to drive home to unnatural, belated meals with a comfortable feeling that the labourers of Little Walsingham and Stibbard, of Great Snoring and Trunch, were, for all their long memories of Joseph Arch, not unwilling to rally in defence of their country's gold. I have no idea how far my intervention helped, but in the event the National candidate won this traditionally radical seat by a decisive majority. The country promptly went off gold, did not starve, and has remained off gold ever since. The sole monetary principle for which, as a result of all my studies, I had been ready to speak out publicly and with utter conviction, was now shown to be a delusion. In addition, I had helped to put into Parliament a member who, conscientious and hard-working servant of his constituents as he was, became a resolute and unshaken supporter of a Prime Minister, Mr Baldwin, whose unconcern over the rise of Hitler and neglect of our defences were to be the cause for me and mine of so many years of foreboding and dismay. I found few enough friends in the City, and still fewer among my Norfolk neighbours, to share these anxieties. It may be that some chance contacts, through my own family,

with some of Hitler's earlier Jewish victims first opened
my eyes to what was going on in Germany, and my
wife's experiences in her untiring and often successful
efforts to rescue these unfortunates steadily fanned the
flames of our angry indignation. But with a few notable
exceptions, my familiar friends and companions in the
City remained staunch supporters of both Mr Baldwin
and Mr Chamberlain. Nor was it easy for me to relieve
my feelings by speaking out even among my own
partners. For one of them was Mr Baldwin's son-in-law;
another his friend and admirer; and there was a genuine
goodness and "niceness" about Mr Baldwin and, in
other fields than defence and foreign affairs, so much
magnanimity and breadth, that his supporters were on
an easy wicket. So when, at a shooting party, I found
myself, glass in hand, sitting by the smoking-room fire
with Lord Chatfield and heard him declare that whenever, as First Sea Lord, he had attempted to impress
upon the Prime Minister the grave shortcomings of the
Navy, Mr Baldwin had yawned, looked at his watch and
said it was time for lunch, I had neither the heart nor
the courage to repeat so damaging a story in our
partners' room. This was moral cowardice, no doubt,
but one has to consider the feelings of the companions
of one's daily work. That my wife and myself were not
so reticent among our friends outside the City is proved
to me by several clear-cut memories. There was the
invitation to a shooting-party with a postscript begging
us not to talk politics, since Geoffrey Dawson would be
there, and was in need of a rest. Naturally we obeyed,
but our hostess had forgotten to warn Lady Violet
Bonham-Carter, and Geoffrey Dawson missed his
repose after all. There were some raised voices in a

breakfast-car from King's Lynn, when a charming
woman neighbour of ours rejoiced over the news of
Hitler's seizure of Prague. There was a letter from a
near and dear relation, who moved in the highest
political circles, begging us for our own sakes to be
more careful, since we were risking the charge of being
"unpatriotic." This was a little hard to bear.

But I cannot think that our views were wrong. In
1919 Germany had been prostrate and disarmed. A
treaty made her disarmament, as far as power to com-
mit aggression was concerned, perpetual. Twenty years
later Germany had the strongest army and air-force in
Europe, and our own armed strength was pitifully small.
It is incredible that our leaders during those twenty
years should have allowed this to happen. But it did
happen. For most of the time the Conservative Party
was in power. The most powerful of the Conservative
leaders, with the most solid and loyal majority behind
him, was Baldwin. Even in 1933 Germany was still weak
and unarmed. Her partial rearmament up to that date
had been secret and furtive. After Hitler came to power
it was public and proclaimed. A Tory majority, whatever else its faults, is never slow to arm if the danger
and the necessities are made clear to it. They were not
made clear.

Chamberlain has been the object of more bitter
reproaches than Baldwin, since it was upon Chamberlain's head that the storm broke. But in fact, when he
took over from Baldwin, there was little he could do,
there was little a Churchill could have done, but to play
for time. Had Chamberlain laid himself out to deceive
Hitler, instead of deceiving himself, until our own rearmament was accomplished, he would have been

playing a distasteful game, but the only possible game for the weak threatened by the strong. It was not Munich, which did give us a further breathing-space, but Chamberlain's beliefs about Munich, which were fatuous, that have brought him so much blame. I do not think Baldwin would ever have gone behind the back of his own Foreign Secretary. I am sure that Baldwin would never have submitted a draft of his speech to the House of Commons for Mussolini's comments and approval. But if Chamberlain refused to read the reports of his own Foreign Service because he did not wish to hear what he knew they must contain, Baldwin neglected foreign affairs altogether.

During Chamberlain's reign we found ourselves, at any rate outside the City, sharing our indignation and our fears with an ever-widening circle. Companionship, even in foreboding, is a comfort. But during Baldwin's reign we met, in our rather restricted world, with little sympathy and much disapproval. Dr Johnson once said that public affairs vexed no man and that he never ate an ounce less meat because of them. I certainly remember no loss of appetite; but I do recollect years of re-current malaise, of gnawing apprehensions. And the measure of our distress is this: that to us, who had lived through the waste, the slaughter, and the destruction of the first World War, this second declaration of war against Hitler came as an exhilarating release, a release from humiliation, from shame, and from impotence.

For there is a sense of impotence in being a private citizen, in being in a minority, and in working day by day in a world that shares none of your misgivings. I was also becoming aware, during this period, of further evidence to illustrate my theme in this chapter, which is the contrast between what I had expected to find in the City and what I did find. One of the legends upon which I had been brought up was that to know the arcana of public affairs, to get to the realities behind appearances, you must go to the City, and in particular to the Stock Exchange. Politicians might know more than the public knew, but the City's information was even nearer the bone. And you must go to the City, it was commonly believed, not only for information, but for judgment. A Prime Minister, a Foreign Secretary, might be reassuring or otherwise, but the test of a situation was: are the jobbers bulls or bears? These admirable traders who, unlike stockbrokers, keep a substantial stock-in-trade of listed securities, and are always ready to buy or sell to a stockbroker's client at a price, perform a most useful function. They constitute the market; without them you or I, wishing to buy or sell an investment, would have to wait not only until a buyer or seller of that same investment, and to the precise amount, made his appearance, but until his stockbroker happened to knock up against our own stockbroker. But the idea that stock-jobbers have secret sources of information and know what a Poincaré is going to say next Sunday before he says it, and mark the prices of their wares up and down accordingly, is of course moonshine. They take the same interest in public affairs as the rest of us, no more nor less, and have the same sources of information, which is usually the press. And as for the prices of their wares, these rise or fall, like other commodities, according to demand and supply. If there is a bull market, with all prices rising, it is not because the jobbers are feeling full of beans; it is because the speculating public, probably far less well

informed than the jobbers, is feeling full of beans. The
Stock Exchange, in short, so far from reflecting the
views of particularly well informed men, cannot help
reflecting the views of the least well informed part of
the community, which is the public at large. There have
been many occasions on which I have known both
jobbers and brokers to be full of concern at a flood of
public buying and a consequent rise of prices, which
they know well enough to be based upon rumour or
gullibility or just fashion. But there is not a great deal
they can do about it. A stockbroker can discourage
and warn, but can hardly refuse a buying order, since
it will merely pass to a rival broker. A jobber can make
prices so high as to be unattractive, but, as the late
Lord Duveen proved in the world of picture-dealing,
there are fools in the world ready to take a high price
as proof of a high value.

No, that mysterious city barometer of which I had
heard so much did not give warning of distant depressions. It merely reflected the day-to-day moods of
widely scattered speculators. There was a constant
stream through our partners' room (where a Samuel
Scott of Westminster hangs over the fireplace, and a
view of Danzig over the leather sofa) or through our
vaulted luncheon-room upstairs, of stockbrokers, jobbers, bill-brokers, industrialists, bankers, insurance-men,
chartered accountants, and so on. Many were lively and
amusing, some were dull; the majority were intelligent
experts in their own line of business. But I cannot
remember getting much enlightenment from any of
them about the profounder movements of public
affairs. It was rare, for instance, to hear the point of
view of Labour. There was a very general confidence

in the Conservative leadership, and a deep suspicion of
all Socialists. Only from our American visitors did we
hear criticism of the powers that were. These friendly
men, mostly bankers or brokers, used to harangue us
throughout lunch in level, monotonous, and almost unbroken monologues. And most of them, although there
were exceptions, did not love Franklin D. Roosevelt.
And I must confess that, in the period when that great
man was engaged in "packing" the Supreme Court, I
did not love him myself. But my most vivid memory
of these American luncheons is of an occasion shortly
after the sudden break in the great American bull
market in 1929. Our American visitor told us of the
number of men, personally known to him, who had
thrown themselves off skyscrapers during the worst days
of the market collapse. I forget the exact number, but
it was sufficient to be horrifying, and to underline the
difference between the British and the American
attitude towards money-making. I cannot believe that a
like disaster in the City of London would have led to
such an outbreak of suicides. Ruin and bankruptcy are
hard to bear, but I do not think the average British man
of business could ever feel that, with a loss of solvency,
all meaning had gone out of life. He would be more
likely to despair if, with his fortune intact, he was to be
for ever deprived of the dear employments of his
leisure. Certain it is that most city men were delighted
when it was time to go home. The bill-brokers, for
instance, whose day ended at three o'clock, were much
envied. Stockbroking, the execution of clients' orders
for a commission, is a non-creative, uninspiring occupation. It is a living, not a life. That is why the Stock
Exchange has to be endlessly cracking jokes, and very

good jokes some of them are, such as calling an unpopular member, whose name was Louis, "Louis the
Fourteenth" because only when a hostess found her
party reduced to thirteen did he get a sudden invitation
to dinner. Insurance has largely become a routine
business, now that the tables of probabilities upon
which the companies make their bets with their clients
have been calculated and re-calculated to the last
refinements. Banking has no doubt its moments of
excitement, for good banking, of the sort that increases
production, involves the reading of character and the
placing of trust in persons. It must be fascinating to
watch the growth of a new enterprise where that trust
has been given wisely; on the other hand, after a
Clarence Hatry had walked into the head office of one
of the Big Five and his character had been misread there,
the directors cannot have had a dull moment for months
on end.

The business of an issuing house comes, on the whole,
into the creative category. The "vetting" of a concern,
in which part of our business I was mostly engaged,
involves enlivening human contacts as well as the
checking of figures. There was plenty of variety in our
days; the one great drawback was the spasmodic
character of the business. It is not every day in the week
that business concerns, or cities, or foreign countries,
want to raise large sums of money, or if they do, that
their agents pass the doors of Rothschild's, of Baring's,
of Morgan Grenfell's, of Lazard's, and of Higginson's
in order to turn in at 41 Threadneedle Street. Not
every day of the week nor, in years of slump and unemployment, in every month of the year. We had idle
months as well as idle weeks and idle days; and these I

found dispiriting. I felt like the young men one sees drooping in those very smart shops in Bond Street, where all the wares are so precious, and every price so high, that only once or twice in a day does a customer drop in. At such times I used to envy civil servants and dons, and all whose work is regular and unaffected by "cycles" and "depressions." And I dare say such dons and civil servants as I was acquainted with envied me, and would gladly have exchanged the regularity of their underpaid jobs for the fitfulness of my overpaid one. I call it overpaid, because in good times my rewards had no relation to my skill, abilities, or character. Financiers—and under this name I include stockbrokers and jobbers and bankers and discount and acceptance houses—are not, like other professional men such as lawyers, doctors, or architects, paid by the job and in proportion to their skill and expertness in doing the job. They are paid by a commission on the volume of business they handle, and while they may quite properly put it to the credit of their own expertise and integrity that business is brought to themselves and not to others, the volume of that business depends upon conditions over which they have no control whatsoever. Their skill and cleverness remain constant in good times or bad; but their earnings depend upon trade cycles, industrial conditions, and all the ups and downs of getting and spending in all parts of the busy world. If you live on rake-offs, as we did, it is the size of the heap, not your skill with the rake, that counts. I was fortunate in belonging to an excellent firm whose name stood high, and have a lively sense of what I owed to the energy and capacity of my senior partners, who could nose out and capture business for which there was much

10

competition. But there would have been a satisfaction I have never known in standing upon my own feet, and in earning, by my own efforts, a living conformable to my deserts. What I have lost, however, in self-approbation, my family has gained in comfort and security. How right Clough was to sing:

> How pleasant it is to have money, heigh ho!
> How pleasant it is to have money.

Among the partners whose nose for business was responsible for so much of the money I found so pleasant I have already written of Nigel Campbell. Another hunting-dog second to none for scenting game was Albert Palache, but since he is still very much alive, and still on the *qui vive*, I must keep to the rules and not praise a live man to his face. Nigel quartered industrial Britain, with gallops into the United States; Albert, in the nineteen-twenties, ranged widely over Europe; he also knew exactly which of the visitors to his private room not to introduce to Bernie Barrington. For that wise, pacific man, with whom no partner ever had a quarrel, has never felt comfortable in a room with a foreigner. His unfailing curiosity as a naturalist, his preoccupation with all living things, suddenly dries up when the living things come from the Department of the Seine, or from Roumania, Amsterdam, or Iceland. He did not disapprove of our handling foreign loans, but did not wish, if it could be avoided, to see or talk to the outlandish borrowers, speaking strange tongues. So it was quite an event in our little world between Adam's Court and Threadneedle Street when Barrington broke with his past and went with Palache to Danzig. How he was persuaded to the journey I no

longer remember: it was in the days when loans were
issued "under the auspices (or was it the aegis?) of the
League of Nations," an empty phrase, for the League
took no responsibility. But it may be that the League
asked for this or that in set terms, and Barrington had
been a lawyer of credit and renown before ever he took
to finance.

As so often happens in this unjust world, our foreign
visitors, whom Bernie would dodge into the lavatory
to avoid, rated him, on the brief occasions when he was
compelled to shake hands, far above his xenophil,
continental-minded partners. For in him they saw the
legendary Englishman, tall, fair, clothed by a High Life
tailor, reserved, phlegmatic, with Justice seated on his
brow, and Cricket, in the highest sense of the word, in
his eye. They took one look at his spats, and adored him.
And so it was in Danzig. The Danzigers with whom he
had to negotiate were not his cup of tea. They had
duelling-scars on their taut cheeks, and grim mouths.
But they fell for Bernie like all the rest, calling him
affectionately "the gentleman-rider" because of the
many riders, all to our advantage, that he insisted on
appending to the contract. And they feasted him, so
that when they returned his visit, bringing their wives
with them, Bernie found himself in honour bound to
feast them in his turn. "It must be done," he said,
"but I'll be damned if I'll be seen with them."

Not Claridge's, not the Ritz, not the Savoy, not the
Berkeley—at any of these places some friend or acquaintance might get a glimpse of Bernie sitting next to a
creature with his hair *en brosse* and a neck like Streicher's.
At last it was decided to order a table at one of those
gorgeous hotels into which it was certain that no living

soul known to Bernie could conceivably penetrate. His partners and his partners' wives were press-ganged, and a big round table chosen next to the band, so as to make conversation with his distasteful guests impossible. The appointed evening came, and we seated ourselves in the great room, beneath the golden splendour of balconies, the glitter of titanic chandeliers. Our guests looked about them approvingly; the gentleman-rider had clearly honoured them with the best that London could give. The dinner was expensive; the champagne was good; the band drowned, with clashing cymbals, every attempt at talk. We beamed and chewed. And then it happened. The band stopped playing. The shaven-headed monster with the duelling-scars turned to me: "And you often come here, yes no?"

"No, this is the first time."

"Zo?" He turned to my wife on his other side.

"But you, *gnädige Frau*, you come here many times. Yes?"

"No, never before. It's nice, isn't it?"

"Zo?" A harder look came into his pebbly eye. He lent across the table to his host.

"You come here very many times, Herr Barrington?" Bernie, unbelievably, was off his guard. He did not actually say "Catch me!" but he failed, shamefully, to tell the requisite, the so indispensable white lie.

"Never been here before in my life."

"Zo-o!" The grim mouth set fast. The eyes went dead. The rest was silence. Our principal guest had divined the wounding truth. This was not where the Honourable Herr Barrington brought his own cronies. Fortunately the loan agreement was already signed and sealed.

But I must return to my Rexinger motif, the contrast between the fabulous and the real City. I could hardly, as a young man, have escaped altogether from the influence of the massive attacks made by Belloc and the two Chestertons on Jewish financiers. At Eton we had all been anti-semites; at Balliol less so; but we admired our Belloc and, on going down, we read the *Eye-Witness*, and passed from hand to hand Belloc's unprinted and unprintable epigrams about Jewish magnates. During my brief career at the Bar I had been shocked by the malignancy and irresponsibility of Cecil Chesterton over the Marconi case, and had shared chambers with a Jew of Jews, George Joseph, whom I much liked and respected. But it was not until I went into the City that I discovered that Belloc and his friends had been boxing shadows. All that wit and savage eloquence had been poured out upon something that did not exist. I do not mean, of course, that there were not Jews who had made vast fortunes on the Rand, sometimes by disreputable methods.

> Tall Goltman, silent on his horse,
> Superb against the dawn

was fair game enough. But Cecil Rhodes was not a Jew and the mere making of millions was not the gravamen of the Chester-Belloc indictment. The rather wilfully uninformed pair of poets accused International Jewry of corrupting our public men to gain some ill-defined but sinister ends of their own. "International Jewry" has a fine conspiratorial sound, but it really means nothing. One of the characteristics of the Jew is his capacity, while retaining all his pride of race and tradition, to become ardently patriotic towards the country of his adoption, nor, after millennia of exclusion from civil rights, is he by nature a political animal. At the period when Belloc was prancing, the head of the House of Rothschild in this country was brooding, aloof from the City, over his lepidoptera. His kinsman at New Court was preoccupied with propagating orchids at Exbury. The financial operations of N. M. Rothschild and Co. were open, conservative, and unexciting. There was much charity to Jewish welfare, but not less to national good causes. The idea of British politicians of either party creeping into New Court by night to receive bribes could occur only to the Poet or the Lunatics of whom Chesterton wrote.

If Belloc was incapable, by some kink in his otherwise magnanimous mind, of crediting Jews with the loyalty and patriotism which is natural in them, he might have considered that the rich men among them, those who had arrived, were the last people of all to engage in subversive activities. Jews are pre-eminently good at enjoying their riches. They like to own racehorses and Old Masters and to eat smoked salmon. And who, after centuries of oppression and dispossession, would not?

The mild, endemic anti-semitism which I found in the City, where Jews have a finger in most pies, if the pie is a good one, had nothing in common with Belloc's. There were no fears of conspiracy: there were no accusations of corruption. There was, and I suppose always will be, an Anglo-Saxon suspicion of cleverness, a schoolboyish contempt for people who cared little for fresh air and field-sports, and a Philistine mistrust of taking the arts seriously enough to spend money upon them. But above all I believe most Anglo-Saxons are subconsciously shocked by the Jew's devastating com-

mon sense and objectivity. We Britons like to wrap up
both our aims and our means of achieving them in a
comfortable vagueness. We hope to attain something,
somehow. The Jew knows precisely what he wants, and
exactly how to get it. And when he comes out with it,
sharply, we are apt to shudder, as if the bedclothes had
been whipped off as we lie in bed. The Jew makes us,
in short, rather uncomfortable; he peers too quickly
through our island mists, and forgets that we have
never lived, as he did, in the clear light of the East.

Mention of this slight cloudiness in our outlook
brings me to a further fallacy about the City. It is inhabited by business men, and before I became a part of
it, I naturally expected it to be businesslike. And compared with America, where every transaction, as far as I
could see (and we had many dealings with New York),
is interminably protracted, no doubt London could be
called businesslike. But compared with the Adjutant's
Orderly Room in any cavalry regiment, or a barrister's
chambers, or a man (not a woman) out shopping, the
City is a place of hesitations and longwindedness. No
doubt there are one-man businesses where decisions are
made swiftly. But in houses where there are many
partners, and at board meetings, the tempo is for the
most part leisurely indeed. There is gossip and chaff and
the latest good story before a conference or a board
meeting gets under way; it is all friendliness and informality; the debate saunters off into by-ways; the real
point is sometimes not reached until we are washing
our hands for lunch. The comfort of our partners'
rooms, the deep leather sofas, the open fires, the
pictures on the walls, all encourage a rather cosy,
lounging method of discussion. Accuracy, punctuality,

and dispatch belonged to the counting-house downstairs, not to the partners' room. They were paid for,
and amply supplied. For the execution of policy we
depended, like Cabinet Ministers, upon a first-class
Civil Service. Those rather dawdling methods, laced
with fun, may be the reason that City men rarely have
duodenal ulcers, unlike their American counterparts. For
the American is unbusinesslike not, like ourselves, from
relaxed attention and mistiness of thought, but because
he likes, or did like, to submit every word of a cable,
every line of a letter, to his lawyers before sending it.
This may sound businesslike, but it results in niggling
and delays. But I dare say all this has changed. Again,
friendship, subject always to unwritten hierarchical laws,
played a part in all our relations with other firms. Not
being a traditionalist by temperament, I was not always
able to appreciate the City protocol, or to feel properly
concerned about the question of whose name should be
printed first on a prospectus. But it was agreeable to
work in an atmosphere where mutual liking played as
large a part as the cash nexus. There was competition,
but it was amicable, even generous.

To sum up, just as in Rexinger I found simplicity
where I had suspected artfulness and almost sinister
complications, so did I find the City, which I had
thought to be economically informed, prescient, and
highly technical, to be a place where men of average
intelligence go about their business with no more
knowledge of, or insight into, the country's monetary
or economic problems than the rest of us. If it was in
some sense disillusion, it was also a great relief, the
relief of a poor swimmer who finds that he is not, after
all, out of his depth.

Soon after the outbreak of the second World War I was "lent" by my firm to the Ministry of Economic Warfare, and on the formation of the Home Guard went home to Norfolk to command a Company until the end of the war. So little do we know ourselves that it was a surprise to me to realise, after some months of absence from Threadneedle Street, that never from the day I left it had I looked at the financial page of any daily or weekly paper. For twenty years I had attentively read the financial papers on my way to the City, and the *Economist* at week-ends. From that day to this I have not turned to the City news of any newspaper or weekly. The stock-markets, the money-market, current issues, rates of exchange—about all these matters, once so pertinent to my daily activities, I found, and find, myself wholly incurious. It is over forty years since I left the Bar, and I still read the Law Reports with attention. Any news about the Army interests me. I feel myself to be a retired lawyer and a retired soldier, who likes to keep an eye upon his former professions, but never a retired financier. The difference is revealing. But if I have been a case of miscasting, I have no regrets. The City not only gave me a livelihood, with jam as well as bread-and-butter, but it brought me valued and enduring friendships. From my firm, captained by Alfred Wagg, a man held in universal affection, I received not only kindness, but indulgence. During many long years of lowered vitality, and one of all but mortal illness, the wind was tempered for me with watchful and rare consideration. I received far more than it was in me to give, but at least my partners had from me, and will always have, gratitude and devotion.

CHAPTER VII

MAX BONN

I TOUCHED, in my last chapter, upon anti-semitism, but not upon its cure. I can think of no better cure than that, unhappily no longer available, of knowing my late partner, Sir Max Bonn.

It would be impossible to be more Jewish than Max. His family were Frankfurters, and although born in America and British by early naturalisation, Max never lost a trace of gutturalness, a precision in the sounding of his "r"s, in voice and accent. But there was a warm timbre, a slight huskiness in his speech which caught the ear most agreeably. All our heads turned expectantly towards Max's desk when he spoke.

Max was nothing much to look at. He was small, with a sad, brown, monkey's face and a toothbrush moustache. But his eyes, sometimes mournful, often pleading, frequently merry, were the most expressive I have known. Every rapid thought racing through that ingenious brain, every emotion stirring that exposed and sensitive heart, was reflected in them. One looked at Max's eyes, listened to his voice, and forgot the rest of him.

Although born to affluence and achieving material success, Max was one of nature's underdogs. Hence that pleading look. Life was always a fight for him, a fight against something, to him, unreasonable and portentous

—the massive obtuseness of Anglo-Saxon habits of thought. His darting intelligence was for ever prodding that great cushion and finding it impenetrable, his nervous sensibility for ever suffering from a sense of bafflement.

Max had been sole partner in his own firm, Bonn and Co, when he joined H. W. & Co. in the middle nineteen-twenties. As a lone hand, his capacity for seeing a hundred sides to a question where the ordinary Briton sees two had handicapped him. How to decide between so many possible alternatives, all with much to be said both for and against them? He wisely decided to become one of a team. There his subtlety, his imagination, his resource, his astonishing memory, could and did clarify, and even create, situations in which slower, less complicated minds could decide and act.

When Max first came to sit in our partners' room, I believed, for some months, that it was going to be the end of my career. For I was not yet a partner, and in no time this strange, vibrant newcomer had all but shattered my nerves. For whenever the telephone rang on my desk, as I was lifting the receiver, I would catch sight of Max grimacing at me and violently shaking his head. His scurrying imagination had made a guess at my probable caller; his mistrust of my diplomacy convinced him that I should make the wrong reply. It is highly disconcerting to be forbidden, by emphatic signs, to react as another man thinks you will react to a situation that has not yet arisen. The result, not unnaturally, was that my answer to the call, whatever it might be, was apt to be stuttering and unsatisfactory. So that Max's subsequent head-shakings were perhaps justified. I have never known exactly which of my defects so irritated Max. I was very large and quite un-subtle, and years later, when we were fast friends, Max spoke of my being "so damned cold-blooded about business." But at the time the strain between us became so serious, and I felt so cramped and inhibited, that for the first and only time in my life I went for advice to a psychiatrist. Mr William Brown had at that time a vast reputation as a psycho-analyst and cost many guineas. In my case they were well spent. He showed no flicker of amusement when I told him about Max and the telephone. He laid me upon a couch and asked for my earliest childhood memories. After one or two visits he said: "I think you will be all right now." It is un-accountable, but it worked. I was no longer afraid of Max; the head-shakings ceased; and we became firm friends. There was one subsequent row, in which I was provoked into telling him that I should have to go back to William Brown. Max was genuinely shocked, and I don't think we ever quarrelled again.

Max, with a business in hand, was like a dog with a bone. However straightforward it might appear to his colleagues' simpler souls, Max would worry it, play with it, run off with it, bury it, pretend to forget it, dig it up again with ecstasy, and enjoy the crunch rather than the marrow. He revelled in complications and elaborations, nuances and fine shades.

Max, whose last card was so often "I feel it in my Yiddish bones," used to explain to us how, in case of doubt, to tell a Jew from a Gentile: you inform the object of doubt that a fly has settled on his right ear. A Gentile will lift his right hand to scare it off, but a Jew will deal with the situation by passing his left hand behind the back of his neck.

He liked to speak in parables. After the Battle of the
Somme, Lloyd George, who hoped the Germans were
reeling from the blow, was disturbed by a speech of
Bethmann-Hollweg's, declaring that never, never, never
would Germany give up Alsace-Lorraine. What sort of
man was this Bethmann-Hollweg? His advisers told
him: "Send for Mr Bonn. He knows the German mind
as no one else." Max was then working in M.I.5 under
Admiral Reginald Hall, but in a junior capacity, and
was astonished to be bidden to breakfast with the Prime
Minister. Lloyd George asked Max if the German
Chancellor had meant what he said. Max wiped his
mouth and replied: "Mr Prime Minister, there were
two Jews, Isaac and Moses, who were bosom friends.
They lived at a small town half-way between Cracow
and Lemberg. They had business in both these cities,
and went every day by train to one or to the other. One
morning on the platform, Isaac asked Moses where he
was going that day. 'To Cracow,' said Moses. The
train for Cracow came in. Moses boarded it. As the
train moved out of the station, Isaac ran beside it,
purple with rage, shaking his fist and shouting: 'Moses,
I will never speak to you again! You and I was boyhood
friends, and when I ask you where was you going you
say "Cracow," and you *was* going to Cracow, you
bloody liar!'"

That was many years before Max joined our firm,
but he did not change his style, and our partners'
meetings were often enlivened, and prolonged, by such
oblique contributions to debate.

Max had the nicest sense of behaviour. I recollect a
visit from M. Arthur Spitzer, the Parisian banker,
bearded, dapper, wearing English tweeds. He tripped

towards Max with both hands outstretched: *"Mon cher Max!"*

"Mon cher Arthur!"

It was a courtesy visit only, and the two men chatted away most amicably, with those minor exchanges of compliments which go so well in French. When the visit was over Max escorted Spitzer out. He came back into the partners' room and almost slammed the door. "That *swine* Arthur!" he said.

"What has he done, Max?"

"Being so nice."

"Why shouldn't he be nice?"

"How much does Arthur care what happens to us?"

Max knew that he and Spitzer liked each other just so much and no more, and was furious at having been compelled by those eager outstretched hands into expressing, in public, a shade more warmth than he felt.

I hope, and believe, that Max grew fond of all his partners, but his admiration, with few reserves, was kept for Bernard Barrington. Here was the man he would have loved to be, tall, fair, equable, and capable, after hearing the arguments for or against, of taking and acting upon a decision without subsequent misgivings. While Max, after some commitment had been taken by the firm, went home to rack himself with doubts, and, ringing up his partners, one by one, to spray them with second thoughts, Bernie Barrington was thinking about partridges, or stretching his long legs in an after-dinner nap as punctual and recurrent as the stars. How much would Max have given for such calmness, such assurance! Yet all the time there was also within him a sense of rebellion against the very qualities he so much envied. How easy to be calm if you were

blind, to be assured if you had no tentacles, no antennae!
What if all this nonchalance, this enviable certitude,
were nothing but obtuseness? Why must his Yiddish
bones ache with forebodings, while Bernie pruned roses
in Suffolk? There were moments when Max would
revenge himself upon the man he so doted on with half-
playful, half-pouting attacks. "What is there so wonder-
ful about this Anglo-Saxon honesty of Bernie's?" he
would ask me. "You never hear *me* say 'Because I don't
want to go to jug.'" Max was referring to a favourite
reply of Barrington, our tame lawyer, when asked at a
partners' meeting why a prospectus might not shed
some of the verbiage required by the Companies Acts.
"Because, my friend, I don't want to go to jug," Bernie
would say, with a characteristic gesture of arm and
hand. Nobody knew better than Max the bubble-
weight of this formula; what he was really grumbling
about was his foreknowledge that whereas his own
obituary would mention his integrity, Bernie's would
take that for granted, and speak only of his cricket, his
love of nature and of shooting, and his charm. Even
praise, to so sensitive a Jewish pride as Max's, could be
tactless.

Max's affections were strong, and there was a short
period when a late marriage seemed to have brought
him a hitherto untasted felicity. The hungry look went
out of his eyes for a spell. But he was tragically disillusioned, and had to face the publicity of a scandalous
divorce case and to fight black perjury and malevolence.
He triumphed, the judge going out of his way to speak
of Max's untarnished honour. But it almost broke his
heart.

In his last years Max found happiness in work of a

new sort. He became chairman of a big industrial concern, the United Glass Bottles Company. Here he ruled; he, the racial, the secular underdog, reigned constitutionally but actively over true-blue Anglo-Saxon directors, technicians, and workmen, and he did it with outstanding success. This salved his sensitive imagination and gave him a sense of fulfilment.

Max, when in spirits, was the best company in the world. He had the gift of laughing at himself and his race while proudly sticking up for both. His Jewish stories, inimitably told, came pat to all occasions. He was charitable, warm-hearted, and courageous.

In a world that has not been kind to Jews, I think the Max Bonns should be remembered. And although the following verses, mainly but not wholly inspired by Max, have already been printed, I make no bones about printing them again.

From sad, demanding eyes his soul peeped out,
 And when a sudden shaft of sunshine took
 Fair heads, and gave to them a burnished look,
He fought again his little war with Doubt.

Pride was his dear companion, and sweet
 It was to savour his undaunted Race;
 Till Doubt came whispering of hangdog face,
Of sloping shoulder, and resentful feet.

Those ancient oracles, his Yiddish bones,
 Faltered in this cold, unresponsive land;
 He waved to friendship with too soft a hand,
And bid for love with too expensive stones.

The light that slept behind his sombre eye
 Warmed to a flame for fantasy and Art,
 As if he felt upon his desert heart
A hot wind blowing out of Sinai.

To guess with subtlety, with skill to plan,
　　Was his by birthright—one that he would sell
　　(On English mornings when he walked in Hell)
To be a tall, blond, striding, outdoor man.

Too circumspect to march, too proud to run,
　　He stood in loyalty that cost him dear,
　　Because he saw a hundred foes to fear
Where his slow blue-eyed partner saw but one.

His raw nerves quivered at a moth-wing's tap;
　　But when a bright-haired woman turned and smiled,
　　He trampled sorrow like a shriven child,
And tossed his heart, unarmoured, in her lap.

Steadfast, tho' wincing at each blow and bruise,
　　And tough as any Maccabee of old,
　　He shook with sudden merriment, and told
A thousand funny stories about Jews.

CHAPTER VIII

RETURN TO NORFOLK

W E all love money, and if it comes in the shape of an unexpected windfall it has a peculiar charm for us; but few can have had my wife's experience of sitting through a sale at Christie's, and leaving the sale-room with the knowledge that she and her young family were no longer dependent upon a salary-earning husband without a penny of capital, but secure from want, with prudent management, for life. The sale was of the Holford pictures from Dorchester House and Westonbirt, and by the will of her uncle, Sir George Holford, my wife was to receive less than a tithe of the proceeds. We had no inkling, in those days, of what such a collection might fetch, and her part of an unknown amount that we had no means of estimating sounded only moderately exciting. So the sale itself, with every tap of young Mr Alec Martin's gavel increasing our future security, was a most exhilarating affair.

Seldom can a legacy have been more opportune. Within a month or so I was struck down, while stalking in Scotland, by a sudden flare-up of old wound-trouble that all but finished me off. After weeks of pain and mishandling in Edinburgh I was saved, at the last gasp, by the great Sir John Fraser; but there followed a whole winter of convalescence in a villa near St Jean-de-Luz and several years of varying disabilities until I had the luck to fall in with the great Dr Jeanneret of Lausanne. This grizzled, simple-mannered genius, who lived in a four-roomed flat, located the seat of a poison that Harley Street had searched for in vain over fifteen years, restored me to health and charged me £10 for doing so.

The legacy not only paid for the villa in the foothills of the Pyrenees, but contributed, on our return to England, to a major change in our way of life. I had been advised to get as much country life as possible, and our altered circumstances, abetted by my firm's willingness to give me my freedom from Friday afternoon until lunch-time on Monday, enabled me to achieve a long-standing secret ambition. I proposed to my father that he should turn out his tenant at my old Norfolk home, Cranmer Hall, and let me have the place on permanent lease. My father, with characteristic generosity, decided instead, with an eye on death-duties, to make over the whole estate to myself.

The tenant of Cranmer for more than a quarter of a century, the late George Lockhart Ross, had fortunately always insisted on a year-to-year letting and took his dismissal in good part. It would be an understatement to call Ross an extraordinary character. The only child of a widow, he had gone to neither school nor college, and had grown to manhood tied to his mother's apron-strings. After her death he went into mourning for the rest of his life, and when out shooting, which was his ruling passion, was dressed in black Norfolk jacket, black knickerbockers and gaiters, a black cloth cap, and black gloves. He was all but inarticulate from shyness, and when he did speak, his words bubbled out in rapid, reluctant, staccato sentences, each one delivered with an air of hoping it might prove to be the last he would ever have to utter.

Mr Ross had arrived trailing rumours, which might have disconcerted my father had they preceded him. There was the story of the bull. It was said that, wandering with a gun, Ross had heard a suspicious rustle behind a hedge.

"Who-are-you?" No answer.

"Speak-or-I'll-shoot." Silence. He shot, killing a dumb but valuable bull. He was a misogynist, having been told, it was said, by a gypsy that he would meet his death at the hands of a woman. (In the event he fell dead, most enviably, in the act of firing at a driven partridge. He and his life's love fell together.)

Ross was a recluse, and during his long tenancy had no visitors except, on occasion, my father, and once a year, an elderly couple from Wales, General and Mrs Hills-John. They were his cousins, and the only relations he acknowledged. A week before their first visit, Mr Ross called upon my father's agent, Mr Woodhouse.

"Have-you-got-a-welcome-Woodhouse?"

Mr Woodhouse always had a welcome for any tenant of my father's, but found the form of the question perplexing. He had no ready reply.

"I-want-a-welcome."

"You are always welcome, I'm sure, sir."

"But-I-want-it-for-the-gates."

After further perplexities it became clear that Mr Ross expected a well-run Norfolk estate to keep on hand a triumphal arch with WELCOME inscribed upon it, which could be erected at short notice over the wrought-iron lodge-gates at the entrance to the avenue. We had

none, but Mr Woodhouse, never at a loss, contrived
one all the same, and General and Mrs Hills-John from
Wales were received as if they had been that princi-
pality's Prince.

On one of my father's short visits occurred the
incident of the mouse. Ross was leading my father,
each with a candlestick in hand, up the stairs to bed.
At a turn of the staircase Ross stopped and turned to my
father.

"Mouse-hold-candle."

My father found himself holding a candle in each
hand, by the light of which he was able to see a mouse,
sitting very still in an angle of the staircase. Ross had
disappeared towards the gunroom. He soon returned
with a ·22 rifle.

"You can't shoot at that mouse," protested my father,
"you'll spoil my panelling." But Ross was already
down upon one knee and taking aim.

"Shan't-hit-panelling-hit-mouse," and he did, very
neatly. He rang the bell. His butler appeared, spectacled
and with a black, drooping moustache.

"Remove-the-carcass." The carcass was removed.

The routine of Ross's life was absolute. Every night
of his life he dressed for dinner in tail coat and white tie,
sitting alone in the panelled dining-room at one end of
a long mahogany table, made to sit fourteen persons
at the least, and set out with a silver centrepiece and its
heavy Victorian satellites. Dinner over, he strode across
the Inner Hall to Philip Webb's elaborate Drawing-
Room, with Italianate barrel-roof, cedar-and-gilt pilasters, Morris wallpaper, tortoiseshell cabinets, and arum
lilies. Here he sat bolt upright, looking at the *Field* or
the *Illustrated London News*, but never at a book, until

ten o'clock precisely. He then went upstairs, put on a smoking-jacket, and descended again to the Study, where, surrounded by glass-cases containing stuffed, partridges and pheasants whose plumage had been found to be eccentric or unfashionable, he cleaned his guns and rifles until bedtime. Above his solitary head a score of bedrooms remained, from January to January, untenanted. On the ground floor his unstraying feet trod but a fraction of the floor-space at his single disposal. Few can have had less cause than Ross to grumble about *Lebensraum*.

The squires of North-west Norfolk in those days, although thin on the ground, were friendly and hospitable, besides being often in need of an extra gun; and Ross, on his first coming among them, was invited to shoot. The Mulhollands at Worlingham were too far off his beat, and as he never stayed away, it must have been at some shooting-party within range of Cranmer that they first encountered this strange, heavy figure all in black, with his turkey's-egg complexion, ragged sandy moustache, and pale eyes. At the shooting-lunch he bubbled out that some gun must have been culpably careless, since pellets had rattled round him at the last stand. Nobody pleaded guilty, and a guest tried to pass it off with a feeble joke.

"Somebody must have taken you for a woodcock!" Ross rose to his feet, purple in the face.

"More-like-a-woodcock-yourself!" and, gathering up his belongings, he called for his loader and his dog-cart, climbed up and drove away. But there was no real fat in the fire until, at some neighbouring shoot and in the presence of the M.F.H. himself, Ross shot a fox. Then there was trouble indeed. The M.F.H., Charlie

Seymour, not only my father's old friend but his banker, who knew well enough that the rent Ross paid was my father's chief source of income, wrote to him none the less to ask, or rather to demand, that Ross be given instant notice to quit. My father, who was, perhaps fortunately, abroad, had to explain that with a large and expensive family he could not afford to make so great a sacrifice even in the sacred cause of fox-hunting.

I do not think Ross himself ever understood what all the trouble was about, any more than he understood his crime, many years later, in shooting a bittern on Sculthorpe Fen. If wild things were within range, you shot them. What else are guns for? But the vulpicide cut him off from his neighbours for many years. Things do blow over at last, and there came a time when Mr Ross, regarded as an incorrigible but good-hearted and open-handed freak, subscribed to the Hunt, attended the meets in his hearse-like car, and followed the hunt by road, with a box of first-aid equipment in case of falls. He was also in demand as "starter" at local fêtes, for his old horse-pistol, charged with black powder, made the biggest bang in West Norfolk, and Ross's boyish pleasure in discharging it was endearing.

When a head gardener, under notice to quit, refused to leave on the appointed day and barricaded himself in his cottage, his trigger-happy master was with difficulty restrained from firing at him with a shotgun through the door and windows; but in the main he was a kind and considerate employer, and ran a most successful Rifle Club in the village with money-prizes, as well as spoons, on a generous scale. On one subject alone was he implacable: poaching. When the local Bench acquitted, for lack of sufficient evidence, a man whom

Ross had prosecuted, he decided that he could never again speak to the Clerk to the Justices, on whose advice the magistrates had come to their decision. Now this was awkward, for the Clerk, Mr Algernon Digby, was at that time my father's agent, through whom all Ross's business with his landlord passed. Algy Digby himself, so enormous that on his visits to Cranmer in my childhood days a special chair had to be fetched from the kitchen, since he had broken too many of the drawing-room chairs to be permitted to risk any more, was the most kindly of men, and although he could hardly apologise for giving correct advice on a matter of law, a lasting quarrel with such a mountain of good nature seemed absurd. So my father was not unduly perturbed at the first news of the break, feeling that a few soothing words from himself would put matters right. He little knew his man. To all my father's pleas for peace, repeated year in and year out, Ross had but one reply: "I-am-a-Highlander-Highlanders-never-for-give." And he never did. Thenceforth, when matters of business arose, my father himself had to deal with those curt letters, written in a nursery hand, in which all words, even those of two letters, were carried relent-lessly to the right-hand edge of the page, and there divided with a dash. With no more than four words to the line, this practice gave a queer look to his in-frequent notes:

> Dear Sir Lawrenc-
> -e, i shall be a-
> -t home on th-
> -e Saturday i-
> -f you can com-
> -e then. But i-

For all his shyness, Ross was fond of a joke and often made one. What the jokes were about, and how good they were, nobody can say, for when joking he was entirely unintelligible. We just joined in the merriment, but watchfully, for it had a way of stopping abruptly; the pale eyes switched into mourning again, and it was judicious to conform. A dying giggle, after high seriousness had been resumed, would have been suspect.

Ross took his notice to quit, as has been said, with admirable good humour, and moved from his park and hall, his hothouse grapes and peaches, to a small red-brick villa in a row at Sheringham. There was plenty of room in it for cleaning guns; a shoot was hired in the neighbourhood, and he wanted no more.

I know of few things more enjoyable than being enabled to do the right thing by an old home. Cranmer Hall, although not acquired by my family until 1751, had been built, in a pleasant local red brick, in 1721, a good date for a middling-sized manor house. But my grandfather had ideas of his own, and very bad ones they were. There was nothing wrong with his earlier extensions in rear of the original block, for they too were in the plain Georgian style; but he entirely destroyed the agreeable face of the house by putting in plate-glass windows, each divided by one clumsy horizontal bar, and by concealing the Georgian doorway behind a heavy enclosed brick porch, roofed with slates. He wanted, my father told me, a place in which to keep the sticks, the spuds, and the umbrellas. The plate-glass gave to the façade a blank, almost a blind stare, and the monstrous utilitarian porch deprived it of its proportions. My grandfather further justified the worst we say about the mid-Victorians by throwing out a bow-window two storeys high, on one side of this long-suffering façade. Around the bow-window he ran a verandah, supported by cast-iron pillars. Later he became more ambitious. Philip Webb, once the partner of William Morris, was at that time the fashionable architect, and my grandfather, who needed more space for entertaining, gave him a free hand. The result, internally, was the fantastic drawing-room, and externally three brick gables to express Webb's impatience with the sober rectangles of the Georgian builders, and a soaring, gawky clock-tower, supported by an immense flying-buttress, which oozed smoke whenever the drawing-room chimney went on fire. High up on the clock-face itself were pinned the sun, the moon, and a few stars, the sun with brazen locks streaming. The chimes were mellow, and remain in memory as cherishable as those of Lupton's Tower at Eton. But the price paid for them, in the outlandish tower itself, touched upon the absurd. Only for the discreetly panelled dining-room, and, unexpectedly, a set of chairs especially designed for it, did Webb exact gratitude from me.

As a child I had taken everything for granted, looking as blindly at the flawed façade as it looked blankly back at me, and much admiring the too heavy coat-of-arms on the pediment. The clock-tower was there, I supposed, for telling the time, and I took pride in the golden sun and moon. As for the drawing-room, redolent of cedarwood and pot-pourri, it had everything, for my young eyes, that Webb could have wished. Mystery in the recess behind the great square solitary pillar; splendour in the gilt that shone from the pilasters; fascination in the birds and arabesques that enriched the bold curve of the barrelled ceiling. The three perfect Georgian rooms in the original block meant nothing to me at all, but that was hardly to be wondered at, for the mouldings had been cut to fit yellow, varnished bookcases or encrusted Victorian looking-glasses, and the fielded panelling was concealed behind layers of Victorian wallpaper.

It is hard, in this changed world, to lay hold again upon the state of mind in which, in 1929, we so gaily fell to and restored this disfigured house to grace. We must, it is clear, have seen ourselves there for life, since we did not spare expense; nor can we have had any misgivings about servants, gamekeepers, and gardeners. It is often said that it was the first World War that swept away for ever the pleasant, privileged life of the English country-house. Yet here were we, more than a decade after that war ended, planning to remake just such a home as the Edwardians had enjoyed. It is true that this time the owner was not to live upon his rents, but to work in the City, repairing to his home only from Friday to Monday and in the holidays—a very big difference indeed, since it cut him off from the public obligations, and left him with only the amenities, of a country squire. There could be no Petty Sessions or County Council activities for me. But what strikes me today as the most surprising, and a rather shocking, thing about my return to Norfolk, is that I was prepared to spend so much upon putting right my grandfather's architectural lapses, before seeing to the state of the many cottages lately made over to me. There were over sixty of these, in the village or scattered over the farms, and, though by no means dilapidated on the whole, many were far from satisfactory. It is possible that had I been less familiar with these small houses I should have examined them with a keener eye. But I had known most of them as a child, and a child walks into the snug living-rooms of his village friends with nothing but admiration for their compact cosiness, for the patchwork rugs, the whorled shells and Toby-jugs on the mantel, the red glow of the small, approachable hearth. If invited upstairs, he finds the steep and narrow staircase an adventure, not a drawback, and the low ceilings and diminutive casements possess, for him, a positive charm. In revisiting, forty years later, the uncomplaining tenants of these same cottages, I was slow to shake off that deep-rooted mood of acceptance, and to see, with a fresh eye, the constrictions and handicaps of their daily lives. To take but one example, I must have sat chatting many a time in the kitchens of a row of small brick houses before I learnt, almost casually, that the wallpaper was peeling off because of the steam on Mondays. For Monday was washing-day, and these cottages had no washhouses at the back, but only coppers built into the wall beside the chimney-breast. If I had noticed these coppers at all, it was only to admire their burnished wells; I had never seen them in action, with the steam filling the room and condensing on ceiling and walls, an intolerable nuisance and a disgrace to myself, as landlord, and to my father and grandfather before me. And even now realisation came too late, for the whole row, although liked by the inhabitants for the warmth of the thick walls, had been condemned by the County Council for containing less than the standard cubic space above-stairs. My remorse did not go so far as the building of washhouses for houses that were to be pulled down.

Whether a single one of my cottage-tenants con-

sciously felt within him that washhouses, not to speak
of whole new houses, ought to come before Georgian
doorways, I have no idea. Probably not. In remote
country places it needed a second World War to put
certain quite simple ideas into the heads of landlords
and cottagers alike. That those who inspected the
alterations at the Hall were surprised by them is likely;
the removal of good thick plate-glass and the solid
slate-and-brickwork of an obviously useful porch must
have seemed to them near lunacy. How far removed
the practical, down-to-earth eye of a cottage-bred
countryman can be from that of his employer is shown
by a plea made to me by a retainer who, in heart and
head, was far nearer to me than any other. He besought
me one day to cut down all the old oaks in the avenue,
in order to obtain the high war-prices for the timber.
"And think how you will enjoy seeing the young trees
you replant coming on," he added. These ancient trees,
dear to the jackdaws, and framing, to any approaching
eye, the mellow house itself, were our pillars of respect-
ability, our Elders of the Kirk, as it were. Of good
height as well as girth, standing in double ranks, and
not too proud to admit a horse-chestnut or two and
even a Scotch fir into their company, they reminded us,
at breakfast in the winter sunshine or at dinner on
summer evenings when their trunks turned red as
pines, that we, like themselves, had roots in that place.
Besides, all old houses should have a respectful retinue
of timber to usher in a stranger. Yet a friend who knew
me well could suggest that these venerable, umbrageous
aisles should be swept away, and that I should console
myself by strolling, on Sunday afternoons, from one to
another of those odious little iron cages in which baby

oaks must be planted, examining the reluctant shoots on the slowest of all saplings! And at my back a house unframed, exposed, unguarded! Decidedly it was not a good idea.

To restore Cranmer's Georgian façade to its original grace was both easy and rewarding; and the rooms behind it, belonging to the same felicitous period, also gave no trouble. It was merely a question of scrapping Victorian bookcases and mirrors, removing cases of stuffed birds, stripping wallpaper from panels, making good broken mouldings, and redecorating in duck's-egg green and white. But Philip Webb's drawing-room was another matter. There was nothing to be done about the gables and the clock-tower; massive structural altera- tions were beyond our purse, and if a house has one agreeable face, and that the one first approached, one can put up with a good deal that is discordant, even grotesque, if it is seen only from one part of the garden. But the drawing-room was the big room, the southerly, sunshiny room, a room for living in. My father, who had so generously given me the place, was very much alive and likely to be a regular visitor; he had been brought up in the belief that Webb's eclectic fantasy was one of the most beautiful rooms in the country, and a feather in the family cap. My boyhood acquain- tance, Hal Goodhart-Rendel, most scholarly of archi- tects, had somehow got wind of our goings on, and had written me a very stern letter, pointing out that Webb's room was a "document," that I held it, not in fee simple, but as a trustee for posterity, and that to meddle with it would be a crime. That I disliked it and had to live in it was not, he said, to the point. But I felt strongly that it was Webb, not I, who was the vandal

and the "aggressor." Had he built for my grandfather
a house from the ground, as he built Arisaig House for
my Nicholson cousins, or Clouds for the Wyndhams,
I should probably have found much to admire, and
certainly nothing to destroy. But for an architect, when
asked to add more living-space to an old Georgian
manor-house, to treat its native simplicity and symmetry with contempt, and to "show off" by being as
exaggeratedly fanciful as he knew how, humiliating the
Georgian moderation and restraint with an overgrown
clock-tower plastered with suns and moons, and a
drawing-room all fuss and fustian, was surely an act of
aggression. As a sop to Hal's concern for the record, I
had Webb's room photographed and sent the photographs to the Victoria and Albert Museum to be laid
up with the Webbian archives, but the room itself was
stripped and transformed into a pleasant, unpretentious
living-room in tune with, if less elegant than, the
smaller rooms in the original block. As for my father,
I left him in my wife's hands. Having no aesthetic
standards of his own, he was the most educable of men,
and in ten minutes' conversation, following upon a
single gasp, he was brought round to a faintly wondering
acquiescence.

All this tearing down and restoring was the greatest
fun, even to the contriving of six more bathrooms; and
because as a small boy I had been able to crawl between
slates and joists to places beyond the reach of the
architect and his men, I was able to demonstrate the
practicability of alterations that had been turned down
as structurally unviable. For intimacy with the uttermost
recesses of an old house there is nobody to match an
active, inquisitive, mouse-trapping boy.

But coming home to live at Cranmer was one thing; commencing landowner was another. My boyhood familiarity with the day-to-day workings of a home farm, seen from the point of view of the labourer, had taught me nothing about ownership or the mentality of tenants. Norfolk people have their own ways of doing things, and I had much to learn. I had not been long at home when I received a letter from the tenant of a smallholding in the village, giving me formal notice of his wish to give up his tenancy at Michaelmas. I acknowledged his letter, with polite regret at losing him (for he was the People's Churchwarden and a man of standing in Sculthorpe), and immediately re-let the holding at a higher rent to an eager, and worthy, applicant. Next Sunday the Churchwarden was not in the church porch to welcome us, as had been his friendly habit; he was lurking in the shadows near the Norman font. The next Sunday and the next it was the same; no good morning for me or my family. After some weeks I heard, in a roundabout way, that in the Warden's opinion "the Major" had treated him in a most "onderhand" manner, and was no longer fit to be spoken to. This "onderhandedness" consisted in having accepted his notice. Above-board behaviour on my part would have been to pay him a visit, personally or through my agent, and beg him to withdraw his notice. This he would have graciously done, in return for a reduction of rent.

As far as the church porch went, I think I was sent to Coventry for about a couple of years, but after that polite, if not very warm, relations were restored. But I was, I fear, ever afterwards regarded by the Warden as inclined to be crooked, especially when the war came and we had to sit, he as Chairman of Parish Defence and I as local Home Guard Commander, on a joint committee. He was ineradicably suspicious of all my proposals, believing, as Lloyd George believed about "the Brass-hats," that I had a kind of vested interest in the war, and was trying to frighten him, unfairly, into absurd and unnecessary exertions. Talking of invasion, for instance, and of Germans in Sculthorpe—pure moonshine. It did not seem credible, to the Warden's mind, that a man of my intelligence could honestly believe in such nonsense. There must be some "onderhand" motive. He stubbornly refused to do anything at all, and how triumphant he must have felt when the war was won and his inactivity proved to have been masterly! A triumph shared, incidentally, by one member of the Home Guard itself who, on the night in the autumn of 1940 when the word "Cromwell" was signalled and all England stood to arms, refused to leave his bed. "I'll get up if he come," he said, "but I know he baint a-coming." And he was right, damn him.

But the lesson of the empty porch—that a notice to quit means nothing at all—by no means completed my education. I was to learn that a unanimous vote in the Reading Room also meant nothing at all. I had stepped, unawares, into Mr Ross's shoes as President of the Rifle Club, but was told, soon after my arrival, that the younger men were taking no interest in it, and that there was a general wish that it should be wound up. Accordingly, in the Chair at the next meeting, I invited the members to say if this was indeed their wish. There was a long silence, broken at length by the Secretary, who expressed his opinion in favour of winding up. Nobody opposed, and I then moved a resolution to that effect, which was seconded by the Secretary. "Those in favour?" Every hand went up. "Against?" Nobody was against. The motion was declared carried and the meeting broke up. On leaving the Reading Room a little later, I noticed that the members had not dispersed to their homes, but were standing in the road in twos and threes, confabulating. A few days later I heard that there was a good deal of dissatisfaction in the village; many of the men were much disappointed at the demise of the Rifle Club.

"But why didn't they say so? Why did they all vote for ending it?"

"Well, you see, they didn't like to go against the Major."

The Major who had had no opinion either way, and believed himself, like Mr Speaker, to be but the servant of the assembled members!

It was becoming clear that I had much to learn; including the lamentable truth that only the privileged, with a background of independence and social ease, have inherited the freedom to speak their minds. But this sad little affair in the Reading Room took place nearly thirty years ago. Nowadays Sculthorpe would, I feel sure, speak out.

My greenness as a landowner, which in the case of the smallholding had merely tarnished my character, was seriously to affect my pocket, and to cause me endless worry, in the case of one of the larger farms. The sitting tenant, known to my childhood, had died after over fifty years on the same farm. He had been the finest type of Norfolk farmer, always doing well by the land, and would in any case have been hard to replace; but, looking back, I am amazed how I ever

came to let this good land to his successor. He had been
pressed upon me, with the strongest commendations,
by a bank manager at King's Lynn, who pointed out
that as the son of one of the biggest and most successful
farmers in West Norfolk, young X would have the
paternal skill as well as the paternal capital to back him.
The father himself brought the young man to see me;
a hulking, tongue-tied, pleasant-spoken young countryman with a rather attractive shy smile, and a public-
school voice. I could not take to his sire, but he talked
about farming like the good farmer that in fact he was,
and promised that his watchful eye would be upon his
son. I remembered that his predecessor had been even
younger than X when he first took over this farm and
expressed, in my fatuity, the hope that X too would
farm that land for fifty years. Young X did not just
farm badly; he did not farm at all. He moved into the
charming four-square red-brick farmhouse, with its
park-like meadow, dotted with oak trees, lying green
before the elegant Georgian doorway and fanlight. He
put on a pair of carpet-slippers, stretched himself upon
a sofa, and read paper-bound shockers. Twice a week
he drove into Fakenham for a fresh supply of reading-
matter. He had no outdoor pursuits. The farm itself he
left to his men. On the first rent-day no cheque arrived
from X. My agent rang him up to remind him that a
half-year's rent was due.

"Rent? What do you mean, rent?"

The rent was paid, of course; I imagine his father
saw to that, although, for all his assurances, he saw to
nothing else. But there was many a Friday night when
the labourers were not paid, and could not be paid until
a calf, or a bullock, had been hastily sold, by torchlight

in the yard, to a neighbouring farmer at an upset price.

By an Act of Parliament enacted in the nineteen-twenties, with the object of giving more security of tenure to farm-tenants, I was disabled from ridding myself of this young incubus unless either I paid him a whole year's rent as compensation, or obtained from the County Agricultural Committee a certificate of his unfitness to farm. At that period the second alternative was not open to me, for our Norfolk Committee had a Labour majority, and refused to grant certificates, on the principle, perhaps, that tenants are always right and landlords always wrong. So I had to watch the docks and thistles take possession of the fields, over which no manure or fertilisers were spread, while the sheep and cattle dwindled and disappeared. I also had to endure a visit from my tenant's papa, who demanded a halving of the rent, shaking his fist in my face and then sitting, arms folded, in one of my chairs, refusing to budge until I should comply. Not till I sent for the chauffeur and gardeners to come and carry him out did he retire, shouting abuse. I must admit that this scene made his shamefaced but nice-spoken son utterly miserable. Had I known enough to assess the rapidity with which good land can deteriorate and foreseen that I should in the end, when the boy's bankruptcy eventually evicted him, be compelled, on re-letting, to lose many hundreds a year, I should have paid him his compensation and let him go. But it goes against the grain to reward incompetence with a round sum in cash, and I hesitated too long.

The experience did bring home to me that land-owning is a skilled job, and that as a City worker in middle life I was most unlikely to acquire the knowledge needed to make a success of it. It was clear to me, as well, that with the only remedy against a bad farmer denied to me, I was not in truth the owner of my own estate. To be compelled to sit by and to watch one's property go bad is not my idea of ownership. So, finding my other farm-tenants, all first-class men, anxious to buy their holdings, and quite willing to relinquish the sporting rights in my favour, I eventually sold the estate to the sitting tenants. I had always believed that ownership of land by the man who makes his living from it had much to be said for it; and as far as my former farms are concerned, twenty years of ownership by working farmers has been, and continues to be, an unqualified success. A man does not let his own fields starve. I later applied the same principle to cottages, offering to sell them to their occupiers on fair terms. Many jumped at the chance, and the improvement in the appearance of the houses and small gardens has been a pleasure to see. A man paints and plants—and now-adays adds a garage—when it is for himself and his children. It is, I suppose, human nature, certainly Norfolk nature, never to stop a draught or a leak, however petty, when there is a landlord to grumble to; but, with ownership, things are made not only watertight and airtight, but smartened up all round. Above all, the cottage-owner has that inestimable comfort, the knowledge that his home is his home, and that he cannot be turned out against his will.

To return, after an absence of thirty-five years, to the scenes of one's childhood, and to visit as Squire, in the shoes of a still-living father, the familiar cottages outside which I had so often tethered my pony before making my shrinking entry on some errand of my mother's, was a somewhat tremulous business. The rather high-pitched Norfolk voices, rising a little at the end of each utterance, were familiar enough, and pleasant to the ear; but I had forgotten, or as a child had never noticed, that if the master of the house is home from work, he does not rise from his chair on the entry of a visitor, not even for a lady, but remains seated, usually in his shirt-sleeves, by the side of the fire. He is pleased to see you, and ready for a chat, but it is his kitchen and his chair, and to disturb himself would be, I suppose, an admission, damaging to his sense of stability, that certain fixed and reassuring relationships might be put in question. It is for the visitor to sit down, not for himself to get up, and in so doing to create an uncertainty as to who is to sit where, and even, who knows, as to the basic independence of one who, although glad to see you, had invited nobody. There are warm hearts in Norfolk, and great fidelity, but too much shyness and reserve to allow of the more superficial graces. And how little these seem to matter in a people capable of the kindliness, even delicacy, shown, in the neighbouring parish of South Creake, to a new High Anglican parson whose ritualistic services outraged a longstanding tradition.

"Yes, we know he antics," said one of his parishioners, "but we loike him, so we antics with him."

One thing that I missed, after thirty years' absence, was the full-blooded Norfolk speech. The lilt and the vowel-sounds were the same, but the idiom was disappearing. Old Dodman, the blind man, could still say "He don't fare to moind that" or "don't yew imitate to dew" this or that, but the younger, and even the middle-aged, had lost the habit. And the general sophistication was greater. When I was a boy an old lady had assured my mother that "Doctor, he say to me, the howl of your constitootion hev gone into your little finger, he say," and many years later my father, when visiting, had found another elderly dame in a state of deep depression. It seemed that a running sore on her leg had, after twenty years or more, healed of itself.

"But what a good thing!" said my father.

"Noo, that it aint. I moind when Lady Jownes she say to me, Mark my words, Mrs Dix, if ever that leg o' yours droy up, you're a dead woman, she say."

My father found difficulty in recognising my mother's gentle and considerate style of conversation.

Gone, too, were the days when so great was the prestige of the Rector that he could cause, by a casual remark, the death of a parishioner. The Rector was my great-uncle, "Reverend Harbert Jownes," and the story was told to my father by the parishioner's widow, who for one believed in it.

"Did you ever hare tell how my pore husband come to doy? Well, yew see, that was this way, Sir Lawrence. My husband he'd been up at the chuch to help carry a gentleman from the Union [i.e. to carry the coffin at the burial of a pauper], and when he come home, he say to me, 'Hew dew yew think oi been a walkin' arm-in-arm with?' he say. 'My dare, how can I tell?' I say. 'Oi been walkin' arm-in-arm with Reverend Jownes,' he say. 'Oh,' I say, 'and how was that?' 'Well,' he say, 'as I was a-comin' out of the chuchyard Rector he come alongsoide o' me and put his arm troo moine. "George," he say, "I'd loike to hev the buryin' of yew," he say. Now why d'yew think he say that?' 'I couldn't say,' I say. Well, that prey on his moind, and he couldn't eat his wittles nor he didn't goo to wuk, and that warnt many days afore he was dead. That's how my pore George came to doy."

Many years later another Rector, the much loved Jack Labouchere, was also the death of a parishioner, but in quite different fashion. The victim in this case was old Lowder, the last Sculthorpe man (and well I remember him) to come to church in a top-hat and a smock-frock, elaborately embroidered. And it was in this Sunday-best that old Lowder attended a church fête held in the Rectory garden. But a tempest that had been growling about over the fen suddenly darkened the sky, the tops of the tall Rectory trees shivered, and down came the rain. There was a scurry for shelter to the Parish Room, and when continuing small rain and a drop in the temperature proved that this particular storm was a weather-changer, and not a mere dust-layer, the Rector, who was an accomplished amateur conjuror, decided that he must come to the rescue with some tricks. The benches were unstacked; the Rector began his patter; old Lowder's top-hat was borrowed, and out of it came the accustomed rabbits. It was too much for the old man. He carried his hat home, set it on the table before him, and muttered, "Thutty-two years I've hed that there—thutty-two years—and I never see no rabbits afore, that I haint." So wrapt was he in wonder, that he too, like poor George, refused his wittles, with the same melancholy result. He died, surprisingly, from surprise.

That there was any falling off in Sculthorpe's humour since my boyhood days I very much doubt, for humour, especially of the catch-you-out kind, is in-grained in the Norfolk character, but caution is there as well, and I have a feeling that the best chuckles are

heard when the Squire has said "Good-night." I had
heard, when a boy, of the farmer's rebuke to his slow-
moving labourer, and believed it then to have been ad-
ministered in our own parish, but now I am not so sure.

"George, did yew ever see a dodman?" (a snail).

"Of course I hev, scores o' toimes."

"Dew yew must'a met it, cos yew never could'a
overtuk it."

But it was certainly a Sculthorpe man who scored off
the gypsies, for he was one of the Winns. Not Jimmy
Winn, who was our own dear "Master," head gardener
at Cranmer, nor Rook Winn, the tall ratcatcher, with
a great hooked nose that held an eternal drop at the end
of it, and ears so thin that you could see the sunshine
through them. I think it must have been Chris Winn,
whom I remember only as a name. He was driving his
tumbril from the village to Hempton, when he passed
a couple o' these hare gypsies who axed him for a lift.
So as they was gooin' along, they want to tell his
fortune. Noo, he say, that you shan't, for he didn't
howld with that. So when they come to Hempton
Splash, where the rood go troo the river, he pulled up
the old hoss roight there in the middle, and he let down
that little ole tumbril so as them thare gypsies goo
slidin' into the river. They did hollar an' all. 'Now,'
he say, when they was a-settin' thare, 'did yew know
that was a-gooin' to happen to yew?' he say. 'Noo,
Master,' they say, 'that we didn't.' 'Well,' he say, 'if
yew didn't know that was a-gooin' to happen to yew,'
he say, 'how could you tell what was a-gooin' to happen
to me?" They hadn't nawthin' to say to that, so he
druv on a-leavin' them pore gypsies a-settin' in the
water. Oo we did laugh.

I found old blind Dodman, as I have said, still talking the true Norfolk, impervious to the accents of the B.B.C. to which he listened all day. (I asked him what was his favourite programme, and he had no hesitation in plumping for the fat stock prices, although he had never owned a calf.) Old Mr Fox, one of my father's woodmen, was talking it as well; so was Mr Groom, the gravedigger and sexton. But they were old men, and it was refreshing to find one woman still in her forties who used the ancient idiom. A racier flow of talk and a wider vocabulary than Mrs Baxter's it would be hard to come by, and although she was disapproved of, not without cause, she fortunately lived in one of my own cottages, and I had every right to sit in her parlour and to listen, with unfailing delight, to her miraculous talk. For she was no reader, and how she had acquired her stock of *mots justes*, one that few of us who are educated could readily draw upon, is a mystery. But Mrs Baxter was a rare bird indeed; and to hear Norfolk spoken today in all its richness you must go to a smoking-concert, or to some village entertainment, where Mr Massey, for long the mainstay of the Faken-ham British Legion, will bring the house down with his Norfolk stories. For it has come to this, that the Norfolk people themselves regard their own dialect as the best of jokes, and like nothing better than to listen to it, a sure sign that its day is over. Let us hope, since it has fallen out of daily use, that its perennial popularity as an entertainment will preserve it, and ensure that it shall be handed down in all its purity from local wag to local wag. It is better, for a language at any rate, to be kept artificially alive than to perish altogether. Although I have learnt, in later life, that few things are more rewarding, so far as daily happiness goes, than the surrender of possessions, the ownership of cottages has, for a countryman, certain advantages. It gives him the right, and even the duty, to knock at many doors which he would otherwise, from shyness, pass by. And although, in prospect, a round of visits could be somewhat daunting, it never failed, in the event, to yield interest and pleasure. I am under no illusions as to how far, if at all, I ever got beneath the polite exchange of commonplaces to the real thoughts of my cottage-tenants. No hearts are worn upon Norfolk shirt-sleeves. But one did catch a flavour of underlying kindliness and, even more strongly, of contentment, born, I think, of an outward-looking habit of mind. Old Dodman's concern with fat stock prices is a case in point. The people had mental, if not active, hobbies, and did not find their laborious lives dull. They never grumbled; and if they had little initiative, they knew how to chew pleasurably the cud of whatever small satisfactions came their way.

After war had broken out, I came, as local Home Guard Commander, to know these people much better, and discovered in them great sturdiness and strength. My command included at least a dozen villages, and on the formation of the L.D.V., as we were at first called, it was natural to appoint as section-leader a prominent farmer in each parish. These busy men took some persuading, not because they had any doubts as to their natural authority over the men they mostly employed, but because they felt that the burden they carried was already too great. And, with a few notable exceptions, they did not persevere.

One upstanding, handsome man of breezy manners

turned out to have the temperament of a prima donna;
several went in for self-pity; one authoritative personality, who might have been a godsend, resigned because
he disapproved of the Ross rifles sent to us by the War
Office. Little by little they made excuses and retired. 1
think these farmers were genuinely thrown out of
balance by the mass of complicated forms showered
upon them. But I noticed that, for all their complaints,
they found time as usual for shooting, and even, on
occasions, for a trip to Newmarket.

With the rank and file it was a different story. When
the master retired, the labourer took over, and it was
remarkable to see the perseverance and intelligence
with which the best of these men turned themselves
into first-class soldiers, with a capacity for command
unbacked by sanctions. For there were no punish-
ments in the Home Guard, even for insubordination.
Only the character and example of the platoon commander or section-leader could hold the men to their
discipline.

There were, of course, failures in the ranks. The
certainty that my gamekeeper, as section-sergeant,
would be busy exercising his men on Sunday mornings,
was an irresistible temptation to Private X, our parish
poacher, not to attend. It was galling for his sergeant to
hear the shots coming from the fen, and to count up,
shot by shot, the morning's toll of pheasants. But there
was nothing to be done about it. And on one Armistice
Day gamekeeper and poacher marched side by side to
church, supporting between them a laurel wreath. I
forget what caused this conjunction; but I have not
forgotten the devout and innocent expression upon
Private X's face. By the end of the war I had in my

Company at least three farm-labourers holding the
King's Commission as 2nd Lieutenants, and they must
have had their reward on a day when they led their
platoons in an attack at the battle school by the sea.
For there was a regular officer there, a brigadier,
lately home from the fighting in France. He stood and
watched our exercise, carried out with real bullets, and
then turned to me to ask to what unit these men
belonged. When I told him the Norfolk Home Guard
his surprise was genuine, and he told me he had thought
them to be battle-trained regulars. It is true that this was
after five years, and we should have been greatly at
fault had we been less than efficient; but for the first
two years we had been short of equipment and instruc-
tors, and throughout the war the men could train only
on Sunday mornings in the field, and one night a week
of lectures in the village schoolroom. Moreover, they
worked long hours throughout the week at laborious
and physically exacting jobs. I am not claiming that
Norfolk had better men than other counties. But I
think it is worthy of record that a class of men who left
school at the age of fourteen, and had, owing to their
work on the land, few opportunities of self-education,
should have been able, by character and natural intelligence, to achieve so much; and that it was on the
sturdiness and devotion of the labourer rather than of
the sporting farmer that our home defence depended.
The service rendered by our farmers in increasing this
small island's home-grown food will never be forgotten;
but they were making money and finding time for
recreation, and the higher good-conduct medals must
be given to their men.

In two parishes the Rectors led the Home Guard

throughout with unfaltering devotion, and that remarkable old character Mr Tatham, the rector of Great Ryburgh, who used "blue-pencilled" for "damned" in every other sentence, gave, with his indefatigable daughter, every assistance short of carrying a rifle. But in many parishes the parsons were aloof and shadowy figures, faintly "grieved," as they would put it, that Sunday mornings were given up to soldiering. In their rambling, unheated rectories, without servants, and with insufficient incomes, they led unenviable lives, shorn of the ancient prestige of their office and regarded at best with tolerance, at worst with indifference.

As the patron of a living, who has had on three occasions to appoint a rector, I have been brought very close to the problem of the Church in remote country places. The lack of scope for a vigorous parson, even more than the unhandy size of the rectories and the inadequate stipends, deters the young, the ardent, and the dedicated among the clergy from applying for these unrewarding benefices. I used, none the less, to receive, on a vacancy becoming known, about seventy applications to sift. But they made sad reading. There were pleadings from impoverished Welsh curates, who began "Honoured Sir" and spoke of wife and child and the two ends that never met. There were enclosers of photographs, showing the applicant, in full canonicals, preaching from a pulpit, with right arm extended. There was the man, far too good for Sculthorpe, who was "directly inspired by the Holy Ghost" as well as being a scout-leader. There were letters of shaming self-praise and letters of Heepish humility. Only one letter, on the occasion of one vacancy, was so simple and straightforward as to lead to an interview and an appointment. On the other two occasions personal recommendations by friends of my own resolved my embarrassment.

When still a greenhorn as patron, I had attempted to discourage unsuitable applicants by inserting an advertisement in the Personal column of *The Times*, specifying my requirements:

> Wanted, for an East Anglian living, a Rector to be guide, philosopher and friend to an agricultural community. Preferably, for this particular parish, a gentleman in the old-fashioned snobbish sense of the word. A liberal Churchman with, if possible, broad views about Bishop Barnes and Psychical Research.

This got me into hot water. The *Church Times* even had a short leading article abusing "Patron," not, as might have been expected, for his heretical softness towards Bishop Barnes, but for his unseemly demand for so unmentionable a thing as a gentleman. "What Patron needs," wrote the *Church Times*, "is not a gentleman but an inspired cad like St Paul." I still think it odd that a church newspaper should have described St Paul as a cad, even in a fit of bad temper. I have always thought of that heroic, ardent soul as a very great gentleman indeed.

When I wrote the advertisement, I had in mind the remark made to me by one of the wisest of my cottagers, a man devoted to his village. "What we want here, sir, is someone to look up to." Also, I was remembering the outstanding incumbency of Jack Labouchere, of cherished memory, who, with his incomparable wife, was "looked up to" indeed.

However, this unpopular stipulation did not affect the contents of my letter-bag. There is a story of the late Lord Birkenhead, in puckish mood, replying to an enquiry by a dubious stranger in the lounge of an hotel: "Go down those steps and turn to the right. You will see a door marked 'Gentlemen'. Do not let that deter you." The applicants who replied to my advertisement did not let the offensive proviso deter them. They appeared rather, to judge from their readiness to supply me with proofs, often touchingly naive, of gentility, to have welcomed a condition which narrowed the field in their favour.

Private church patronage, looked at dispassionately, is a remarkable survival. There is no provision, either in law or practice, that it should be exercised by a churchman, or even a believer. But it seems to work pretty well. An old friend, a High Anglican parson and a devoted admirer of his own bishop, once said to me: "Never leave the disposal of a living to a Bishop. Bishops are the worst of patrons, for the poor men are always at their wits' end how to provide for a bunch of misfits."

Many years later I had proof of the wisdom of this advice, when a Bishop, sadly agreeing that a resigning vicar had been unfitted to cope with a parish of five hundred souls, promptly appointed him to another parish in the diocese with a population of two thousand five hundred. He was perforce concerned with the fortunes of one man; the private patron is interested in the fortunes of a whole parish.

But a patron, if he is to function satisfactorily, must know the character and needs of the parishioners. For that reason, when compelled, thanks to Hitler, to abandon my old home, I transferred the patronage to a man ideally placed for exercising it. Colonel Peter

Labouchere is not only the son of an outstanding Rector of Sculthorpe but is now living in the Old Rectory in which he was born, among the very people he knows best.

If I never had a farmer's eye for my land, and could see it pass into more expert ownership without regrets, that is not to say that I was not intimately acquainted with every field and pightle, every hedgerow and spinney. But my close friendship for these quite un-distinguished features of a rather flat countryside had nothing to do with agriculture; I loved them partly for their looks, and partly for their indispensable contributions to sport. Their looks, to the eye of a visitor from county after county boasting of downs, of moorlands, of majestic trees, of salmon rivers, amounted to nothing at all; but the very meagreness of the black-thorn and the early primroses in the Claypit Lane, of the precarious bluebells in Fox Hill Wood, enhanced the excitement, which never grew less, of their recurrent and expected discovery. And we did possess, for our pride and delight, half a dozen trees of rare quality. These were wych-elms that stood unattended in the park, lofty and symmetrical. They flowered only every other year, but when covered, in early April and before any leaf had appeared, with bunches of delicate seed-pods, between green and yellow, these immense yet ethereal-looking cones were things of singular and moving beauty. Seen against the still black woods, they shone as if with a brightness of their own, and appeared to dispense, rather than to reflect, the thin pale light of a cold Norfolk spring. But these beauties were rarities; as were our group of Scotch firs near the sandpit, whose trunks signalled the sunset to our front windows,

13

and one huge Insignis pine that darkened the flank of Primrose Walk. We are an oak and ash country, and although the underlying chalk favours beeches, the long years when there had been no money to spend on the woods had left their mark on what we had of them. They had been crowded and jostled by young sycamore, such of them as had survived the great gale of '95, and never given the elbow-room a beech must enjoy to achieve its native nobility. There were good oaks in the park, and here and there a mighty ash with its twisted old roots exposed, and half its great limbs missing. Most of our ashes remained leafless until June, and I have often wondered from what part of England came the old rhyme:

> Oak before ash,
> In for a splash.
> Ash before oak,
> In for a soak,

for in North Norfolk I have never seen the earliest ash in leaf before the latest oaks or, indeed, anything but lagging far behind. But this tardiness is welcome, for it prolongs the spring; and we are still admiring the young, tufty shoots of our ash-trees when in Surrey all the various greens of budding woods are already merging into uniformity.

There is no better exercise than swinging an axe, and provided you have a professional woodman to keep your axes sharp for you, few things are better fun. The planter of trees needs infinite patience, and if he plants hardwoods can never live to see them in maturity, but a man with an axe can give himself the exquisite pleasure of adding full-grown trees, oak and ash and beech, to his visible possessions. He can do this, that is to say, provided his woods and spinneys have been, like mine, neglected; for in that case all but the tops of his trees are likely to be hidden by undergrowth and saplings. Now a tree that you cannot see from the ground up is hardly worth possessing; all its majesty depends upon its stance, all its poise and strength upon the height and girth of its trunk. Besides, if the trunk is hidden you cannot judge of a tree's spread and symmetry, or mark its habit, which depends upon the outward or downward trend of its limbs and branches and the way in which it holds, or allows to droop, the leaf-bearing twigs. So I had the satisfaction, by clearing away thickets of elder, or of self-sown sycamore, both easy prey for an axe, of bringing into full sight again the lost trunks of oak and ash, of Spanish chestnut and beech. It must be admitted that nettles, the curse of our soil, were apt to clog and conceal, except beneath the beech-trees, the point of departure, where the trunk swells and broadens at ground level; a real loss to the eye, since a trunk, like a stone pillar, needs a base. But where, as in Fox Hill Wood, the oaks marched, fairly spaced, up a grassy slope, and were revealed by the cutting down of an old thorn hedge, the result was entirely satisfactory, and the pleasure of walking to church, even when the gorse was out, permanently enhanced.

Beyond the woods, on the land itself, thoughts about shooting were uppermost. Our light, dry, friable Norfolk soil is the very thing for partridges; their small feet do not get clogged, nor do lethal cracks appear in times of drought, as in clays, to swallow up the chicks. And our hedgerows, mostly of thorn on the top of a bank, make good nesting places; the herbage on the banks is thick and the foundation sandy. But because the estate was long and narrow, it was not well adapted for driving, since in a high wind the birds, in certain places, were likely to carry on too far and cross the boundaries. For this reason the annual rearrangement of the crops was of vital interest to me, and in walking over the land in early spring, I was, I fear, more concerned with the position than with the condition of the sowings in this field or that. The coveys, once sprung, seek shelter, and what mattered most to me was the future situation of the crops that afford most cover—the roots, the potatoes, or the clover. High clover is the most holding crop of all, too much so for driving, since the birds, once settled, cannot run in it; but turnips, kale, and potatoes offer perfect concealment to a partridge, yet allow him to move freely beneath the green shade.

Upon the position, then, annually changed by rotation of the cover-crops and the stubbles, our October tactics must depend, subject to the last-minute intervention of a high wind. Gamekeepers, especially on a narrow terrain, dislike high winds, naturally enough, for they reduce the bag; but for those who believe in one crowded hour—or rather five minutes—of glorious life, there is a great deal to be said, in our flat country, for half a gale. Our good farmers nowadays have cut down the old hawthorn hedges, often twelve feet high or more, and on a quiet day driven birds skim over a low, neat hedge in the most unsporting way. Before the war there still stood, here and there, strung out along the trim-banked hedges, some hedgerow oaks; and partridges do not care for flying under or even between trees, and will often rise steeply rather than do so, even when the air is still. But with half a gale behind their tails, the birds appear to fly high for the sheer excitement of it; they begin to climb as soon as they feel the wind, and come over the tree-tops, high and headlong, in the most reckless fashion, overshooting the known and comfortable root-fields which would, on other days, have been their objective, and coming to rest well beyond the boundary, scattered and confused in strange surroundings. Then begins the calling—most familiar sound of late shooting-afternoons—and the short, lone flights of single birds rallying to the covey. For come home they will and must, but not for us again that day. Their casualties will have been few; but I think Guy Benson, for one, will remember a windy morning when a few minutes were worth the rest of the day. For there was a stand where our usually cautious birds, committing themselves joyfully to the gale, came rocketing over the trees, and he, alone among the guns, and using sixteen-bores, shot like a man inspired.

But even on still days, when there is hope of driving and re-driving the birds, much planning is required, first for emptying the stubbles into the roots, and afterwards for ensuring that each drive plays into the hands of the next. And the most careful plans can go awry if the actual driving is mismanaged. Quietness is all; partridges take quick note of the human voice, and I once saw an obtuse head keeper (not mine) empty half a field by shouting: "Stop that hollerin' and bellerin'" to some beaters engaged in conversation. The beaters' objective should be to induce the coveys to rise, one by one, from their respective hiding-places in the roots, in a purely precautionary, not a frightened or startled mood. If the birds are unduly alarmed, as by human voices, they tend to run together or into the hedges; but the mere rustling and whispering of the roots brushed by the beaters' boots appear to suggest to a partridge not running away, but stopping to listen, and when the sound gets too close for comfort, a flight into the next field for prudence' sake. And so the birds rise, covey by covey, without having lost their heads, and can calmly observe, once they are above the roots, that there is a line of men in one direction, and a flag or two in others, and so choose the one unguarded hedge to cross. Partridges that have lost their heads from fright will fly almost anywhere, as can best be seen when a kite is flown, and a covey no sooner leaves the cover of the roots than it scatters in all directions, each bird flying low, singly, and in panic to some hedge or thicket. And the sight of the men and the flags will be quite enough to add pace and determination to their flight; it is no longer a matter of skimming gently into the next field, but a purposeful rush to get well away from the neighbourhood of these disturbers of their peace. So if the guns, too, have moved quietly to their places, with no coffee-housing on the way, the drive should come off.

The ways of partridges, however, are not quite so predictable as the foregoing might suggest; and a shooting-host's anxieties are never over till the end of the day. In my own case, they were far greater when it came to the pheasants. For the waywardness of par-tridges is so well known that everybody makes allow-ances, and while partridges coming high over trees are far more exhilarating to shoot at than partridges skim-ming low, it also takes skill and judgment to kill, safely and cleanly, the bird that comes straight at your head like a cannon-ball, with a line of beaters not far behind him. Besides, there is a charm about the terrain in a partridge-shoot: the yellow corn-stacks in the corners of the stubbles; the hips and haws and splashes of golden maple on the hedges; the rainbow hues of the kale and the cabbages; the matt grey-green of the swedes relieving the faintly vulgar glossiness of the mangolds and sugar-beet. And the whole day is full of movement and manoeuvre; there are sudden changes of plan, consultations, ruses, victory alternating with defeat. And always the fascination of guessing what tricks the impulsive and empty-headed little enemy will be up to next. Had partridges a little more brain it might be an easier thing to ambush them, as the Boers used to ambush our generals long ago. The moves of those simple minds were calculable; the reflex actions of unreasoning birds are far less so.

But pheasants, to be flushed from small flat coverts encircling a small flat park, set a more difficult problem to a shooting-host. Ours were wild pheasants, it is true, not the pampered birds whose first impulse, on peeping out of cover and seeing their dear foster-father, the head keeper, in his bowler hat, is to gather round his boots for food and praise. But all pheasants, wild or tame, share one disadvantage as against the partridge: whereas once up in the air, and in full flight, their size and power enable them to outstrip the smaller bird in speed, they are slow and lumbering starters, and the problem is to get them well into the air and into their best stride before they reach the guns. Nobody, except the late Mr Lockhart Ross, wants to shoot at a slow and lumbering object. It smacks too much of murder. Really high birds, what are known as "crackerjacks," it was quite beyond our powers to produce. You need falls of ground, hanging coverts, valleys, or depressions in which to place the guns, to achieve these. The most we could do, here and there, was to induce our active wild birds, of whom a fair proportion wore those old English black neck-cloths, to rise, on shooting-days, to a reasonably sporting height. There was only one way to do this. Pheasants are home-loving birds; although, late in the season, the cocks will leave the woods and range freely enough to the outlying pit-holes and hedgerows, they keep, on the whole, to some familiar wood, not too dark, not given over to brambles, but having both cover and clearings in which they can warm and dust themselves in the sunshine. If driven, with care and circumspection, and preferably on their feet, away from their homes, and to a sufficient distance, and there flushed, they will, once in the air, make for home with determination, and should trees, or even a line of guns exposed to view in the open, stand between the pheasant and his home, he will respond to the obstacle, not by altering his direction, but by rising to what must seem to him to be the height of security.

What makes this manoeuvre, although full of risks, practicable is the fact that the pheasant is essentially a running and walking bird. Left to themselves, both he and the partridges use their wings only for the shortest and most utilitarian flights, as a secondary means of escaping danger; wings contribute nothing to the main preoccupation of all birds and animals, that of earning their living. In fact it has always been a puzzle to me how birds that would enjoy the life of a barndoor fowl can on occasions show such signal prowess in the air. But, always thinking first of their legs as a means of escape, pheasants, if alerted rather than alarmed, will run considerable distances in front of a line of discreet and soft-stepping beaters, tap-tapping here and there a tree-trunk with their sticks.

Using these tactics, I was able, for two stands at any rate, and in the place where the bulk of our pheasants dwelt, to give my guests some very fair shots. But whereas in one stand, where the running birds were made to break out of the Square Wood on a broad front, from which they took low flights or ran down a hedgerow to the solitary Bramble Clump, there were no special anxieties, the other stand was a much more delicate affair. It could, and on one occasion did, end in fiasco. The birds in Bramble Clump always came back, and because they saw the guns plain with tall beeches or elms at their backs, they naturally flew high. The problem there was of flushing; but a single keeper or beater, using circumspection, could usually nudge them quietly enough to avoid the dreaded flurry.

But in the View Stand the preliminary footwork involved a right-angled turn, a promenade down a belt not fifty yards wide, and a final assembly in an oval-shaped bulge. The host at a shoot should not draw for a place with the other guns, but swim loose, and I had a tremulous moment when I went forward to stand outside this bulge, to hear the rustle of little feet in the dead leaves, and to see an occasional small head peep out, meditating escape. For there had to be a dangerous delay while a band of wire-netting, suspended from side to side of the neck leading to the bulge, was lowered to the ground by the silent beaters. Once this was accomplished, the beaters filed out of the belt on to the park and quietly showed themselves, unspeaking, in a half-circle round the bulge. The peepers decided that a park full of men, however tranquil, was no place for

them, and when a single keeper entered the bulge and
began his tap-tapping, the birds either rose from where
they sat, or, running back through the belt, came up
against the wire-netting and took to their wings. In
both cases they were for the Square Wood, which was
home, and the shortest way there was across an open
field, for their walk had taken, as I have said, a right-
angled turn. Across the field were strung the guns; the
pheasants, according to their wont, relied upon climbing,
not a change of direction, for safety, and some reasonably high birds resulted from this rather ticklish manoeuvre. And I had a right to be tremulous, for on one
occasion something, it may have been a fox, caused a
premature panic in the bulge, and the pheasants, folded
there with so much care, burst out squawking in all
directions, and were lost for the day.

Certainly a shooting-host has his worries, but he has
his rewards as well, for he gets on terms of intimacy
with the ways of the game and with every wood and
field, and if, like myself, he is a poor shot, he can forget
his misses in the satisfaction of seeing his plans go right.
And one preoccupation I was spared: the amount of
the bag. For we had no records and no ambitions, and
if, after a successful drive, the bulk of the birds were un-
scathed, it meant so many the more for another day.
No gun was ever invited for his prowess, but for his
good company. We went out shooting for fun.

And how pleasant the shooting-lunches could be, on
a brisk October day, with hot potatoes in their skins
rolling out of a napkin, and the girls, looking like hen-
pheasants in their tweeds, gently deriding our shooting
"shop." My daughters, after passing through the inevitable period of horsiness in their early teens, were

never dryads; music and charades, a beribboned guitar, a deft pencil, *New-Yorker*-like jokes were their Saturday-to-Monday pleasures; but they liked young men and they liked peach-brandy, and both were provided at our shooting-lunches.

But my best memories are of Saturdays, when there was no house-party, spent on the Fen, alone with two keepers or a single companion. Sculthorpe Fen lies within a wide bend of the River Wensum, and is a quiet, unfrequented place, mostly reed-beds between deep open drains, impassable to those ignorant of the hidden, unsteady planks. But there was a wood of oak and alder within it, and a Black Clump of Scotch fir and poplar, and areas of dry, tufty soil where birch trees grew, a likely spot for woodcock. Wild pheasants abounded there, for the pheasant is a marsh bird as well as a wood bird, and finds, in the small damp-loving snails and slugs, a diet much to his liking. Except from the Black Clump, which I learnt by experience to beat out away from the guns, so that the birds, emerging on the far side, would rise and, turning, come over the tree-tops to make for the alders in the loop of the river, there was no question of driving on the fen. We killed pheasants there for the pot, as we came across them; what we were out for were duck and snipe. The duck were mallard and teal (I once shot a shoveler) and one could count, in those days, on seeing both; but once the teal were up, whether from the river or from the flood-water which lay in the rushy meadows that spread out between the arable land and the marsh, a shot was likely to scare them away for good. Teal disturbed, but not shot at, will circle far and at speed, rising and falling, and eventually returning to their starting-point; the spectacle alone is worth a morning's walk; and if they come within shot, and one or more should fall, your day is made. The instantaneous uprush, seemingly almost vertical, of the whole wisp when the shot is fired, is a fine display of air-acrobatics; but it used to be the end; they did not return that morning. Wild duck, on the other hand, are more persistent in their will to come back, and, even after a shot, and an apparent departure for the coast, will sometimes reappear, mere dots in the northern sky, which swiftly grow bigger as they circle round, looking all neck, and drop suddenly, legs down and braking hard, into river or drain. Also, unlike the teal, they will at times lie close in the reeds and give an easy shot as they rise, but that, again, is pot-hunting.

After teal, driven snipe gave the best fun. If flushed from the flooded meadows, where there was no cover at hand to encourage a low-flying, jinking escape, the snipe used to go wavering up skywards, and although the chances of a single or a couple of guns were small, there was a line which, on the whole, they seemed to prefer. A high snipe offers a very small target but a very vulnerable one; he does not fly at one speed like a teal, or even in a straight line, but in short jerks, weaving this way and that, and at moments giving a misleading appearance of almost standing still, but to be misled, and to check the swing of your gun, is to miss him. His small body drops like a stone when killed, not turning over in the air. You needed a good dog to gather him from these reed-beds. Our game-bag, after a morning on the Fen, was never heavy, but it could, on a lucky day, include pheasant, partridge, woodcock, duck, teal, snipe, pigeon, and a hare. And if the day was unlucky, there remained the moments of keen expectation, the watching and hoping, the gleams of sunshine on the feathered bulrushes, Fakenham church-tower tall in the background, and the wide Norfolk sky.

Things were not too prosperous in the City in the early thirties, and for a few years I used to let my shooting. And thoughts of the Fen remind me of Mr Judkin (which is not his real name). Mr Judkin headed a syndicate from the Midlands who hired the shooting for two years. I had reserved the right to shoot pigeons, and one day late in January when the Syndicate had finished shooting for their first season, I went down to the Fen with Ben Pollen to stand for pigeon in the wood. A single teal came high over the trees and Ben Pollen, who is human, shot it. Teal do not breed on the Fen, so that it could make no difference to Mr Judkin and his friends whether the bird lived or died. But, for correctitude, I wrote a note to Mr Judkin informing him of the death of the teal in the course of a pigeon shoot. I got, by return, a furious letter, in which the word "stealing" was used. I returned the letter, with the following note:

"No, no, Mr Judkin, I cannot accept this letter. I enclose a draft of the note which I expected, and still expect, to receive from you." The draft was as follows:

"Dear Major Jones, I am delighted that your friend got a teal, and only wish I had remembered to tell you to shoot what wild fowl you liked now that the season is over."

Mr Judkin did not actually sign and return my draft, but his apologies were prompt and abject, and I am not sure that the technique of supplying draft replies to one's own letters might not be more widely practised with advantage. At any rate my game-book shows that the following year, on the second of February, I shot, without a companion, two snipe, six mallard, five teal and a shoveler.

The most agreeable change in country life, to one coming back to it after thirty-five years, was the enlargement of our range by the motor-car. The North Sea is only nine miles from Cranmer as the hoodie-crow flies on his way, as our local name for him suggests, from Denmark, but in my childhood days nine miles, along the gritty Holkham road, was an expedition not lightly undertaken. And the sea at Holkham, when you got there at last, was sometimes so far away that you could not see it. Moreover, the vast expanse of sand was in itself intimidating to a child; there were no rocks, as at Hunstanton or Cromer, to break the monotony, no pools or seaweed, no crabs or sea-anemones, while our minds were haunted by thoughts of quicksands, and of the drowning, not so long ago, of two nursemaids from Holkham Hall. We were not supposed to know of this, and knew, as children do, that we were not supposed to know, so could not bring our fears into the open and have them laid to rest.

In a car it was no longer necessary to strike the coast at the nearest point. Some miles west of Holkham lies Brancaster, most delectable of playgrounds. For here are not only broad sands and safe bathing, but a strip of turf, gently undulating, firm and dry, designed by Nature, with uncommon prescience, for an eighteen-hole golf-course. Nine holes out, with a grey-green marsh on your right hand, to the ninth green on a little hummock, from which you look across to Scolt Head; nine holes home, with tees from which you survey the sea, and wave your club to the family bathing. The marsh, submerged only by the spring tides, turns purple when the sea-lavender is out, and is full of birds and bird-noises; curlew, whimbrel, and redshank cry or bubble in the spring. But the prime, the all-important function of Brancaster Marsh is to protect the golf-course and the beach for all time from the encroachments of builders. An artificial causeway carries a single road from the village of Brancaster to the shore, a distance of a third of a mile or so. On each side of the causeway the marshes, profoundly unstable, have saved this fortunate stretch of foreshore from the fate of Cromer, of Sheringham, of Hunstanton—indeed of every seaside place where bricks and mortar, pressing relentlessly towards the sea, can find a secure footing. From the North Sea itself, when a gale backs up a spring tide, our strip of turf, and especially the club-house, stand in intermittent jeopardy, for their foundations are on sand; but the erosions resulting from the attacks of the sea, being gradual and inapt to catch the eye, as well as being Acts of God, are a hundred times more bearable than the raids of the speculative builder.

Brancaster is lovely and tranquil; the land declines with gentle contours from the wooded arable fields above the red-tiled village to the grey-greens and sage-greens of the marsh; and the clean-washed sands, pale gold to white beyond the bronze of mud-banks, contrast sharply with the solid, matt blueness of the distant sea. For Brancaster faces due north, a rare aspect for a seaside place in England, and there is never a dazzle to make you shade your eyes when looking seawards. One eyesore alone mars the prospect: the club-house.

The late Victorians had a knack of doing the wrong thing, which, in the heirs to so many examples of happy marriages between artifact and landscape, is almost unaccountable. The horizontal lines and quiet undulations of this stretch of coast might have suggested, one would have thought, a low, long building, crouching to avoid the gales, hugging the marram-grass among the dunes. Instead, a tall, narrow, lop-sided, defiantly hideous object was erected, built of brash red brick, gabled, gawky, dominating, and shameless. It was sited on a hump of sand exposed to the attack, by battering-ram or by sapping, of the high tides; a choice which has already cost the members thousands of pounds for defensive plates of steel. It is both a folly and a monstrosity.

And yet, and yet—so strong is the spell of Brancaster, so pleasant were the luncheons in that large light dining-room on the first floor, with coffee on the wide balcony overlooking the first tee and the last green, so comforting the leather arm-chairs into which one sank, sighing for toast and tea, at the end of a second round, that I recall a building that would have disgraced even Surrey with nothing but affection. If our grandfathers had no eye for beauty, they did understand comfort, and on the north coast of Norfolk, between which and the North Pole there is no intervening land, there are many months of the year when comfort, even in the intervals of playing a game, can never be despised. Nor is it possible to think about the clubhouse apart from the people who laughed and gossiped in it, of whom must stand first, by common consent, the late Major Gilbert Legh.

Major Legh ("Joey" to his contemporaries and "the

Major" to the rest of us) was at all points what is known
as a "character." To a stranger his appearance all but
touched the comical. He was small, with a jaunty
carriage, a canary moustache, a monocle, a slightly
receding chin, and little feet that turned out as he walked.
One had a feeling that, in his youth, he must have been
pursued down Piccadilly by the *Punch* artists of the
eighties. But a very short acquaintance with the Major
dismissed all such ideas. For he possessed uncommon
"bite" and originality, combined with humour and
humanity. The Major had thought out everything for
himself; "*il avait vécu*" and his conclusions were his own.
He could be dogmatic, especially about currency reform,
one of his hobby-horses, but loved disputation, and his
good humour in argument was unshakable. He was a
gardener, and his garden at Thornham was crowded
with rare trees and shrubs which he loved almost to
caressing point, while despising herbaceous borders—
"all that fustian." But most of all he liked to entertain
his friends, to hold forth as the port went round, to
exchange chaff, to throw out ideas, to deride, to
contradict, to be puckish and unexpected. During the
years that he shared his home with Archie and Doris
Jamieson, to stay or to dine at the Drove House was
not only to be spoilt with the best of everything, but
to be amused and stimulated, chaffed and cockered up.
The Major drove to his golf in a pony-cart. He played
a short but canny game; put the committee to rights;
gave his caddy the statutory fee and no more; called
us all "me dear"; and found something fresh to say
about all topics, however trite.

How, in the dim past, the Major came to transplant
himself from his native Cheshire to the Norfolk coast

I cannot remember, but the pull of Brancaster is almost
magically exercised, and the Major was only the first
of a whole colony of Brancastrians. Trees, Cory-
Wrights, Jamiesons, Leslies, Harveys, Gilliats—all fell
under the spell. The fathers strode magisterially over
the springy turf, hitting golf-balls immense distances
over the marshy inlets, while the mothers and children
spread themselves over the sands or caught shrimps for
the fathers' tea. These spirited invaders, whose rights of
conquest were never disputed by the natives, brought
gaiety and wit and friendliness to this tranquil and
sequestered spot; they bought or built cottages for
themselves in the village; they founded a freemasonry.
Fresh airs blew about those people, mentally as well as
physically; they were vigorous and purposeful, and
their boys and girls took after them. During the latter
years of the period I am describing some of us had our
forebodings, but our anxieties were general, not con-
crete, and we could not then know how many of those
gallant children were doomed. In the event Hitler's war
dealt hardly with the young Brancastrians; they were of
the breed of front-liners, and many had to fall; but in
our memories they still cluster about the bathing-huts,
vivid, athletic, and full of promise. Of the survivors it
is a comfort to think that one still inhabits the Drove
House, an outstanding winner of the Victoria Cross.
Brancaster could hit back, as well as suffer.

In spring a boat from the Staithe carried us across
the tidal estuary to the bird-sanctuary at Scolt Head, a
promontory of dunes and marram-grass, of beach and
pebbles, where the terns and ringed plover nested.
Common terns, little terns and Arctic terns abounded,
but the excitement was the occasional nesting of a pair

or more of roseate terns. Whatever stamp-collectors may say, there is something absurd in valuing a thing for rarity alone, irrespective of its intrinsic beauty; but the roseate tern is not only rare but beautiful, excelling the others both in the delicate rosy blush upon lower breast and underparts, and in the extra length of its streamers. Only its voice, a harsh croak, is ugly, but serves a useful purpose in enabling one to pick out more speedily this graceful rarity when flying in a noisy crowd of commoners. But the best sight of all, to my mind, is that of the newly-hatched ringed plover, who turn themselves into small mottled stones when approached, while the mother-bird drags her wings distractedly as she darts about, hoping in vain to draw attention from her brood. The shelduck, biggest and brightest of the many obstacles to concentration which beset a Brancaster golfer, do not nest on Scolt Head, but farther inland, on the hither side of the marsh itself, and are even met with on the high road, leading their ducklings in the first long march to the mud-banks and the salt water. Birds have always had a peculiar charm for me and, if it had not been for Brancaster, I must confess that I should have felt something starved at Cranmer, for there the bird population of our immediate surroundings was singularly lacking in variety. A hawfinch nesting in the orchard was an event; so was a redwing on the lawn, or a goldcrest in the Wellingtonia. All the years I was there I never saw a red-backed shrike (of which kind I once counted fourteen on the telegraph-wires alongside the railway from Pangbourne to Oxford) or a spotted woodpecker, greater or lesser, or a reed-bunting, or a cirl-bunting, or a wryneck. We had to walk half a mile to hear a nightingale or a nightjar, with no assurance of any reward, and the single appearance of a peregrine falcon in the Avenue, of a rough-legged buzzard over the Rookery, could not make up to me for the flatness of discovering that my own home fell far short, where birds were concerned, of the villa gardens at Gerrards Cross, or Beaconsfield, or Farnham Common. For birds with whom to live at close quarters through the nesting and singing season, give me the Thames Valley or the Chilterns; but for birds to go visiting by car, Norfolk is the place. At Brancaster I have met with snow-buntings on the golf-course itself, hanging in the gale and rising and falling like enormous snowflakes; I have had to pull up the car upon the causeway before a gigantic, solid carpet of bramblings, orange flecked with white, which lifted, undulating, and relaid itself a hundred yards along the road. And there were crossbills in the avenue of Scotch firs at Congham; and the bearded tit in the reeds on Hickling Broad. Hickling, where the late Duke of Portland enjoyed the duck-shooting so much that, as his valet told Lord Desborough, he buttoned up his own braces three mornings running, and where the great Jim Vincent himself escorted us in the punt.

But the show-piece, the sight with which we used to entrance the least bird-minded of our visitors, was the rise of the black-headed gulls from their nests at Scoulton Mere. This inland water, thirty miles or more from the coast, is in fact a natural moat, not thirty yards broad, surrounding an island on which these gulls have nested since the fifteenth century at least. The nests are crowded together, all but touching, on a tussocky, well-drained acre or so at one end of the elongated

island, and at the approach of visitors beyond the
defensive moat the birds rise together in their thousands.
If the sun is shining and the sky is blue (and your day
should be picked with care) the moat will take on the
colour of the sky, and, backed by the upper, reflected
in the nether, blueness, the multitudinous shifting,
wheeling and interweaving of the gulls, like a gigantic
snowstorm in a crystal ball, is a truly breath-taking
spectacle. It seems impossible that so many wings,
beating the air in so small a space, should never touch
or collide one with the other, but they never do; the
instinctive calculations of these navigators are infallible;
climbing, banking, gliding, volplaning, crossing and re-
crossing, the gulls manoeuvre without thought of
narrow shaves. There is no appearance, in their complicated gyrations, of evasive action or of dodging;
each bird follows with confidence and certainty his own
invisible path, and yet the total effect is one of con-
tiguity, not separation, of a close, not a loosely-knit,
assembly. And this moving mass, remember, is one of
whiteness against blue; of a dazzling whiteness if the
sun be behind you, for the black heads and narrow
mourning-bands of tails and wings serve only to enhance
the prevailing brightness. The screaming that goes on is
harsh and almost deafening, but it adds to the excitement and reminds you that all this airy movement is
not a ballet designed for your pleasure, but a spontan-
eous display of resentment, probably anger, at your
disturbing presence. The gulls are alarmed, but not to
the point of retreat; their weaving and circling is done
directly above their nests; their clamour is the sound of
scolding, not of complaining. These are wild birds with
their protective instincts at full stretch, and for that

reason you do not stay long; the incomparable beauty
of the spectacle must be enjoyed at a gulp, not dwelt
upon, lest the eggs get cold. And as you move away, the
clamour subsides; the pace of the agitated fliers slackens;
the white cloud loosens and dissolves as gull after gull
alights, and when the last of your party is out of sight
behind the alders, quietness descends. If the season is
early enough, you can find consolation for the fall of
the curtain, as after other theatrical occasions, by buying
a basket of gulls' eggs from the keeper. They are all but
as good eating as plovers' eggs. But it is time to change
the subject. For many people bird-lovers are, not unreasonably, equated with bird-bores.

For a Norfolk man, I am deplorably ignorant of my
native county. In childhood our range was that of a
pony or pony-cart; in later life I was a mere week-ender,
owing to the necessity of earning a livelihood in the
City. We visited Norwich as tourists, and were not
even members of the club where the squires met at
luncheon to talk partridges and the crops. I have never
set eyes on half the famous churches and ancient houses;
I have only a nodding acquaintance with the Broads.
At the Fakenham Races or the West Norfolk point-to-
points, where the County turned up in full tweeds, we
did not know the horses or the riders, and there was
something faintly out of keeping, that called for a
second quick look over a shoulder, about our own
house-party. A don from King's, perhaps, or young
Jasper Ridley from Balliol in the wrong sort of trousers.
It did not matter, because we knew Humphrey Barclay,
and, once seen joking with this most sporting and
popular of all squarsons, we were upon an unassailable
footing, house-party and all. Besides, friendliness is the

rule in East Anglia. But while I still retained memories of Norfolk interiors from my early manhood, when I danced or shot with Gurneys and Buxtons and Straceys and Lombes round about Norwich, we did not, thirty years later, have many opportunities of renewing acquaintance with subfusc wallpapers, dark, heavily-framed landscapes of the school of Crome or Vincent, cases of stuffed birds, dog-and-gunpowder aromas in stone halls and passages, deep mahogany-cased baths. Perhaps all this had changed; perhaps, if we had not been so engrossed in our own home and friends and those of our daughters, we should have discovered white paint and light colours and the airy, bright, uncrowded look of room and passage known to the eighteenth and twentieth centuries, but never to the Victorians. If so, there would have been something to regret; for, given a home to one's own taste, there is far more interest and pleasure to be had from other people's houses if they preserve some tradition, illustrate some period, even if, aesthetically, the tradition or period is a faulty one. In such cases I am on the side of Hal Goodhart-Rendel. And so it was an added pleasure to our shooting-visits to Harry and Sybil Birkbeck at Westacre High House, to find that hospitable pair and their family still living among the massive, even stately, furniture and hangings of a Victorian squirearchy at its most dignified. Harry, when in his late fifties, still hunted his pack of beagles, and it was only to be expected that he would be impervious to the draughts that froze less hardy ankles in his stone-floored study, where the men smoked and gossiped after shooting while the dogs dreamed and twitched before the fire. But the rigours of the great hall, which ran the whole length of the house, had to be faced in evening clothes; the fireplace was enormous, and piled high with mighty logs, but even as we crowded round it till our faces reddened in the heat, icy currents from outer space lapped against our necks and chilled our thinly-covered spines. But if old Anthony Hamond, whose splendid full-length portrait by Samuel Lane, Sir Thomas Lawrence's deaf-and-dumb pupil, looked down upon us as we sat, with two pairs of evening socks and a woolly under our boiled shirt, in the lofty formal dining-room, had been able to flourish and survive in a low temperature, his descendants could do the same. And they did, betraying no awareness of their own enviable hardihood. As for their guests, it was only a question of taking special precautions in the matter of underclothes; and in any case a few shivers were a small price to pay for so much charm and cheerfulness. Harry farmed ten thousand acres, all in hand, an enormous task demanding, in those years, an enormous overdraft; but so equable was his temperament, so profound his natural contentment, that neither responsibility was any burden to him. His was the smiling philosophy, and his quiet, companionable ways were a pleasure to watch. He had some of the best partridge-shooting in the county, with long, matured belts over which the birds flew high, and his keepers were masters of the art of showing pheasants. Harry himself, out shooting, while directing everything, might have been a carefree guest; he strolled, and was amused, and enjoyed himself. Red-headed Sybil diluted the fur-and-feather atmosphere of that home of sportsmen with the flavour of books and music; she had never been a Buxton and did not rise from a sickbed, as did one gallant huntress of that clan, to go rat-hunting in the barns; and her daughters divided their interests, with impartial liveliness, between West Norfolk and the world.

If I have given to Westacre High House a special place in these memories of Norfolk, it is not from forgetfulness of other houses and other hospitality. It is rather because the way of life at Westacre seemed to me to preserve to an unusual degree the tradition, peculiar to Norfolk, of an alliance between banking, land-owning, generous living, and sport. Barclays, Buxtons, Gurneys, and Birkbecks, for the most part of Quaker origin, have been for many generations the backbone of the Norfolk squirearchy. Originally private bankers confined by Quaker principles to the peaceful pursuit of riches, they later acquired land in many parts of the county, and their descendants, while retaining the banking and dropping the Quaker connection, became complete countrymen. To be born a Gurney or a Buxton is almost to be born a naturalist, with a special turn for birds; their responsible Quaker blood may still take them daily to the bank at Norwich or at King's Lynn, but their hearts are out of doors. If some were fox-hunters, all were rat-catchers; if some were horsy, all were doggy; they had unnumbered cousins in common; their occasional black sheep were even better company than the white, and they went to Kenya as you or I would go to Scotland. I have heard a character-istic voice in a London shop and said to myself "a Buxton," and turned to see a lady quite unknown to me; but, sure enough, she gave the shopgirl the name "Mrs Buxton," thus doubly confirming my suspicions. For it is a further characteristic of the clan to marry their cousins. Only shyness prevented me from accosting a

stranger, who had so unconsciously proclaimed to the
loiterers in Hatchard's her own enviable status, for it is
enviable to be born into the freedom of East Anglia;
to recognise, in such a home as Westacre, one's own
familiar background; to have an inherited affection for
all wild things, including those so lovingly bred up to
be so skilfully killed; to be inured to east winds and
chilly houses; to enjoy an easy, unassuming mastery
over one's native fields and the unassailable regard of
one's own people. So to taste the essential flavour of
Norfolk, and in particular its characteristic self-suffic-
iency, you must go to the Westacres rather than to the
more ancient Holkhams and Houghtons and Melton
Constables. For these great houses, with their stately
saloons, their pictures, their libraries, and their ac-
cumulated treasures, are haunted, inevitably, by memories of the eighteenth century and of a more cosmo-
politan society. It is true that there was a prolonged
reign at Holkham when the owner might have been
regarded as Regent for the Partridges, the real lords of
those broad acres, and when damp and neglect put the
great library itself into jeopardy. But Mr Charles James
came to the rescue in the nick of time: little Johnsonian
Mr James, as good at botany as at books, erudite,
musical, kindly, sensitive, and cantankerous, who paid,
like a latter-day Creevey, immense visits to immense
houses all over England and lived on nothing a year.
Mr James cherished the Holkham books for thirty
years, and was sacked in the end for wearing a shawl
at the dinner-table. But he had done his work, and in
the all-too-short reign of the late Lord Leicester, Tom,
the possessor of Leonardo's sketchbook and the other
Holkham treasures, knew and delighted in them all.

Chamber-music, after a hundred years, was again heard
in the Sculpture Gallery, with Tom himself playing
the fiddle and Lionel Tertis the viola. Tom's fiddling
had not been popular under the Partridges, and even
when a grandfather he was obliged, when dining out,
to leave at ten o'clock because he was not entrusted
with the keys of the Holkham park gates. Sixty years
as an out-of-door man, a good shot and a good golfer,
could not win a latchkey to his old home for one of his
artistic leanings. And when at last he succeeded to his
great inheritance, the constrictions of the war-years
delayed, yet again, his blossoming into the type of
owner for which a place like Holkham was designed.
But at least his things of beauty were cherished and
displayed; the intelligent and the gay, as well as the
sporting, were made welcome to his home; and the
devotion which that great Lord Lieutenant, Mr Russell
Colman, had lavished upon pictures, was given by his
successor to the cause of music, not merely at home, but
throughout the county. In these days it is unfashionable,
if not actually reprehensible, to draw attention to a man
who, but for the laws of primogeniture, might not have
made any particular mark in the world. But so long as
there are Holkhams, and Holkhams in private hands,
the cause of what I like to think of as civilisation is also
to some extent in that keeping, and virtues which are
ordinarily recorded only in the hearts of a man's friends
can be of general interest when found in a curator,
however fortuitously appointed, of precious things. The
late Lord Leicester, civilised to the backbone, might
have been chosen by acclamation, had he not been
born, to be the guardian of so much that has counted,
and ought still to count, in our hours of leisure.

But if Holkham stands for a tradition that is independent of locality, that is not to say that the Coke family are less deeply rooted than their neighbours in Norfolk soil. Few men can have brought more of that soil into the house on their boots than Dick Coke at Weasenham, or have been on more intimate terms with it. He knows it, by birthright, as the sustainer of partridges, of which he has shot his thousands with accuracy and zest. But he has known it best, through long years and long days that would have been more than laborious to men less tough and dedicated, as a forester. He is a planter, preserver, and lover of trees, and if rhododendrons are not trees, then he is a consummate gardener as well. He has worked, unconscious of meal-times and impervious to climate, with his own hardened sinews, and he has allowed a share in the enjoyment of his life's work to all passers-by. The only warning to these visitors is a notice: TRY NOT TO BE VILE. That is the notice of a civiliser, who has embellished the place of his attachment, and whatever his wife may say, wistfully pondering in the wilds of East Anglia the refinements of her former Franco-Irish background, a civiliser must surely be, however old his clothes and irregular his meals, himself civilised.

I have also mentioned, as a contrast to the Westacres, Melton Constable. Here the Astley family has been settled on the same land from time immemorial, but here again, as at Holkham, the associations belong to the history of England rather than to the history of Norfolk. And although Delaval, the late Lord Hastings, was untiringly devoted to the service of his native county, he was not so typical a Norfolk squire as Harry Birkbeck. There was a touch of the eighteenth century in his gift for oratory, which was remarkable; of the speakers I have heard, I can think of none to equal him for ease of diction and rightness in the choice of words. For those with an ear for good English it was a pleasure to listen to him. And just because a temperamental impatience had often failed to win for his own quick, clear mind the appreciation of slower minds, it was the more to his honour that, in the crisis of Hitler's war, he subdued that impatience to the necessities of his new responsibilities. I served under him, as my Battalion Commander in the Home Guard, for five years, and was deeply impressed by his consideration and helpfulness, as well as by his unmeasured devotion, in spite of physical handicaps, to the frustrating task of making bricks with little or no straw. It is true that he had the help, as Adjutant and Quartermaster, of his brother, Melton Astley, whose unrattled competence was in the top class. Disparate as the proverbial chalk from cheese, these two combined to make of stately Caroline Melton a centre of support and sympathy, not of barked-out orders, to the harassed Company Commanders. Understanding of the problems of subordinates is none too common at any military headquarters, and while it was to be expected, perhaps, in the easy, friendly Adjutant, it was no less full and generous in that reputed autocrat, the Colonel. And a commander, as I had learnt in the first World War, is none the worse for being a man of the world, with a touch of the statesman in him. There was no danger of our bringing away from the conferences at Melton any impression that the Norfolk Home Guard was the main prop of Home Defence, and that the War Office, by their slowness in equipping us with modern arms, was our chief enemy. Hastings, who

had a sense of proportion, could understand his super-
iors', as well as his subordinates', difficulties. A great
house has links with the great world which can be, on
occasion, most serviceable.

I have been writing, with some freedom, not only of
the childhood home to which I returned after thirty-
five years, not only of the familiar Norfolk landscape,
but about people. For myself, in spite of the change from
boyhood to middle-age, there was a strong element of
recognition in my re-encounters, both with the people
of Sculthorpe and with our neighbours in North Norfolk. From the moment I heard the light sing-song
voices of the porters shouting out the names of the
stations between King's Lynn and Fakenham, or
between Fakenham and Norwich, I knew that I had
come home. But except in Sculthorpe itself the recognition was entirely one-sided. There was nothing in
myself or my family for any inhabitant of Norfolk
beyond the boundaries of my own small estate to
recognise. We were Londoners, escaping pure Cockney-
ism only by the grace of our country origins and the
cleansing effects of holidays in Scotland, visits to
Howick, and summers spent in villa gardens within
easy reach of the City. The head of this family pur-
porting to be "returning natives" belonged to a species
unknown to Norfolk, that of "City man," and his
daughters brought with them more guitars and music-
cases than shooting-sticks. How did we look to our
neighbours? What tit-for-tat should I get if one of them
were to be as free with his pen as I have been with
mine?

The only authentic verdict which ever reached us was
"nice, but a pity they have no sense of humour." (I am

afraid the *New Yorker* must have been seen lying upon the long table in the Cranmer drawing-room.) To hazard a guess, where friendliness and good manners so effectually screened the evidence, I should say that we were judged to be, if not so insoluble as the sulphur superstitiously dropped into a dog's drinking-bowl, yet not easy to absorb. The village, it must be admitted, did not find us indigestible; on the contrary, after a speedy and inevitable capitulation to my wife, it went on to discover, at the wave of my eldest daughter's baton, that it could sing; and later, after watching the present Master of Pembroke (Cambridge) pass by as Mr Pim, that it could act. And there would be more than a handful of middle-aged men today, had they not been killed in the war, with rather rueful memories of long, hot, August afternoons of enslavement to the insatiable, the implacable Sculthorpe schoolchildren. Francis Cochrane, for one, could hardly have forgotten a morning spent in inflating, by lung-power alone, a hundred balloons, only to be asked to untie them all and to release his own precious breath, imprisoned with such pains, so that the balloons might be carried home without risk of premature burstings.

But to be assimilated by one's own village is one thing; to fit snugly into the neighbourhood at large is quite another. It cannot be denied, I fear, that we were, as a family, either engrossed with the friends of our pre-Norfolk era, or much taken up with the fascinating, but hardly native, colony at Brancaster. To those who have tasted country life, on the spacious and not the Beaconsfield or Gerrards Cross scale, only as guests, the sudden possession of a sizeable country-house is an exciting experience, and one to be shared with their

oldest and most familiar cronies. It is not surprising
that the names of the guns in my game-book are the
names of men whose company, tested through the
years, was most enjoyed, and are not, for the most part,
Norfolk names. The bare return of hospitality enjoyed
at Grogarry or Balbirnie, at Buckhurst or Underley, in
this kindly home or that, was a debt which, though
never paid or payable in full, had first call upon our
modest resources.

If there was peace between our yew-hedges and old
red walls, pleasure in the sight of bright tulips studding
the long grass beneath the apple blossom, of great
chestnut trees billowing, like cumulus clouds, beyond
the lilacs, they must be first savoured, we felt, by old
friends. And so with the partridges, the wild pheasants,
the duck, and the snipe: their lives must be delivered up,
first of all, into the hands of those whose own birds I
had so often and so enjoyably missed. In addition to
these pleasant obligations, there was the centripetal pull
of my elder daughters upon young men and girls from
far beyond our lone East Anglian horizon. My children
had no roots, as I had, in our Norfolk soil; their tastes
were musical and theatrical, not sporting or horticul-
tural; they were anything but rat-catchers, and their
reputed lack of humour was, fortunately, unnoticed by
the uproarious young people, or the maturer Cambridge
dons and musicians, who sprawled upon our warm turf
or acted, with all but professional virtuosity, in highly
sophisticated charades. Exhilarated by so much im-
ported wit and talent, it was small wonder that, as a
family, we were self-sufficient. All the same I should like
to think that, had there been no war, we should, in the
course of years, have grown more roots, pushed out

more tendrils, and mulched, tended, and East Anglicised
by Anthony Hamond, have flowered at last as a genuine
Norfolk family, known by and knowing our own
county.

But there was a war. Its shadow began to dim our
gaiety a year or more before it broke out. A daughter
returned from Vienna, from Munich, with sinister
reports of things heard and seen. My wife was deeply
engaged in the heartbreaking task of extricating, in
spite of the tangled confusion of visas and permits, a
score or more of Hitler's intended victims. Some of
these refugees found temporary asylum with ourselves,
and we had the humiliation of being unable to reassure
or comfort them. The monstrous persecution of the
Jews and of all who refused to shout *"Heil Hitler"*
appeared to make no impression upon Mr Chamberlain
and his advisers. It was not easy to explain to men and
women who had lost everything, whose families were
in concentration camps, who had watched the Nazis'
massive and relentless preparations for war, why our
Government was so soft towards the dictators. Even
the true excuse, that we were compelled by Baldwin's
neglect of our defences to play for time, carried no
conviction—for had not Mr Chamberlain waved a piece
of paper to a cheering mob exclaiming "Peace in our
time"?

The war broke out. Marriages, bereavement, war-
work dissolved and scattered our little group; Cranmer
became a Red Cross convalescent hospital under my
wife's command, and the headquarters of a Home Guard
Company under mine. For myself, the war years
brought an intimacy with, and an enduring admiration
for, the Norfolk labourer of which I have already

15

written. Together we stood to arms when the Holkham geese, descending at dusk upon the Morston marshes, were taken for parachutists; together we watched a dummy shell, fired by a Blacker Bombard, pass a foot behind the head of the bicyclist towing the target; together we held our tongues about it. In my leisure hours I pushed a perambulator containing my eldest grandson about the lanes, everlastingly picking up diminutive gloves thrown overboard for the sport of hearing me curse, and being chaffed by my men from the top of the strawstack beyond the hedge.

"That's a rum job you got there, Major! Hover, we all hed to dew it, haint we?"

And when peace came at length, it was all up with the English country-house. Had I been told, in 1939, that the destruction of Hitler and Mussolini would cost me my old home, I should have thought the price ridiculously cheap, and when pay-day came I thought the same. Since then I have come to wonder whether, personally, I paid any price at all. Possessions can give pleasure, but to be free of them is even more enjoyable. Looked back upon by the liberated, possessions have the aspect of chains. But a family home could never have been parted with voluntarily, for the sake of the owner's personal manumission. To my daughters and their children the lack of a country parking-place for relentless infants, and of a standing holiday house, is a dead loss. By cutting loose, with a consequential release from the bondage of the City, I have increased my own pleasure but am deprived of the power of giving it. Such reflections must have quenched the exhilaration of my new-found liberty had not the surrender of my possessions been made to *force majeure* alone. Thanks to

Hitler, I am, on a cool assessment, better off than before, but at the expense of others. It is a dreadful thought, so I do not think about it.

I left Norfolk in disgrace. I had been uneasy when Mr Churchill, for whom my admiration and gratitude are boundless, accepted the leadership of the Tory party, the party that had so firmly supported, in spite of all Churchill's warnings, the disastrous administrations of Baldwin and of Chamberlain. It was an unpalatable thought that so many members of the House of Commons, convicted by events of either folly or blindness, should be able to return to that House under the great man's umbrella. But I do not think I could have brought myself, in the election that followed so closely upon victory, to vote against Churchill but for one over-riding consideration. Great as was the triumph and the relief, the hour of victory had for many of us been darkened by the shadow of Russia. Stalin, who had been an ally but never a friend, was now poised, huge and menacing, to threaten our very existence. Unfortunately this sinister apparition in the East was unnoticed by millions, and politically powerful millions, in this country. The rank and file of trade unions, and many of their leaders, had been shouting "Hands off Russia" so regularly and for so long that they had shouted themselves out of any power of objective judgment where Russia was concerned. Russia's military achievements in the war had enormously, and deservedly, enhanced her prestige.

Accordingly it seemed to me that the first task of a new Government, first because concerned with the very survival and not merely the welfare of this country, was to persuade the workers, the men and women who had and have it in their hands to cripple or to maintain our powers of self-defence, that Stalin, to put it shortly, was not a good chap but a bad chap, and not only a bad chap, but a desperately dangerous one. Now it was idle to expect that Mr Churchill, or any Tory Government, could ever hope to convert the workers to this view. Mr Churchill, still remembered by Labour for his encouragement of the White Russians after the first World War, and lately compelled by the exigencies of the war-alliance to exchange toasts and pleasantries with "Uncle Joe," was of all living statesmen the least fitted for such mission-work. Fortunately there were Labour leaders available who had no illusions whatever about Stalin and Russia. Pre-eminent among these was Mr Ernest Bevin, and however reluctant the rank and file of the trade unions might be to hear the Word preached by an Attlee or a Dalton, what Ernie Bevin said went. I voted for the Labour candidate in North Norfolk in the hope that a Labour Government, with such stalwarts as Bevin among them, would be able to bring the mass of the working-people, skilled and unskilled, men and women alike, to a realisation that victory had not brought safety, and that in Stalin and his gang we had an enemy as ruthless and far more powerful than Hitler himself. In the event, that Government, and Bevin in particular, did achieve this. I have never had a moment's uneasiness about the rightness of my vote on that occasion.

But so lively were my fears of what might happen if the people of this country went on cherishing illusions about Stalin's Russia, that I could not be content with a secret, silent vote. I wrote to Mr E. C. Gooch, the Labour candidate, explained my views, and offered my services. As a result I was asked to take the chair and speak at several village meetings. This was occasionally embarrassing. In my own village school I had to begin my speech by repudiating everything the first speaker, a raw young Socialist, had said. He believed that, thanks to our brave Uncle Joe, the world was now safe for democracy and that nationalisation of everything would make us all rich and happy. But on the whole, by sticking to foreign affairs, I was spared any heckling, and was able to see myself as a patriotic, reasonable man "doing his bit," in an obscure corner, to enlighten the voters.

To my surprise this was not how my neighbours saw me. They were not present at the meetings and did not hear my arguments. But they read in the *Eastern Daily Press* that I was taking the chair and speaking for Mr Gooch, and the picture they saw was not merely the picture of a wrong-headed, but of an unpatriotic, man. A neighbour, for whom I had much liking and admiration, cut me publicly in the market-place at Fakenham. A charming retired naval officer with whom I was on the best of terms accused me, in a letter to the press, of the basest motives. Except for a couple of years before the first World War, I had passed my life among people for whom private friendships were not frayed by political differences. We might think our friends mistaken, but not ignoble. So it came as a shock to me to discover that in North Norfolk the estimation of a human being, and his fitness for social intercourse, depended upon his support of the Tory party, the party of Baldwin and Chamberlain. It is only fair to say that with the passage of time the breaches have been healed, and the animosities of that election forgotten. Had I not spent a lifetime as a "floating" voter, who liked to judge political parties upon their performances, I should no doubt have been prepared for the assaults upon my honour. For dogma, political as well as theological, breeds anger and anathemas, and at my time of life I ought to have known this. Not that I have any alternative to offer for the party system. It works, but would it work any less well if the parties, even at election time, could credit their opponents with personal integrity?

Today two-thirds of Cranmer have been pulled down. The garden is a jungle. The great oaks in the avenue have been felled. Gigantic American bombers fly incessantly over the park, drowning all country sounds. But in the village life is pleasanter, more prosperous, more sociable, than ever before. Television has enormously multiplied the topics for thought and for talk, as the cars that now stand here and there before the council houses have enlarged their owners' range. The young girls who used to go into service at the Hall as kitchenmaids and under-housemaids are now smart cashiers, elegantly dressed, in the Fakenham shops. The late squire gets a warm welcome on his annual visits as an old friend. But he is not missed.

If there is much to be said for being rooted in one's native soil, there is also much to be said for swimming loose. For all the feeling of homecoming I still have when I get under that wide Norfolk sky and hear the light, ascending tones of the Norfolk speech, I have other homes to revisit. There is enough of the Celt in me to account for this same sense of homecoming whenever I set foot on a Scotch mountain or moor. Indeed, to be candid, I believe the pull of Scotland to be the stronger. And it was not for nothing that I spent part of my boyhood in Provence. The umbrella pine and the cistus, the myrtle and the cork-oak, are not foreign to me, but native. I have even lived long enough in London to feel domesticated, like the pelicans, in St James's Park. There is something about the South Downs, about any bare, grassy hills, with folds and hollows, that persuades me that I belong to those as well. And mountains everywhere, although I cannot climb them, give me the illusion that I possess, and not only enjoy, the landscapes over which they preside. With so many places of my own to frequent, it is not surprising that I feel neither homeless nor an exile.

CHAPTER IX

PEN AND INK

"AND after Oxford, what next?"

"I want to be a writer."

The answer came from an Eton boy who knew that he would have to earn his own living. That was on the Fourth of June before last, and I am told that it is nowadays quite a common thing for young men, and young women as well, with their way to make in the world, to decide to be "writers."

Fifty years ago such an ambition would never have entered our heads, once childhood was over. We thought of writing, not as a profession, but as a gift, a vocation; you were born to it or you were not, and even if you were born to it, there would be long years, as R.L.S. told us, of apprenticeship, of "playing the sedulous ape," before you could hope, or dare, to give yourself the name of "writer." We would not, I think, have thought of journalists as "writers," but even journalism was rarely, if ever, a pre-selected profession. It was a thing you drifted into from the Bar, perhaps, or from schoolmastering, or the Civil Service, approached in the first place as a means of earning a few guineas on the side.

My first appearance in print was in the pages of the *Amphibian*, one of those ephemeral magazines which are published at Eton on the Fourth of June. I sent in verses

and skits and epigrams, and the two editors, of whom I
was one, were delighted with them; indeed, together
with the contributions of the other editor, Cecil Charrington, they made up the whole of the *Amphibian's*
contents. We had agreed not to refuse each other's work,
but to reject all other contributions, as the best way of
maintaining a high standard throughout; but it led to
some heart-burnings, for my friend Maidstone had
covered two sheets of foolscap with a long poem which,
in spite of faulty rhymes and a complete disregard for
scansion, he very much admired. I can still see him
following me down Keate's Lane, waving his manuscript
and begging, with beseeching eyes, for reconsidera-
tion; while I cruelly reiterated my poor falsehoods
about "lack of space" and "too late for the press," for I
had not the heart to tell him how bad it was. We sold
enough copies of the *Amphibian* at sixpence each to pay
for the printing, and I had my first secret sip of pride in
authorship when Mr Arthur James, a retired Eton
housemaster, translated one of my epigrams into Greek.
He addressed his letter containing this piece of flattery
to "the Editor" and, as bad luck would have it, it was
handed to me and not to Cecil Charrington. If only, I
thought, one other person could have known about it,
even, perhaps, mentioned it at large! As it was, I was
too shy to show it even to my co-editor, or to anyone
at all; and this is the first time I have disclosed the
matter to the world. Authors are notoriously conceited;
but my own boyish pride must have been inordinate so
to compel me to silence, for nobody else would have
given a second thought to the fact that a kind old
scholar had amused himself with my four lines.

At Oxford my mind was wholly taken up with work

and rowing, and only on one occasion did I sit down, on a sudden impulse, and write some verses, which I sent to the *Oxford Magazine*, then edited by J. L. Stocks. I wrote them *currente calamo*, and took no pains about economy or polish, but to my surprise Stocks printed them and even put the title, which I have forgotten, on the poster of the magazine. They were signed "X," but Stocks told Cyril Bailey of their authorship, and Cyril gave an amused pat on the back to a rowing-man breaking out into verse. But the College chaplain, Henry Gibbon, who had been a Major in the Indian Army, thought them beautiful. This would have been more gratifying had not Henry Gibbon thought everything beautiful. I remember no inclination to try again.

When reading for the Bar in London I made my first guineas by writing for the press, and promptly got into hot water. I was quite ignorant of the etiquette of journalism and when, on consecutive days in Boat Race week, I was asked first by Hilaire Belloc, for the *Eye-Witness*, and secondly by the editor of the *Saturday Review*, for a signed article on the Boat Race, I gladly accepted both commissions. Belloc gave me five pounds and the *Saturday* three guineas, but the editor did not print my article and I returned his cheque. He then wrote to say that he could never have believed that an old Oxonian would play him so ungentlemanly a trick as to write on the same subject for two periodicals. Since one article had been a review of the prospects before the race, and the other an account of the race itself, it had not crossed my mind that I ought not to do both; but that, it seems, is the rule. I apologised, and he forgave me, even insisting that, having done the work, I must accept the fee. He even invited me to write about

the coming Olympic Games, of which he spoke with
enthusiasm. I did so, but condemned the Games out of
hand as causing nothing but international bitterness. He
printed my piece and wrote to me that I had converted
him, and he himself attacked the Games in a short
leading article. I picked up a few more guineas when
J. A. Spender accepted three or four short stories for the
Saturday Westminster. The *Westminster Gazette* was an
evening paper printed on green paper; it had carried
cartoons by Harry Furniss deriding the Tory Government in the last days before its fall, including the
celebrated drawing of Joe Chamberlain as a fox carrying
Arthur Balfour as a rabbit in his mouth. With the
Liberals in power it took on a most superior tone, and
Spender, who wrote many of the leading articles himself, went on hectoring what was left of the Tory party,
night after night, in what I felt to be a rather petty
and spiteful way. However, Spender enjoyed a reputation for high-mindedness, even nobility; he had a dome-
like head, and was in the confidence, it was said, of the
Cabinet; and it was undeniable that his green evening
paper was, apart from its self-righteousness, far better
written and more readable than its pink, Tory competitor, the *Globe*. And on Saturdays it relaxed and went
in for short stories, literary competitions, and so on.
Only one of my stories was in any sense an original
composition; the others were anecdotes of real life
worked up with frills. I rediscovered these little tales
lately; they had a great deal of style, all borrowed from
Belloc. I had forgotten how much we young men must
have admired, in those days, Belloc's handling of
English. The story with an original idea was called
"St Judas" and was signed with my initials. On the

Saturday that it appeared I travelled down to Royston to visit my cousin and godfather, Mr David Bevan. I travelled third class and he travelled first; but as we drove from the station I saw that he had a copy of the *Westminster* in his hand. He said rather gravely: "There's a story in this paper signed L.E.J.; you didn't write it, I hope?" I confessed that I had. "I am surprised," he said; "your mother used to be such a good church-woman." That was the first scrap of literary criticism I received; all the same, he showed it to his wife and daughter, who solaced me with their secret approval. They, too, must have had a taste for Belloc.

I was pleased with the guineas, but the appearance of these stories, even in the *Saturday Westminster*, did not put any ideas into my head about being a "writer." Indeed, apart from a few obituary notes in *The Times* and a review in the *University Magazine of McGill*, I did not appear in print again for nearly thirty years. I forget how it was that Mr Andrew Macphail, the editor, came to invite me to review a volume of poems by a young Canadian, Miss Marjorie Pickthall, but it was in 1913, and my wife was still in touch with Canadian friends. On re-reading this review, in the beautiful large type of that impressive grey magazine, where I appear in company with A. D. Godley and Stephen Leacock, I find myself surprised at the assured, magisterial, and booming style in which I highly commended the young poetess, while advising her to be more fastidious when selecting poems for publication. She must have seen, I think, behind those authoritative, balanced periods, that kindly, avuncular criticism, a ripe and elderly *littérateur*, sitting among his bookshelves, accustomed to being listened to. I hope Mr Macphail did not let out to Miss Pickthall that it was the first review ever written by a young man engaged in selling prismatic glassware.

A life of getting and spending, of stalking and shooting and playing golf, of being blacksmith to five daughters who all in turn imagined themselves to be ponies in need of shoeing, of an incurable addiction to deep arm-chairs and books, did not turn my thoughts towards writing. It may be, too, that the more a man reads the less inclined he is to write; everything seems to have been said, and better said than he could say it. And when, in my middle fifties, I did at last go out into the revolving garden-shelter at Cranmer, turn it round with its back to the wind and settle myself with writing-pad and fountain-pen, it was not from literary ambition. It was to write a play with a leading part in it suitable for a beautiful actress with a foreign accent.

We had made the acquaintance of Sybille Binder in the late summer of 1937 at Altaussee in the Austrian mountains. Sybille, who had then reached the top of the tree in her role as the Empress Elizabeth of Austria, to whom she was said to bear a striking resemblance, was on holiday, hiding her Titian hair under a scarf, bare-legged, wearing flat canvas shoes and no make-up, trying to escape notice. She approached my wife in the post-office, to enquire about some English lessons. Sybille's beauty is in the bones, in the curve of the cheek, in the eyes; her voice is a contralto, vibrant and warm; and her attempt at disguise availed her nothing. My wife invited her to drink coffee and wrote to me, detained in the City, to promise me a rarity in the Saltzkammergut, for she knew my horror of places where relentless phalanxes of fir-trees descend from all the hills, sombre and bird-forsaken, to hem you in. It rained every day but one during the fortnight we spent beside that zinc-coloured lake, and we saw little of Sybille, but that little was enough. Six months later Hitler marched into Vienna, and Sybille, whose detestation of the Nazis was no more a secret than her Jewish origin, had to make her escape in a matter of hours. She came first to Cranmer, and our friendship began, but with no presentiment that it was to lead me, after thirty years, to a return to authorship.

Twenty years ago a name that was a household word in Vienna could mean nothing at all to those who control the affairs of the London theatre, and there were few open arms upon our stage for foreign actresses. Sybille moved from celebrity to total obscurity in the time it took her to travel, with every worldly possession in a cabin-trunk, from Vienna to London. Even the personal friendship and goodwill of a John Gielgud and a Peggy Ashcroft could not open by more than a chink a door so firmly closed against intruders. Moreover, at that time Sybille's accent, although remarkably good for one who had never lived in England, disqualified her from a part in most plays upon an English stage. And so it was that, after a year of frustration, I told Sybille, half in fun and half in earnest, that I must write a play for her myself, and went out into the garden one summer morning to do it.

My problem was to invent a part for a leading lady whose beauty was of the exquisite sort, touched with mystery, withdrawn as well as alluring; for an actress who had triumphed in the role of Oberon. My play had to be a fantasy, but I was neither a Barrie nor a Bridie and whatever I had to say—and a playwright must,

after all, find something to say—would inevitably be
about present-day manners and morals. I decided therefore, with Sybille's enthusiastic approval, to bring an
Immortal of sorts into an average British, Philistine
home, where her uncorrupted sense of values should
make hay of their conventional morals, and her beauty
betray a philosopher into teaching her, to her and his
own cost, the meaning of earthly love. There was
nothing original in the idea, but it was none the worse
for that. I think the whole play was scribbled upon a
pad in that revolving shelter which looked down the
long herbaceous border, backed by the blue and silver
of ceanothus and silver willows, to the great rounded
horse-chestnuts. I could work on it only at week-ends;
but Sybille was mostly there to listen to each scene and
to approve or condemn it. It was delightful, on a June
morning, to be taught by a lovely actress how she made
love and how she liked to be made love to, even
though it was humiliating to discover how little I knew
about the business. That, said Sybille, was because I was
an Englishman; but I was an apt pupil, or rather a wax-
like and malleable playwright, for on looking through
The Visitor again I recognise that the love-scenes,
economical, reticent, and veiled in evanescent wisps of
poetry, were dictated, almost word for word, by
Sybille herself. Not that I did not kick or wriggle; it is
hard to have to tear up pages full of masculine passion,
and we occasionally went into lunch as enemies, but I
recognised the sureness of her touch, and always gave
way. The satire, such as it was, she left to me, as well as
the melodrama. For my heroine, always with the
purest motives, murdered an old lady, burnt a fortune
in Treasury bills, tortured a Member of Parliament by

sticking a pin under his finger nail, attended a wedding believing it to be a funeral, and a funeral dressed for a wedding, interfered in a pending suit for divorce, urging that gluttony was worse than adultery, and that lobsters, not Lydia, should be cited as co-respondents, and all but married a wicked Press Lord. By the end of the summer we had giggled together, with the whole family joining in, enough to half-believe in the play, which was duly despatched to a firm of theatrical agents, Messrs Christopher Mann.

In September war broke out. Sybille married Dr Gerald Shirlaw. In the strains and public preoccupations of that autumn the play was forgotten. But shortly after Christmas Messrs Christopher Mann wrote to say that Mr Basil Foster, who was managing a "try-out" theatre at Richmond, was taken with the play and would like to discuss it with the author. Plays at Richmond were put on only for one week and with severe economy, and frequently escaped the notice of both West End managers and critics. The message in reality meant very little; but it filled Sybille and myself with excitement. I asked Foster to lunch to meet Sybille, for he was not, I think, aware that the play had strings to it, and I felt, rightly as it turned out, that Foster had better see the strings before hearing about them. Foster's capitulation was instantaneous, before the hors d'oeuvres were consumed; rather embarrassingly so, for he decided upon the spot to play the leading man himself. Basil Foster in his younger days had been a *jeune premier* in comedies of the lighter sort; he had fair hair, blue eyes, a graceful figure, and charm of manner. The actor on whom he tried to model himself, he told me, was Gerald du Maurier; but whereas du Maurier never failed to be du Maurier in whatever role he was cast, Foster could only be Basil Foster. Sybille and I had intended her to be made love to by a shy but ardent philosopher, as far removed from a matinée idol as imagination can stretch. Foster's fair hair was faded and very thin on the top; there were few lines of thought upon his brow and as much ardour in his love-making as it takes to shake hands with an aunt. But there was nothing to be done. At least the play was to go on, and under a manager whose penury was made up for by his genuine enthusiasm.

The producer was Peter Powell, all tact and gentleness, but not to be deflected from his own views. So ignorant was I of stage matters in those days, that when Peter asked if I would care to look in upon a rehearsal, I had no idea that he was doing me a favour. I thought that authors had a right to attend, and even to make suggestions. I had been led astray, no doubt, by stories of Shaw and Barrie walking on to the stage and showing famous actresses how to move and to speak their lines. I was soon to learn my mistake. At the first rehearsal, in some small, unheated, empty room, I intervened once or twice when an actor seemed to have missed a point. I fortunately noticed that Peter had turned red in the face before I had gone very far, and at the end of the rehearsal he told me that he could not continue if the author was going to take a hand. After that I sat in silence, but Peter never failed to give generous attention to my notes.

Except for the miscasting of Basil Foster himself, whose perfect tea-table manners were a poor response to Sybille's airy flittings, like those of a blown leaf in moonlight, the cast was good and workmanlike. I

16

wonder if all playwrights feel a warm and instant affection for the actors and actresses who give life to their play? I felt myself to be curiously beholden to them, with an impulse to apologise to those with small parts for having somehow maltreated them. To have created a footman and left him at that seems, when you see an eager young man in the flesh, a shabby thing to have done. On the other hand their pleasure when they got a laugh was most rewarding. I felt as if I had tipped a schoolboy. We had one bad moment. Two days before the first night the play was returned by the Lord Chamberlain with a letter asking for sixty "cuts" before he could give a licence. Foster had regarded the play as being Lord Chamberlain-proof, and the blow was quite unexpected. The "cuts," if made, would have left the play in ruins. By telephoning to Sir Alan Lascelles I obtained not only the address of the Lord Chamberlain's reader, but an appointment with him. He had rooms in Windsor Castle, and Peter Powell and I travelled down, in a total black-out, to Windsor. The snow was deep on the ground; the precincts of the Castle were deserted; it was ten o'clock at night, and we had great difficulty, flashing our torches, in finding the reader's lodgings. The reader, however, thanks to Lascelles, received us kindly. He was recovering from influenza, and wore a suit of thick brown Jaeger pyjamas. He had not seen the play himself; he had relied upon the report of a sub-reader. I sat down by his side, and we flipped through the pages of the typescript. He could not have been nicer. He hinted that his subordinate must also have been suffering from influenza. Apart from some perfectly loyal references to Queen Victoria, who, with God, is unmentionable upon the stage, and a third

"bloody" (the allowance is two), all the cuts were
restored. But what would have happened if the author
had not been at Oxford with Sir Alan Lascelles?

Our second panic overtook us on the very morning
of the first night. Mr Battersby M.P., a key character,
was reported to be down with pneumonia. There were
no understudies at Richmond, and without this actor
the play must, at the best, have been postponed in-
definitely. Here Dr Shirlaw, Sybille's husband, stepped
in. He walked, unannounced, into the player's flat and
bedroom, produced a syringe, and plunged it into the
astonished invalid. Whatever the dose was, it worked
wonders. Mr Battersby M.P. rose from his bed and was
his gross and bounding self not only that night, but for
the rest of the week.

There was no question, of course, at Richmond of
having the setting for the play specially designed. I had
fortunately, with an eye to economy, written all three
acts to be played in one set; but the drawing-room at
Richmond was not the drawing-room I had seen in my
mind's eye. It was a most unlikely room for a modern
tycoon to have inhabited; the carpets and curtains were
shabby, the furniture was massive Victorian-Gothic,
and if an audience can have its temperature lowered
by the scenery, this was the scenery to depress it.
All the same, my friends had gallantly rallied through
the snow and fog and the black-out to the first
night; a row of officers from the R.A.F. in the first
row enjoyed all the jokes, one of them with a pump-
handle laugh loud enough to warm and reassure any
playwright's heart; the good people of Richmond
applauded; and there was a satisfactory feeling of
enjoyment and success. And Sybille, who had never

before had a line to speak with a laugh in it, being intended by nature for romantic and tragic roles, declared that the novel experience of having to pause for laughter was most exhilarating.

But a "try-out" is pointless unless London managers or critics are there to see it, and they were not. So that when I went down to Richmond on the last night, the full house and Sybille's personal triumph and many "curtains" did not bring any feeling of elation. It had been fun, but it was all over; our main purpose seemed to have failed. But as we were slowly trooping out into the snow, a messenger asked me to go to the manager's office. There I was introduced to two gentlemen with cigars, a tall one and a short one, and both rosy with good humour. They were Mr Tom Walls and Mr Leon M. Lion. It seemed that Mr Tom Walls had a young friend in the cast; he had braved the wintry night to please her, and had persuaded Mr Lion to come too. They were both much tickled by the play, enchanted with Sybille, and inclined to do something with it. The end of it was that, although Mr Tom Walls dropped out, Mr Lion decided, on conditions, to take the play on tour with a view to an eventual production in the West End.

Leon M. Lion was a curious character. A small, bullet-headed Puck, he combined a genuine delight in poetry and some romantic enthusiasms with ruthless egoism and a disconcerting habit of sudden rudeness. His conditions were dictated: the play was to be revised by himself and myself in collaboration, his name was to appear as joint-author, and a fresh character was to be introduced suitable for himself to act. I naturally accepted, since it was a matter of sink or swim for

Sybille, and the "collaboration" began. I was by this time working long hours in the Ministry of Economic Warfare, and our collaboration took the form of our dining together at restaurants, where he was often highly entertaining. But as "joint-author" he was a disappointment. He was as incapable of invention as he was of expressing himself on paper, and when the revised version was complete, and the play re-christened *Miss FitzNewton* by L. E. Jones and Leon M. Lion, the second author's contribution was exactly one disastrous adjective on which he had insisted: "pachydermatous." It is true that he was helpful on matters of stagecraft, and the new scene, in which Lion had a lengthy duologue with Sybille in the character of an unscrupulous Press Lord, added some salt to the third act. All the same, his claim to "authorship" was brazen.

I do not think Lion ever suspected how much my study of his own character, in our many interviews, helped me to write the additional scene. Lion was a good actor, and although he attempted to "hog" the duologue at Sybille's expense, he undoubtedly played the part to the life, and no wonder, since I had largely made him the model for the buccaneering Lord Muckleton. He had only to be himself in his less agreeable mood. When spring came, the play went, with Lion as producer, to the Arts Theatre at Cambridge; to Edinburgh; to Golders Green where Mr James Agate slept through it and gave it what must have been the most withering notice ever printed, although, "in the kindness of his heart," he mentioned neither play, author, producer, nor cast by name. The fall of France and the fear of invasion now gave Lion the excuse which his pride as joint-author required for bringing the tour to an end. He spoke of the West End in the autumn, but when autumn came the bombing of London again saved him from having to admit the truth: the play was not good enough. It is hardly surprising. It was written, not because the playwright had a play in him, but because a lovely and distinguished foreign actress was out of a part. It asked the public to believe in, and to care about, the opinions and emotions of an unearthly being who had materialised on an English lawn as the result of an experiment by Sir Isaac Newton. All the characters in it were puppets designed by the author to express his private criticism of modern manners and morals. The action was melodramatic, and did not flow from the characters or situations of the people in the play; it was arbitrarily imposed upon them by the author to make a curtain, to get a laugh, or to illustrate an argument. Spurts of poetry were injected here and there because the leading lady, in looks and temperament, was a poetic person. To make a successful mixture of moral satire, broad farce, fantasy, and poetic romance requires a Bridie or a Christopher Fry, and I am neither.

All the same I had tasted blood. I do not know what professional writers regard as the most rewarding moments in their vocational lives. Probably those in which they complete a line or a paragraph and feel that, while it precisely expresses what they sought to express, the sound of it also falls sweetly upon their inward ear. And if that is the first prize, the second prize is probably the public praise of a critic whose judgment and integrity they respect. But for the play-writer there are sweeter moments still. Nothing, I think, can be more fascinating for an author than to hear, for the first time,

his own words given life by an accomplished actor or
actress; nothing more intoxicating than to hear a roar
of laughter from an audience. There is no value in the
laughter; the joke may be a cheap one and the audience
ninnies. But none the less it is delightful to listen to.
And what with the novelty, the professional tricks and
jargon of rehearsals, the unexpected human warmth of
the actors and actresses, the sense of being admitted to
the secrets of an esoteric group whose members live
strange, double lives—what with all this, play-writing
brings rewards more various, less personal, and far more
amusing than the satisfactions to be had from other
kinds of composition. It could be corrupting, of course;
every time the playwright hugs himself over an empty
laugh at a trivial joke he loses caste in his own eyes, for
being pleased with praise from people whose praise is
worthless. But so long as he keeps his head, and enjoys
it all as fun, and does not confuse himself with Mr Noel
Coward, still less with Shaw, there is no harm done,
and very good fun it is.

So, having tasted blood, I was determined to try
again. Our reverse had not been such as to leave
Sybille and myself utterly discouraged. And Sybille, too,
had tasted blood, in the unaccustomed experience of
getting laughs. So, after two summer days when Miss
Ellen Pollock, who had acted in *Miss FitzNewton*, sat
with Sybille and myself in the Cranmer rose garden,
and we three had sketched out the plan for a comedy,
I wasted much time over a ridiculous and futile play
called *The Pink Angel*. I can remember nothing about
it except that it included an *enfant terrible*, because Ellen
Pollock said a child on the stage was good "box-office,"
and was written round a series of situations and jokes

contributed by three persons possessing disparate types
of imagination and humour. I think *The Pink Angel* was
sent to an agent, but nothing more was ever heard of it,
reasonably enough, considering its genesis. A writer
who tries to please anyone except himself is lost.

So I tried again. This time I was determined to write
a straight drama where the action should spring from
character, where there should be no satire, but a love
story sufficiently poignant to give full play to Sybille's
gifts for tenderness and tragedy. And since I am incapable of inventing a story, I based myself upon the
story of Joseph and Potiphar's wife; but twisted round
for my own purposes. The play was called *The Truth
about Joseph*, and was preceded by a prologue in which
Mrs Potiphar, in her old age, confesses to a young
journalist that the story of her affair with Joseph as told
in the Bible (and in the two-volume life of the late Sir
Jacob McNab) was her own invention, contrived, at
the cost of her own reputation, to save that of her much-
loved Joseph. The play itself tells what really happened
between them. The setting is entirely modern; Sir
Jacob and his sons are rich Scotch farmers, and Joseph a
rising young politician.

The play never reached the stage. Curiously enough,
it was never actually rejected by a manager. Sir Bronson
Albery kept it for months, hoping to use it "when I have
a theatre available." Mr Anthony Hawtrey, then
managing the Embassy Theatre, kept it for a year or
more, declaring he liked it immensely, until my agent
and only whole-hearted "fan," dear Joan Ling, asked
for its return. She sent it to the B.B.C., and after further
long delays it was boiled down, with what I thought
extraordinary skill, to run for an hour and a half, and

produced with a first-class cast, in Saturday Night Theatre in the Home Service. So I did make sixty pounds, and had the fascinating experience of sitting in a glass box in Portland Place and watching a rehearsal, while a young man at an enormous switchboard turned knobs to make various "noises without." The "listeners' reactions" were peculiar. There was, they told me, a higher proportion than the average of high marks, but also more than the average of protests. These were from listeners who held that since God had himself written the truth about Joseph in the Old Testament it was sheer blasphemy to give another version. So it has not been repeated. In any case Sybille was no longer available to play the part written for her, and to that extent I had failed in my purpose in writing the play.

All this play-writing was done in such time as was not taken up by commanding and training a Company of the Norfolk Home Guard. I found it a great refreshment, and began to be bitten with word-spinning for its own sake. So when Sybille's husband, Dr Shirlaw, was sent overseas at short notice after beginning a book about how to deal with a defeated Germany, I was in the right mood to be persuaded to finish his book for him. Gerry Shirlaw, a Pole by birth, sent himself to school in Scotland at the age of thirteen, became a British citizen, and took his medical degrees at Edinburgh. He combines warmth and affection for his friends with a forcible and outspoken dogmatism. Although his experience with a Military Mission to Roumania after the war gave him a near view of Russian behaviour in a satellite country that sickened him for life of the Russian form of Hitlerism (still so ineptly called Communism), Gerry was in 1943 still trailing fogs of idealistic misconceptions about both Russia and Socialism. He had boomed at me from the hearthrug often enough and long enough to convince me, not of the rightness of his opinions, but of the quality and vigour of his intelligence, and I had gladly obeyed his commands (for all Gerry's requests sound like orders) to correct his headlong, racy, but in-accurate English style. And when he asked (or ordered) me to complete his book for him, I agreed to do so in the rather unusual conditions, as between joint-authors, that I was not to be bound by any views expressed in his part of the book.

What had happened to me by the summer of 1943 was this: that the practice of writing, even plays, had gradually induced in me a habit of ordering my thoughts upon all sorts of subjects as if they were to be put down on paper. Like most people who are not in politics, I had spent my life talking, and grumbling, and deriding, where public and international affairs were concerned, without ever troubling to reduce my views, which were often positive and rarely nebulous, to orderly and communicable form. It would be too much to say that the habit of writing made me think, but it did give me a quite novel impulse to express my thoughts, and so to "think" them more purposefully.

It is, for me, a curious reflection that an accidental encounter in the post office of Altaussee in 1937 between my wife and a Viennese actress should have resulted in my becoming a writer not only of plays but of a serious book on politics: for my share, which amounted to two-thirds, in *You and the Peace*, published by Macmillan in 1944, dealt, except for one chapter on Africa, almost entirely with the future of the United Nations after the war. The argument was that war can never be prevented until there exists a World Criminal Code, enforceable by a Police Force, so overwhelming as to be an absolute deterrent, at the disposal of the United Nations; that the nations should contribute arms and men to this Force according to their wealth, but otherwise, except for keeping order at home, disarm; that when the Code is infringed, action by the World Police against the offender must be automatic (as is the action of civil police) and not subject to a vote. On all other matter votes in the United Nations must be weighted according to wealth and population, and there should be no veto on the decisions of a majority. There is nothing original in these ideas. They are plain common sense, and the world will remain under strain and apprehension until they are grasped and acted upon. Unfortunately "Nationalism" and various so-called "Ideologies" carry, with their emotional appeals, much more weight with the majority of human beings than does common sense, while those most devoted to the cause of peace continue to put their faith in an unarmed, lobby-ridden, futile, and impotent Assembly. To make matters worse, Russia, formally a member of the Comity of Nations, is at heart as much concerned for the welfare of her fellow-members as a wolf for a flock of sheep.

The book, as its title shows, was intended for popular reading, and was written in a colloquial, "snappy" style. But it did attempt to face all probable objections, and to make its case by practical, down-to-earth arguments. Its tone was businesslike, not idealistic. About six thousand copies were sold and, considering the profound obscurity of the authors, it won surprisingly satisfactory notices. It also brought me an

invitation from the then Master of Balliol to lecture
upon its thesis to a gathering of young men and women
from the armed forces of the Commonwealth. I found
that lecturing, provided there is room to walk up and
down for a few paces each way in front of your reading-
desk, holds something, pale shadow though it may be,
of the pleasure of play-writing. There is a living
audience; its responses are visible; and the eager, con-
senting looks of a pretty girl in uniform are more
stimulating, more provocative of a lively phrase, than
the four familiar walls of a writer's study. At the final
discussion in the Junior Common Room the Sage of
All Souls, Lionel Curtis, appeared, snowy-haired and
benign, to preside and to speak. It was a disappointment
for me, and I think for my pretty girl and her companions as well, to hear him dismiss the idea of putting
force into the hands of the United Nations as moonshine. He believed that "moral leadership" and "world
opinion" would prove to be more efficient than armed
forces. But that was twelve years ago.

When *You and the Peace* was published early in 1944
we had not yet heard of an atom bomb. When the first
of these fell on Hiroshima I was greatly excited. "Now
at last," I said, "wars can be ended." It seemed to me
that a terror, the only known restrainer of wicked men,
could for the first time in the history of the human race
be manufactured in so devastating a shape that no
Hitler, no Stalin, would dare to risk its unleashing. The
concentrated form of the new weapon, the futility of
defences against it, seemed to make it an ideal armament
for a World Police. The nations had only to agree to
put this new bomb into the exclusive hands of a Police
Force, and to define such breaches of good behaviour

on the part of a nation as would oblige the Police, automatically, to dangle it, and armed aggression would be a thing of the past.

In the days before I had taken to what George III would have called "scribble, scribble" I should have contented myself with boring my family and friends at the dinner-table with these reflections. But now, of course, having lately launched a book about these high matters, I must be out with my fountain-pen and writing-pad and tell my thoughts to the world. And, with the feeling common, I suppose, to all apprentices that they "can do better next time," I decided to give my momentous message to the public not in a book but in a play. No doubt I was subconsciously pining once again to attend rehearsals, to hear my own words thrown back to me, alive and kicking, by accomplished actors and actresses, and to hear that heart-warming laughter in the stalls.

This time I was no longer hampered by the necessity of writing a part for an individual actress. I must have known by now that a play for the English stage has a better chance of success if it contains one or two "star" parts, since the public are more interested in actors and actresses than in ideas. A manager, when reading a play, is naturally more inclined to produce it if he can see some well-known "box-office" personality in this part or in that. But a play in which the scene of all three acts is a Peace Conference does not lend itself to star parts. It was to be a play of satire, argument, and propaganda, and although I had the sense to make room at the conference table, or at any rate among the gilt chairs behind the plenipotentiaries, for a Miss Kay Bannerman and a Miss Avice Landone, even these ladies had, for

most of the time, to put politics before allure. And
because it was a play with a purpose it suffered, like
my first play, from the grave defect that all my characters, try as I might to disguise it by their sex, nationalities and accents, were in the last resort spokesmen for
myself. It is the defect of Shaw as a playwright, but
in Shaw the brilliance, wit, and range of the talk
more than compensate for an audience's lack of concern
for the fate of his puppets. On a more commonplace
level the audience tires of argument and of verbal exchanges, however neat, and longs to laugh or to cry
with sane creatures of flesh and blood.

I forget whether I had the Arts Theatre in mind
when I sent *The Dove and the Carpenter* to Joan Ling; I
think it is probable, for I knew that this theatre took a
less commercial view of new work than the usual run
of West End managements. At any rate, after the
customary long months during which aspiring playwrights at first school themselves for disappointment
and end by forgetting their lost child altogether, I was
one day called in from the garden to take a long-
distance call. The call was from Alec Clunes, at that
time managing the Arts Theatre. Would I care to come
to London to talk about my play? "The first act is
inspired"—my heart leapt—"but the third act is no
good at all. I can make no promises. Come if you are
prepared to do some rewriting." Of course I was
prepared; and I hastened up to London and called
upon Alec Clunes at his office, so small that it would
hardly hold us both. He was charming, but not particularly encouraging; there was no more talk of "inspired,"
and no very precise guidance as to how the third act
ought to go. I came away, none the less, with the

comfortable feeling that here was a manager none of whose criticisms had anything to do with "box-office"; they had all been directed towards making the play a better thing in itself. And if his alertness and intelligence had been a little alarming, his warm friendliness restored my self-confidence. In the end the re-written play was given a month's run at the Arts, with Peter Powell once again as producer, to my great pleasure. It was all most enjoyable.

I was again lucky in my cast. Harold Scott as a Labour Foreign Secretary; John Ruddock as a Stateless waif whose many wives and children had been machine-gunned in every corner of Europe; James Hayter as a foretaste of Mr Dulles; Clement McCallim as a Russian off whom Harold Scott, who had shouted "Hands off Russia" for years, could not keep his hands; Bertram Shuttleworth as a disillusioned, wise-cracking China-man; Oliver Burt as an Austrian savant dressed up as an English archdeacon in order to penetrate the mysteries of ecclesiastical thinking about bombs; Alan Trotter as the elegant and imperturbable Civil Servant —each one of them, as far as I was concerned, not merely represented, but filled out and enlivened, the character assigned to him. And that, for a playwright, is the ultimate thrill: to find his puppets more con-vincing in the flesh than they had been in his imagina-tion. As for Avice Landone and Kay Bannerman, I am too susceptible to be quite trustworthy; I can only say that when writing the parts of Ma Godwin and Frau Frühling I had no inkling that I was to fall in love with both these creatures.

For all the admirable acting and Peter Powell's lively production, the play did not succeed. I recall the first

night: after the first act Alec Clunes dropped into the
bar where the critics were gathered to do a little innocent eavesdropping. He came back to me to say: "It
has failed. They haven't a clue." A few rows ahead of
me my friend Rupert Speir, now Member of Parliament
for Hexham, slept soundly in his stall. The critics said
it was amusing in parts, some even spoke of "wit";
but not one treated it as a desperately serious piece of
propaganda on a matter of life and death.

One incident is worth recording as evidence of the
climate of opinion just after the war. Clunes had real
difficulty in finding an actor willing to take the part of
Barashkov, the Russian delegate to the Peace Conference. I had done my best, on Clunes's advice, to give
this character some not unattractive personal traits to
set off against the fundamental ruthlessness of his policy.
But it was not enough. More than one young actor
had preferred to remain out of work rather than play
the part of a Russian who was less than all sweetness and
light.

The failure of this play, which after all had been
thought good enough for a trial by an Alec Clunes,
should have taught me that theatre audiences do not
love satire, or relish a mixture of jokes and verbal
fencing with propaganda for a cause. The brilliance of
Shaw can, as I have said, compel them to enjoy
argument and disputation in spite of themselves. But
the effective way to have moved a British audience to
think seriously about the atom bomb and its consequences would have been through an emotional drama,
such as Mr Graham Greene might have written. And
for such a major work of feeling and imagination I am
entirely unequipped. Not that the result of thoughts

provoked by emotion is by any means certain to lead
to wisdom. On some high matters feeling can darken
counsel.

Taking stock with my family of our situation at the
end of the war, we agreed that it would be impracticable to remain at Cranmer. Taxation had reached such
a height that even if I were to return to the City, I could
not hope to earn enough to keep going a country home
of even Cranmer's moderate size. Servants were no
longer to be had; it needed an invested capital sum of
£10,000 to maintain a single gardener. The end of an
age had arrived, an age of leisure and pleasure, and of
living on the backs of men and women who were no
longer of a mind to bear our weight. Had it been
possible to find a buyer able to preserve that mellow
old house, the lawns and yew-hedges and warm brick
walls that had seen so much gaiety and happiness, it
would have been a great comfort to us. There were
momentary hopes that the County Council might take
it over as a training college. But they came to nothing.
A public auction attracted no single bidder. In the end
the place was sold for a song to a farmer from another
county, whose ambition was to live in "a Hall." He
spoke grandly of the pride he would take in its preserva-
tion, but after changing the decoration of the Georgian
rooms from white and duck's egg to yellow and black, he
tired of his "Hall." He removed the top floor, made three
houses out of one, and finally pulled half of it down. For
a time fowls scratched and moulted where there had
been green lawns, and then gave place to a wilderness.

However, Hitler and Mussolini were dead, and since
the City could no longer support Cranmer, I was under
no obligation to return to the City. We already had

"rooms with a view" in St John's Wood, a view to the Surrey hills that consoles us, so exhilarating is its sweep, so various its colours, lights and shadows, for the loss of our Norfolk skies. And the itch to be writing, now that I was liberated from possessions, increased. On more and more subjects my thoughts began to take shape as sentences, and to "fall in," like men on a parade-ground, in squads and sections that could be marched away from head to writing-pad.

The winter of 1947 was so cold, and the "power-cuts" so frequent and prolonged, that the first problem for a would-be writer was to find a warm corner in which to write, for cold fingers can be the death of authorship. But I was lucky, for the Travellers' Club kept a blazing fire in that spacious and classic library where Thackeray's chair stands to remind us that books must be written before they can be read. In front of the fire is a leather sofa, and in a corner of that sofa I wrote, upon my knee, a book called *The Bishop and the Cobbler*, only interrupting myself, from time to time, to drop a lexicon upon the table in order to wake up a late member, whose snores, in range, variety, and cacophony, exceeded anything yet attempted by the most modern of musicians. The purpose of my book was described in the preface as follows: "Moved by a kind of lifelong bewilderment at some of the things that good and high-minded people believe and say, I have attempted in this book to apply what may be called 'moral common-sense' to a few of the religious, ethical and social questions which tease us." I was, I suppose, getting things off my chest. At any rate I wrote at speed, with no thought of style, concerned only with the matter, not the manner.

I naturally took the book to my old friend Daniel Macmillan, who had published both *You and the Peace* and, in this same year, a book of mine for children called *Jesus: Discoverer and Genius*, in which I had attempted, remembering my own childish distaste for the meek and mild figure presented to us, to bring out the heroic qualities of the Man "who turned the world upside down." Dan sent it to three rather distinguished readers, and all three advised him to publish. With great kindness he broke a publisher's rule and showed me these opinions, but declined, none the less, to publish. Had he been, he said, on his own, he would have published a book he had much enjoyed, but a book that "goes for" good and high-minded people must of necessity be heretical, and the traditions of the great firm of Macmillan are orthodox. But he sent me, in a happy hour, with a letter of recommendation to Secker & Warburg. They decided to publish, and I made some new and rewarding friendships.

On the book's appearance I naturally sent an inscribed copy as a present to my father. A few days later I went to tea with him. He greeted me with unwonted gravity. He then rose from his chair, unlocked a drawer, and took from it my book wrapped in a brown paper cover. "My boy," he said, "what have you to say about this book? I could not leave it about where the nurse or any woman visitor might see it." I was a grandfather in my sixties, but I felt like a schoolboy discovered with a paper-backed book printed in Alexandria. It appeared that a chapter called "Sex and Sin" had shaken him to the core. That any child of his should have written a book about sex, a volume to be hidden in drawers, had been a dreadful shock.

Fortunately my father was the most persuadable of men. I explained that this particular chapter had been written in the hope that it would be read by adolescents and curates and suchlike innocents, and after five minutes' talk the brown paper cover was torn off and the book prominently displayed on the table by my father's chair. He came to speak of it as "your fine book" and recommended it to all his friends.

Unknown authors are in need of strokes of luck. Mine was that Mr Nigel Nicolson spotted my book in a batch sent to his father, Sir Harold Nicolson, for review. Sir Harold was at that time reviewing books in the *Daily Telegraph*, and his favourable notice gave *The Bishop and the Cobbler* a good start and the publishers a moderate profit. My private satisfaction in it is founded, not on any public recognition, which has been of the very slightest, but on a handful of private letters from persons, even including parsons, who have found in it the answer to troublesome, even corrosive perplexities. To one like myself who, except in times of war, has borne no public burdens, to be assured that he has been of use, and even a comfort, to a single fellow-creature is a most acceptable sop to conscience.

An appetite for preaching grows with practice, and a year later I had produced another small book, of still more serious import, called *Beyond Belief*. I was provoked into this remonstrance by a paper-covered pamphlet called *Towards the Conversion of England*, being the Report of a Commission on Evangelism appointed by the Archbishops in 1943. The doctrines there set out so horrified me that I next turned to the *Report of the Commission of Christian Doctrine appointed by the Archbishops of Canterbury and York in 1922*. The report of this Commission, which sat for thirteen years, mostly under the Chairmanship of Archbishop Temple, is a much less repellent document than *The Conversion of England*, but disturbing enough. After once again searching the New Testament books to see what authority could be found for the extraordinary "Plan of Salvation" expounded in these Reports, I was driven to conclude that the answer, so far as the Synoptic Gospels and the teaching of Jesus himself are concerned, is "None at all."

The preface to this essay was as follows:

> The argument of Part I of this essay is that the doctrines taught by the Christian Churches are "beyond belief," because they impute to God a failure in Goodness. It suggests that for this reason they are being, and will be, rejected by increasing numbers of thoughtful people. Part II discusses how the wisdom of the historical Jesus, going as it does far beyond "Belief," can be disentangled from these rejected doctrines and restored to power. This essay has been written out of a profound conviction that that wisdom could even yet save a distracted world.

The book fell completely flat, and went almost un-reviewed except for a few angry barks from the church newspapers. I had not realised, nor presumably had my publishers realised, how right the French editor had been when he rejected an article on the ground that "*Question de Dieu, cela manque d'actualité.*" The vast majority even of the literate public no longer take any interest in religious matters, while church-people accept, without curiosity or reflection, what they were taught at their mother's knee. My own lifelong preoccupation with the *question de Dieu* has been shared with few, and those of my friends who are most faithful to their

Church are the last to sympathise with it. Nor are they concerned with Biblical criticism, since "the Church" and not scripture is the authority for their beliefs.

The failure of *Beyond Belief* induced in one of the partners of Secker & Warburg a feeling that I owed his firm three hundred pounds, a feeling which he had no difficulty in persuading me to share. Strictly speaking, I imagine that a publisher's acceptance of a book is an acceptance of the risk of loss, but in my childhood and youth the importance of not wasting or losing money had been almost an obsession, and I have never grown a shell hard enough to enable me to say "*Caveat emptor.*" So, with a troubled conscience, I cast about for some means of redeeming myself. The swings on which the loss was incurred had been grave and serious; what about a little frivolity for the roundabouts?

For some years I had been a regular competitor in the literary competitions run by the *New Statesman*. I had originally subscribed to this weekly newspaper on the grounds that induced a Liberal friend of mine to read the *Tablet*. "Nothing is so healthy," he said, "as to have your blood made to boil once a week." It was good advice, and I still derive benefit from my Friday blood-boilings. But I have also enjoyed, and continue to enjoy, the literary, artistic, and musical pages of that paper, traditionally edited without respect to politics. When I began to compete, the literary editor was Raymond Mortimer, who not only himself set us problems but required, from other setters, a standard which justified the word "literary." I owe to him the discovery that I had a certain facility for pastiche, rhyming, and translating, which has given me a great deal of fun, and even enabled me, for five or six years, to "mulct," as I saw it, an often reprehensible newspaper. Raymond Mortimer liked to ask competitors to deal with some topic of the day "in the manner of" the classic writers of prose or poetry. I believe the secret of success in this game is, rather paradoxically, not to refresh your memory of, say, "the manner" of Tennyson or Dr Johnson by turning again to particular poems or passages of prose, but rather to shut your eyes and try to imagine what Tennyson or Johnson, as men, not writers, would have had to say about the topic set. Having made a plausible shot at this, with your mind's eye filled with pictures of the Doctor's great rolling head in the scorched wig, or of the gruff, pipe-smoking, bearded Bard, their "manner" seems to come of itself. To put it briefly, to achieve manner look first for matter.

By the time I had been, as I have said, gently "brainwashed" (although not by the partners at large) into thinking that I owed money to my publishers, I had quite a substantial collection of prize-winning entries in these competitions, enough, with a handful of unbespoken verses, to make up a small book. Secker & Warburg were more than willing to publish it; and Mr Roger Senhouse in particular took much trouble over the format of the little volume, to which Mr John Banting contributed some graceful and witty decorations. Indeed, if writing books can never bring to an author the enchanting by-products that accrue to the playwright through that whole delightful business of rehearsals and making friends with producer and cast, there is still a deal of ancillary pleasure to be had through dealings with a sympathetic publisher. I shall never forget my visits to Roger Senhouse's room in John Street, hung with exquisite modern pictures, but with floor, tables, sofas, and chairs concealed under layer upon layer of books, papers, manuscripts, and galley-proofs. The work of a bulldozer had to be done before I could sit down, and the process of making room for my cup of tea upon the round table was like a prolonged game of spillikins. Roger himself did not look in the least like Messrs Chapman and Hall in Chesterton's portraits; the corners of Chapman's flannel collars would never have curled up towards his ears, nor Hall's ties peeped out from the gaps in a half-buttoned jacket. But if Roger and his room were untidy, his mind was not, and when my particular business, to every detail of which he gave attention, was finished, he would entertain me with talk about books, and fine printing, and Colette, snatching up *pièces justicatives* from the surrounding chaos to illustrate his points. Had I possessed only half a memory, which I do not, I could have enriched my mind at each one of these so-called "business" interviews.

À la Carte, as the book was called, had excellent notices, one in the *Spectator* by Mr C. E. Vulliamy being beyond the dreams of authorship. Even the sales, moderate though they were, soothed my own sense of guilt and enabled me to climb the stairs to Senhouse's rooms without going on tiptoe. But the inestimable blessing that came to me through *À la Carte* was the friendship, for the years that remained to him, of Max Beerbohm. A friend had sent him a copy and Max's reaction to an imaginary passage from his own Autobiography was to send me a drawing, in pencil and wash, of King Edward VII at the Boat Race, with an inscription which modesty, to my own loss, forbids me to quote. Correspondence followed, and an annual

visit, brief but entrancing, to the Villino Chiaro at
Rapallo or, if the weather were still too hot, to the
Albergo at Monte Allegro. It is probably true that
writers encountered in the flesh rarely come up to
expectations. Max more than came up to them. It was
not just that his conversation was on a level with his
prose, and that the elegance of his clothes, the perfection
of his manners, were precisely suited to both. The
qualities which, though always to be detected in them,
are not on the surface of his writings, were his warmth,
goodness, and simplicity. Max the writer used artifice
and fantasy, but as a person he was transparent. Benevo-
lence, laced with humour, informed him, and although
he had often bitten, and I imagine was still able to bite,
he admitted to us, in his mellow eighties, that there
were some bites he regretted. "They were such *good*
people," he murmured, shaking his head over some
celebrated lines, written long, long ago, about a royal
couple. And there was a cartoon—"The Infant School"
—he wished he could have recalled. But he soon cheered
up, and sitting beneath the leafy trellis in his "Vining
Room," eating less than a canary eats but sipping his
red wine, he would tell us, in gentle tones and with
precise articulation, about Henry James and his incurable innocence, that caused him to throw up his arms
in utter despair when told over the port wine that things
looked black in the Balkans. The stories and reminis-
cence flowed, but always in the select vocabulary of his
writings; and he had the knack, for all that he must
have repeated his tales a hundred times, of making his
hearers feel that the words were fresh-minted for this
special occasion, for this much-looked-forward-to visit
of the Joneses.

18

Max's eyes, wide open under their rounded canopies, were blue as forget-me-nots, and gave to him an air of child-like ingenuousness which made a telling foil to his sophisticated wit. But above all he inspired affection, a quick response of the heart; he was a touching, as well as an admired figure; and it was easy to understand the unresting yet unstressed vigilance with which Lady Beerbohm hovered about her fragile but still exuberant charge. For those of us who knew him only in the last years, Max will not be thought of apart from her; it is the pair of them, he little and unruffled, she like a poplar in a breeze, upon that sun-warmed terrace, beneath that Italian sky, who will live undivided in our memories.

Rhyme and metre are out of fashion today, but they are fascinating to play with, and present problems for solution which prose, and that anarchic stringing of words called poetry by the moderns, do not. There was a good deal of versifying in *À la Carte*, and, having still things in my head begging to be let out, I next tried my hand at a volume of verse. I have far too great a respect for poetry to call anything I have written a poem; nor am I capable of writing one, for poetry is born of imagination and passion, not of reason and sentiment. But having failed, in prose, to draw attention to my personal quarrel with dogma and with what I have always regarded as the moral obtuseness of the dogmatic, I tried once again, through fables and satires expressed in concise, traditional verse-forms, to make my protest. I ought, of course, to have known better. The orthodox few are no less offended by, and the indifferent multitude no more concerned with, heresies expressed in verse than in prose. Nor did an admixture of light-hearted pieces about people and places and sport and pleasures, together with a sprinkling of epigrams, win any but negligible notice from reviewers or nine-and-sixpences from the public. But I have never regretted the year I spent wrestling with rhyme and metre, and, if my thoughts were commonplace, at least they were neatly turned out. There is great enjoyment to be had out of mere craftsmanship, the fitting and the polishing and, best of all, the cutting-down. To reduce six lines to four without loss of content has the thrill of doing a "birdie" at golf. And I was not to go without some private satisfaction, such as Max Beerbohm's appreciation of *Stings and Honey*, and the fact that a most distinguished critic keeps his copy "*là où le Roi va seul.*"

Roger Senhouse once again took infinite pains in reading and criticising and selecting from the verses I showered upon him and, although they must have foreseen a loss, Secker & Warburg, acting, I believe, from mere friendship, were prepared, if I would wait a year, to publish the little volume. The best sorts of publishers are not entirely governed by considerations of profit and loss, but the amount they are prepared to lose in any year on non-commercial books must obviously be limited, and I was proffering my unsaleable wares at a moment when their quota was already full. But I was impatient, and also embarrassed by my sense of their own misgivings. So I withdrew the book, to their and my relief, and went elsewhere. But I can never forget the encouragement and friendliness I received from Fred Warburg and Roger Senhouse and their partners. They have been real godfathers to me.

I find it remarkable, on looking back, to find how incapable I am of learning by experience. After my failure in the theatre with *The Visitor* and *The Dove and the Carpenter* one would have supposed that I might have done with play-writing and especially with satire, which inevitably calls for argumentative puppets to make the author's points, rather than for characters of flesh and blood. But I could not forget the fun and excitement I had had, even with my failures; besides, the suppressed preacher in me kept on nagging. There had been a chapter in my book *The Bishop and the Cobbler* called "Sex and Sin" (the chapter that had so disturbed my venerable father) in which I had written things I still believed worth saying to a people, like the British, who are reluctant to look sex in the face. And since moral essays in prose-form do not sell, why not, I thought, put my thesis on to the stage, and attempt to dissolve with laughter the rather murky clouds which envelop, in these northern latitudes, our thoughts about a natural and insistent impulse?

Accordingly I wrote *Sex and Seraphim*, and sent it to Joan Ling. A West End manager was interested, but had no theatre, and, while waiting for one to turn up, sent it to the Lord Chamberlain, who promptly refused the play a licence. After my experience in the snow at Windsor Castle, I did not take this rebuff too seriously; might not the Reader of Plays be once again suffering from influenza? Through the good offices of Sir Terence Nugent I obtained the Reader's telephone number, and put through a trunk call with the intention of asking for an interview. My old acquaintance, who had been so affable, was dead, and the new Reader was irritable when called to the telephone.

"This is most irregular," he said. "What do you want?"

"I want to know your reasons for turning down *Sex and Seraphim*."

"I can tell you that. Because it is the most pornographic and subversive play I have ever had in my hands."

Not being a Press Lord, I reacted violently to the word "pornographic."

"What the hell do you mean by such language?"

"Well, you take the sin out of sex, don't you?"

"At least you have seen my point."

"But if sex isn't sinful, what is?"

I am afraid I banged down the receiver. The Report of the Archbishop's Commission on Christian Doctrine, presided over by Archbishop Temple, had declared:

> The belief that the process of human generation is in itself sinful . . . is not a necessary part of the doctrine of original sin, and we are agreed in repudiating it. We believe that it is totally unwarranted. . . . That the sexual nature is necessarily or inherently sinful must be absolutely denied.

Those are plain words; yet here was the representative of the Lord Chamberlain, a great officer of State, laying down as axiomatic the precise opposite. To be refused a licence because I took the same view of sin as the Church of England was maddening.

As for the ugly word "pornographic," I had a clear conscience. It was what lawyers call "mere vulgar abuse," and not the faintest suggestion of anything of the sort was made when, a few years later, another Reader passed my play for production.

The Lord Chamberlain—and needless to say the gentle Lord Clarendon had no personal part in the affair—is a law to himself, and the play had to be thrown into a drawer, where it remained for several years. But

Joan Ling remembers what even her clients have forgotten, and there came a day when I was approached by two clever ladies who were then running the little Watergate Theatre in a kind of cellar in Buckingham Street. The Watergate Theatre was a club, and as such did not come within the Lord Chamberlain's jurisdiction. The underground room in which plays were staged held about a hundred people at most, had no ventilation, and a very small stage. For a drama in which two acts are played in Heaven and so require plenty of wing-room, no stage could have been less suitable; but a playwright's avidity to see his play produced is insatiable, and I threw prudence to the winds. Besides, Miss Ellen Pollock was enthusiastic, and prepared to produce the play upon what the stage calls "a shoe-string," and to take a leading part herself. To say that my characters once again lacked flesh and blood would be an understatement, since about half of them were seraphs and angels, in whose concerns no audience could possibly take an interest; they were there, of course, to argue, seraphically. The scene of the first act is the Ministry of Creation, where the plans for the creation of Man are under discussion. A competition is being held for the best system of procreation, and a complacent Seraph is confidently awaiting, among his angelic assistants, for the result to be announced. Splendidly winged himself, he is all for beauty, and, not above plagiarism, has been taking hints from the Department of Flora. And to fill up the time of waiting, he displays to his chief competitor, and to the audience, his animated models of Adam and Eve. In Eve's forehead is a rose, in Adam's a lily, and nothing can be prettier than their mating, when Adam gently inclines his forehead to hers and the pollen falls like golden dust. Even his competitor is charmed, although asking, with an air of innocence, about the expense. Then the blow falls. The too-confident Seraph has been Highly Commended, but the award has gone to his competitor. It seems that the Treasury stepped in; the rival, and winning, system was infinitely more economical. The crestfallen loser asks for details; a blue-print is unrolled, and the winning Seraph proudly points out his dual-purpose gadgets, economically combining drainage with reproduction. The loser is horrified, and insists that the human race, who are to be endowed with an aesthetic sense, will never stand for it. The winner points to the high coefficient of pleasure involved, and maintains that it will work. Bets are exchanged and it is agreed to hold an enquiry after so many aeons of experiment on Earth.

The second act is played out in Putney. A "muddle-class" British family is disrupted and made unhappy by prudery, shame, and the sense of sin. Only one clear-sighted Frenchwoman is unembarrassed by "the system," and has come to terms with it.

In the last act the celestial inquest is held. The events at Putney have taken place during the war, and a lucky bomb had enabled all the human characters to be present and to testify in the witness box. An Arch-seraph is umpire; the rival Seraphs are represented by Counsel. Only the Frenchwoman's evidence prevents a condemnation of the system: if she can work it, why not the British? It is permitted to continue.

Miss Ellen Pollock set about assembling a cast; but how, I asked her, can any human girl be equal to playing Eve? Under the trees in Cornwall Gardens she confronted

me with Miss Mercy Haystead, and there before me
was Eve. The cast was youthful but talented, and I
had the fascinating experience of watching Ellen Pollock
at work, taking, with great virtuosity, each role in turn.
I also, had, on two occasions and in the oldest stage
tradition, to sit patiently at my coffee while my leading
lady rose majestically, threw up her part and swept
from the room, to return five minutes later, in even
greater majesty, to forgive and forget.

But as the agreed date for the production of my play
drew near, the two ladies were no longer to be seen in
the Watergate Theatre Club. Even their diminutive
manager was difficult to get hold of and, when button-
holed, was curiously dumb and distrait. When the cast's
weekly pittance was due, the manager was not to be
found, and I had to put my own cheques into their
envelopes. At the eleventh hour the small manager,
dreadfully embarrassed, came clean. There was no
money at all, and the ladies had transferred the management to new hands. The new hands were interested in
the excellent restaurant and bar, but had no intention of
producing plays. But they would let out the stage for a
percentage of the takings.

I was accordingly faced with the alternative, of
letting down, on the one hand, producer, cast, and the
young man who had painted all Heaven on the backcloth, and the young woman who had winged my
Seraphim in the colours of the rainbow, or of paying,
on the other hand, for the production out of my own
pocket. If the ladies had relied, when they found themselves suddenly penniless, upon their knowledge of the
vanity of authors and upon the unlikelihood that I
should have the courage, or the hard-heartedness, to

abandon a devoted producer and cast, how right they
were! It had never crossed my mind that I was to
spend three hundred and fifty pounds on backing a
play, but that, in the end, was what I was forced into
doing.

Thanks to Ellen Pollock, who was a superb Seraph,
and to the verve and talent of the young actors and
actresses, the thing went well enough. I had managed
to persuade the Lord Chamberlain to send one of his
readers to see the performance; I sat behind this envoy
and saw his shoulders shaking, and on his report I was
granted, after making two or three face-saving alterations (of which I never saw the point), the licence so long
and so unreasonably withheld. But the Watergate
Theatre Club was then small and obscure; not many
critics and few managers came to see the play, and one
who did, and held out hopes of a West End production,
was struck down with a serious illness which put an
end to the negotiations.

I do not think the play would have succeeded even at
that time in a West End theatre unless some professional
playwright could have been persuaded to rewrite the
second act. I cannot manage human beings on the stage;
they remain puppets, mouthpieces for their creator,
types, not individuals. And in the five or six years which
have elapsed, there has been a perceptible change in
popular thinking about sex. I am inclined to believe
that if a further celestial enquiry were to be held today,
there might be found witnesses even from Putney to
testify, like my Frenchwoman, that the system can be
worked without shame or embarrassment. The play
already "dates."

I shall be very much astonished if I ever again

attempt either verse or playwriting. I have found, and hope to find again, a great deal of amusement, interspersed with moments of frustration and despair, in translating French poetry. I have enormously enjoyed writing my recollections. And because writing has now become a habit, almost an addiction, and is the perfect hobby for a man over seventy, I all the more regret my lack of imagination, of inventiveness, which would have enabled me to go on enjoying myself. How pleasant it would be to spend the evening of life in writing a novel! Unfortunately the things that pre-occupy me most of all, the questions that seem to me of profound importance, hold little interest for the public. A minority believe that they know all the answers, and to the majority the questions themselves are of no concern. To find a public I should have been writing sixty years ago. But then I could never have found a publisher.

POSTSCRIPT

R EADERS may well heave a sigh when a writer, at the end of a third volume about himself, announces that he proposes, even now, to tack on a personal note. But it is just because I have said so much, that I feel impelled to say a little more. For there have been omissions and reticences which cover more poignant experiences and profounder satisfactions than any that I have described. That I have wanted to write little or nothing about my own family goes without saying. But I do feel that it would be a little shabby to make no acknowledgments to some people and places hitherto unmentioned. To Howick, for example, my wife's old home—to Howick and its inhabitants, young and old, who for nearly half a century have added so much to the sum of our contentment. Howick, among its beech-trees, is lovely in itself; but the happiness dispensed there is the real point of that delectable home. There has always been fun at Howick and, far better than fun, an ethos that envelops all who go there like a benediction. It has been, like Cranmer, a house we went home to.

Besides, Howick has been a starting-point for other friendships. There is nobody alive today to receive my thanks for days of exhilaration at Underley, a place of shining memories; but although Blackmoor, Gothic among its pines, has passed away, its younger inhabitants have not. They survive, old only in affection, to take

267

my bow, and will know, I feel sure, how low a bow it must be.

Stanway in Gloucestershire is linked with Grogarry in South Uist as laughter is linked with loving-kindness in the memories of both. Can it make any difference to a man stalking grey lag geese as the sun rises over the shoulder of Hecla, what sort of people inhabit the Lodge? It can, and it did. Few rods or guns got round the table at Grogarry who owed no debt to Buckhurst, to the Buckhurst of fifty years ago, the Buckhurst of the bluebells, gay and untroubled. From Buckhurst many roots ran out to sprout elsewhere as at wakeful Courteenhall in Northamptonshire, with its military tang and constancy, and Norton Hall in Gloucestershire, that shakes hands again with Stanway, from which a younger rootlet runs northwards to Gosford and the windswept woods on Aberlady Bay. And across the Forth, below the Paps of Fife, lies hospitable Balbirnie, where talk hit all the nails upon the head. With all these places our ties have been stable and unfrayed by time, but not more enduring than those first knotted in the corner of the Master's Field at Oxford and pegged down near Hughenden, where the buds of the whitebeam shine like blossom at the edge of the April woods. To Hatfield, whose may-trees with the yews of Naboth's vineyard still haunt our memories, are due thanks for rare consideration to a youthful pair, as well as for an offshoot of never-failing liveliness; and there is a high, round room in a corner-house of Hyde Park Square where old friendship never dulls the eloquence and wit. Number 8 Scroope Terrace, in Cambridge, is an unforgettable address. I should have felt the same had it been at Harrow. Terling must be remembered, both for itself and its colonies; open-eyed Terling that stretched out in a second generation the hand that welcomed my youth. There is a home near Rogate where humour and good-humour go hand-in-hand; and there remains, after half a century, steadfast and distinguished, the rock-like friendship of Moon Green. So buttressed and fortified, it is little wonder that an obscure life has been a happy one. And if I have preferred affections to activity, and put contentment before usefulness, I can only plead, in extenuation if not in excuse, that the temptations were irresistible. If I failed to hitch my wagon to a star, it has been drawn by a hand that I could not, and would not, let go.

THE END